The Theatre Art of BORIS ARONSON

The Theatre Art of
BORIS ARONSON

Frank Rich with Lisa Aronson

Alfred A. Knopf New York 1987

THIS IS A BORZOI BOOK
PUBLISHED BY ALFRED A. KNOPF, INC.

Photographic credits appear on page 323.

Library of Congress Cataloging-in-Publication Data
Rich, Frank.
The theatre art of Boris Aronson.
Includes index.
1. Aronson, Boris, 1898–1980.
2. Theaters—Stage-setting and scenery.
3. Set designers—United States—Biography.
I. Aronson, Lisa. II. Title.
PN2096.A76R5 1987   792'.025'0924   86–45354
ISBN 0-394-52913-8

Manufactured in Japan
First Edition

For my parents,
Helene and Joel, Frank and Anadel,
who always took me
to the theatre
F. R.

For Marc
L.A.

CONTENTS

Preface

I studied painting, but I always liked toys, tinsel, cut-outs, and an empty stage.

This is a book about an artist who worked in the theatre—Boris Aronson, a painter and sculptor who, from the mid-1920s through the late 1970s, designed over a hundred productions, many of them landmarks of originality, for the American stage.

Our book is not a biography, although it contains a biographical accounting of Aronson's life. Nor is it a nuts-and-bolts book about the craft of set design, although much about that craft will become clear, we hope, in the pages to come. Rather, we are attempting to explain how an artist of exceptional gifts—and with strong ideas about both his own art and the theatre in general—helped shape the dramatic works on which he collaborated. By looking in detail at how Aronson created his designs, we also hope to help illuminate, from an unusual and little-understood perspective, the theatrical process as it has been practiced in New York, especially but not exclusively on Broadway, during much of this century.

This would be an impossible task had not Aronson's career been so varied and his own aesthetic convictions so strong. There have been other outstanding designers in the American theatre—some of whom will make brief appearances in these pages, as their careers intersected Aronson's—but there has never been a designer for the American stage whose body of work is so varied. In fact, there may not be another major figure in the American theatre who, as Aronson did, traveled all the way from revolutionary Russia to the avant-garde Yiddish theatre in the Bronx to the big-budget Broadway musicals of Harold Prince and Stephen Sondheim—with stops along the way at the Group Theatre, Radio City Music Hall, *Three Men on a Horse*, and the epic theatre of Jean Giraudoux and Archibald MacLeish. There are some major figures in the American theatre whose paths did not cross Aronson's—most notably, perhaps, the American playwright he most admired, Eugene O'Neill—but many more did: from George Abbott to Elia Kazan, from George Balanchine to Jerome Robbins, from Clifford Odets to Arthur Miller.

Although the majority of Aronson's productions will be illustrated in these pages, we have chosen to focus, after an introductory essay, on a select, representative group. These productions have been singled out because we consider them to be either Aronson's best work or the most revealing about how he and his collaborators functioned. We do not pretend that every Aronson design was a success.

When a failure is of unusual interest in Aronson's development—or unusually instructive about the workings of the theatre—we have included it. With every design, however, we try to answer the same question: Why and how did Aronson create the setting he did for a given theatrical piece? In all cases, the productions we've chosen for detailed discussion were selected on the basis of the design—*not* on the basis of how successful the production was, as measured by critical approval, box-office receipts, or length of run. In an appendix, we have listed all of Aronson's productions, and a reader should not be surprised to find that some important Aronson designs were for fast Broadway flops and that some Aronson hits have not been discussed in the text.

To piece together the aesthetic process by which Aronson created his designs, we have relied in part on a wide variety of journalistic and other published sources, which are listed in the Bibliography. Because set design was sometimes regarded as a trade rather than an art by the commercial theatre—though never by Aronson himself—information in some instances is sketchy. We have attempted to unearth any documentary materials extant, even including scribbled notes from production meetings. We have interviewed, in person or by letter, collaborators who might have memories about how decisions regarding the design of Aronson's projects were made. In many cases, the design process is the last aspect of any production that anyone remembers. And, of course, many of Aronson's collaborators had died before work on this book began. While some of those theatre people left behind memoirs, rarely do such theatrical autobiographies go into the matters that concern us here. Yet, in more instances than we had at first expected, we were able to track down the essential information we sought to reconstruct a somewhat neglected corner of theatre history.

We wish to thank those Aronson associates, friends, and family who were so kind as to rack their brains and share their memories with us—in some cases, of sets that were carted off to the junk heap (as all sets are in the commercial theatre) a half-century ago, or of productions that expired on Broadway in a very few nights. They are George Abbott, Stella Adler, Avram Aronson, Yanya Aronson, Bob Avian, Frith Banbury, Michael Bennett, Uta Hagen, Peter Hall, Sheldon Harnick, Garson Kanin, Elia Kazan, John Keck, Florence Klotz, Ming Cho Lee, Burgess Meredith, Arthur Miller, Robert Mitchell, J. J. Moore, Tharon Musser, Kazuto Ohira, Richard Pilbrow, Harold

Prince, Anthony Quayle, Norman Rosten, Otto Schenk, Irwin Shaw, Matthieu Slachmuylder, Oliver Smith, Stephen Sondheim, Maureen Stapleton, E. J. Taylor, Robert Whitehead, and Patricia Zipprodt. We also wish to thank other theatre historians who shared research or otherwise assisted us: Betty Corwin, Thor Wood, Dorothy Swerdlove, and Diane Bruning of the Library of the Performing Arts, New York Public Library at Lincoln Center; Dr. Leonard Gold of the New York Public Library; Mary Henderson and Diane Cypkin of the Museum of the City of New York; Margaret Brenman-Gibson, the Clifford Odets biographer, and her associate, Virginia Rowe; and Jeanne Newlin of the Harvard Theater Collection. And those who supplied or tracked down photographic material: Mary Bryant, Susan Cook, Zoë Dominic, Robert Galbraith, Elu Gausmann, Tony Holmes, Mikio Sekita, Frederick M. Stone, Martha Swope, and Arnold Weissberger. Other invaluable assistance was provided by Marc and Kristin Aronson, Doris Blum, Arlene Caruso, Carol Coburn, Jay S. Harris, Lore Lindenfeld, Elizabeth Lomas, Sterling Lord, Ruth Mitchell, Remi Saunder, Richard Stoddard, and Jan Younghusband. Lisa Aronson would like to thank John Beaufort, Lynn Feller, and Gail Merrifield. Over twenty years ago, Harry Stein and Joseph Stein gave the non-Aronson collaborator on this book the opportunity to watch the designer at work.

It was Bob Gottlieb who had the imagination and temerity to insist that the book be done, who brought its authors together, and who waited patiently for the results. We are eternally grateful for his support of a work far from the mainstream of commercial publishing. At Knopf, we also wish to thank Eva Resnikova, Mary Maguire, Paul Hirschman, Martha Kaplan, Eric Simmons, and Ellen McNeilly for their expert help. Our special thanks to Dorothy Schmiderer for her unflagging interest and sensitivity in designing the complex layout of the book.

This book's real author—without whom it could not and would not exist—is Boris Aronson himself. Although he, too, died (in 1980) before work on this book began, he had dreamed of writing it for many years. Luckily, he made various attempts to assemble it. To this end, he had assiduously saved a remarkable array of material that had passed through his studio—not just production photographs and renderings of his sets, but also preliminary sketches, models, research archives, discarded designs, and memorabilia. Though seeing a two-dimensional reproduction of a set on the page of a book is not the same as seeing the set in a theatre with actors moving within it, the wealth of visual material available makes it possible to offer more than the usual department-store-window tableaux in many (if not all) cases.

Aronson had also attempted on several occasions, with future publication in mind, to record his theatrical ideas and his thoughts about the specific productions he worked on. Although he regarded the theatre as an "organized calamity," "a collective art where the strongest man wins," and although he distrusted any "system" for creating theatre (or any art), he codified what might be called his own anti-system through the years. These philosophical credos, constantly refined and sometimes sent forth to the public in interviews and published essays, are the most eloquent verbal expressions of his artistry available. Some of them appear as epigraphs to the book's chapters.

Many more of Aronson's observations, polished and unpolished, can be found in the text. They are the backbone of this book.

In working on this project, Lisa Aronson has taken primary responsibility for the visual part, while I am responsible for the sentences that are not attributed to others. But every such sentence is the result of lengthy discussions between myself and Mrs. Aronson, who was her husband's assistant for most of his career and who has painstakingly taught me how to look at the theatre, as best I can, through his all-seeing eyes. In any case, we have tried to remain invisible presences as much as possible throughout. Boris Aronson's art and his own words about that art are so powerful that we couldn't upstage them even if we were so foolish as to try.

F. R.

The Theatre Art of BORIS ARONSON

ABOUT BORIS ARONSON

It's a miracle when you succeed in the theatre. The only thing is, in order to have it happen, you must prepare the miracle.

For Aronson, the preparation began in Russia, where his ideas about both art and the theatre were forged before, during, and immediately after the Revolution. As one of ten children of the Grand Rabbi of Kiev, he enjoyed the privilege, denied to Jews of less exalted status prior to 1917, of living in a relatively sophisticated city. He was a witness to the social cataclysms of his time—from the pogroms he saw as a young child to his peripheral involvement, as a teenage art student, in the Soviet state's new official socialist culture. Yet the identity Aronson carried out of his homeland—and clung to for an eight-decade lifetime—was not parochially Jewish or ideological in the political sense. He was less a provincial child of the Russian Revolution than a cosmopolitan student of the century's international revolution in art. It was the birth of modernism, not the triumph of the proletariat, that captured his imagination during the brief and exciting period of aesthetic experimentation that swept through Russia after the Revolution. "I grew up at a time of revolt—both a social revolution and a revolution in the arts," Aronson was fond of saying. "Billboards saluted Cézanne as a painter and Einstein as a scientist." Once he had absorbed Russia's particular contributions to modernism—Con-structivism in art, the anti-naturalism of Meyerhold and his contemporaries in theatre—he traveled on, eager to absorb and join the concurrent artistic upheavals of Europe and America.

His official birth date is 1900, though some sources suggest it was a year or two earlier. From the beginning, Aronson never quite fit in with either his family or his community. Decades later, he loved to tell a story about waking up early one morning in the room he shared with his three brothers in Kiev. Boris began to concentrate on the shiny brass doorknob of the bedroom door and asked his brothers just what they saw when they looked at it. Their answers were uniformly direct and abrupt. They saw a doorknob—nothing else. For the young artist, however, there was much more than that: reflected in the small brass knob was a fantastic collection of colors, lights, and shapes. "I knew that morning that I would have trouble in this world," Aronson said. "If you have any imagination, it can cause you a lot of difficulties."

His was a precocious talent. "I used to draw pictures of my buddies in school when I was a kid. They poked fun at my drawings because they didn't see their likenesses in them. Occasionally, our teacher, the Rabbi, would leave his Gemora [a large volume of commentary on the Scriptures] open on his desk, and once, before class began, I seized the opportunity and drew a fly on the white margin of the open page—life-size, with shadow and highlights on the eyes and wings. During the lesson, the teacher noticed the fly, cupped his hand, and with a quick swipe tried to swat the fly. There followed a tense moment of silence. When he realized he had been fooled, he asked, almost in a whisper, 'Who did it?' The boys pointed at me. The class was dismissed, and the teacher decided to inform my parents. But he was so enthusiastic about my skills, he pronounced me a 'genius.' Everyone was elated—my standing in the classroom soared. It was my first encounter with naturalism. And I learned two things. First, that it is easy to fool people in art, and, second, if you can make a fly look like a fly, you're in." Soon the boy was in rebellion against the orthodoxy of his father's way of life. During a visit to the family's rural *dacha*, his father caught him sitting on the roof of the house, whittling away on a cane, on a Saturday when he was expected to be in Hebrew school. "When I faced him," Aronson remembered, "I cried out in desperation, 'It's not *me!*' "

A love of the theatrical soon blossomed as well. With his siblings, Boris was fond of acting out his father's ceremonial work rituals—the making of divorces, for instance—that could be observed within the Rabbi's official chambers in their Kiev home. "I frankly don't understand what was the first thing which made me drunk with theatre," Aronson later said. "Perhaps it was the Purim plays I put on for my very large family—to get their holiday money. Perhaps it was the day I wandered into the Kiev Opera House and saw its magnificent curtain with a large peacock painted on it. I don't know if it was the curtain or the curiosity about what was behind it that made me run home and complain, 'Here I am, ten years old, and I have not yet seen an opera!' This was where I belonged, that's all I knew, and I kept on crying."

Aronson thought of his father as "a very educated man who knew Dostoevsky's and Tolstoy's writings very well, but had nothing to do with the visual arts." The boy received more encouragement from his grandmother, who lovingly called him a *mujik* (peasant) and who would make up elaborate stories about the images she could pick out of his drawings. Boris chose his own nickname for himself—"The Outlaw"—and periodically ran away from home. Once, his father sent one of his brothers, Yanya, to find him. "It was known that he hung out at the Café François, an artists' haunt," Yanya recalled. "I found him there—expecting that he'd surely be in questionable company or imbibing hard stuff. But Boris was sitting by himself, drinking tea with milk. At the time, I couldn't understand why he had run away when he could have had the same tea at home."

Aronson enrolled at a Kiev art school where he could also get a general high-school education. His father greeted his son's career choice with a parable about a magician at the fair: "The magician has a large audience, and he pulls not only rabbits and flowers out of his hat, but also gold coins—much to the amazement of all. But after the applause dies down, he passes around the same hat to collect pennies as a reward. When you are able to do the tricks without having to pass the hat afterward, then you'll know you are doing the right thing and have chosen the right profession."

At school, Aronson's work was disliked by his instructors, who had been trained in the old French tradition. The boy discovered that to be praised, "one had to paint Russian trees as French trees." During a summer vacation, he began to move away from the realistic models of his teachers and exhibited the results in the school's fall show. At some point after that, he managed to get to Moscow, hoping to see firsthand some of the French modernist paintings he had seen reproduced in art magazines. He had heard rumors about a private collector, the textile merchant Sergey Ivanovich Shchukin, who had a large stock of canvases by Cézanne, Gauguin, Matisse, Monet, and Picasso—none of whose work had yet been seen by the Russian public. Beginning in 1909, Shchukin had opened his house to visitors on Sundays as an informal "Museum of Matisse and Picasso." Because Jews were not allowed to live in Moscow prior to the lifting of restrictions in 1917, the young Boris slept in the street with the hansom-cab drivers overnight, then went to the Shchukin mansion. But it was not a Sunday, and, upon being turned away by a servant, Aronson decided to plead his case, as an art student, for a private appointment to see the treasures inside. Suddenly, Shchukin himself appeared at the gate and, taking pity on the young man, gave him a tour of his collection; the merchant and the art student discussed each painting in detail, whetting Aronson's appetite for further contact with the new art of the West.

With the arrival of the Revolution, Aronson began to find his way as an artist—and his growth coincided with that of Kiev, which soon became the center of the Jewish avant-garde. Aronson participated in a new modern-art center there, one of the many "Museums of Artistic Culture" formed around the country during the short-lived post-revolutionary boom, and by 1920 he had helped organize a "Jewish Art

Exhibition'' which featured innovative works by Iosif Chaikov, El Lissitzky, Nisson Shifrin, Alexandr Tyshler, and himself. ''There was the most breathtaking and fascinating throwing off of the old forms of expression and the seeking of new ones,'' Aronson said of the period. ''Sheer size was the order of the day in art.'' Along with other Kiev art students, he was mobilized in 1918 to extend building façades artificially, in the manner of movie sets, so that they could accommodate monumental slogans like ''Religion is the opium of the people.'' Aronson was ambivalent about the Revolution's overall drift. ''Tragedy,'' he said, ''was a view from my window in Kiev. . . . In the first months of the Revolution, the Red Army was not in any uniform. They were a shabby mob in beggar's garb. Such a mob I saw marching with an arrested aristocrat. Although this was his 'last meal,' although he walked to his doom, he represented centuries of good behavior—something you could not kill, it was too well made. Valor was imprinted in his every step. The members of the police looked, in spite of their victory, defeated. It looked like the aristocrat was the distinguished leader and his captors the prisoners. He had generations behind him. Here was the tragedy of our time—power on both sides that made the suffering unbearable.''

Aronson had few doubts, however, about the merits of the revolution sweeping through the theatre. Its leader was Vsevolod Meyerhold (1874–1940), a director who had been trained under Konstantin Stanislavsky at the Moscow Art Theatre but who now challenged the precepts of Stanislavskian realism. Though Stanislavsky had himself reformed Russian theatre at the turn of the century, his once-iconoclastic principles were regarded by Meyerhold as stifling dogma. ''The artists must throw down the brush and compass and lay hold of the ax and hammer for the shaping of the new stage,'' Meyerhold said. Aronson vehemently shared this rejection of Stanislavsky. ''By the time I was fourteen,'' he claimed, ''I was past crying over *The Cherry Orchard* and no longer cared whether the three sisters arrived safely in Moscow. At the Moscow Art Theatre at that time, in one of Chekhov's plays, a picture was removed from the wall and one could clearly see on the wall the dust and the cobwebs that had accumulated behind the picture. But now new theatrical ideas blossomed and began to develop—the theatre of theatricality.''

Meyerhold drew his theatrical ideas in part from the creative manifestos of two European innovators, the English theoretician, designer, and producer Gordon Craig and the Swiss designer Adolphe Appia. In a Meyerhold production, the director imparted his own strong imprint on the text. In place of flat, painted scenery—which simulated reality with trompe-l'oeil effects and backgrounds ruled by strict perspective—was a plastic, three-dimensional setting, subtly lighted, that stylized reality. No longer was the audience watching a picture framed within a rectangular proscenium arch; artificial barriers between theatregoers and performers were meant to be removed. Mimetic depiction of reality was banished; ritual, commedia dell'arte, and dance were welcomed; stage artifice was revealed rather than camouflaged. The goal was a unified production—and one in which a designer played a role as prominent as that of the director and playwright. As Meyerhold wrote in a statement cherished by Aronson, the designer shares the director's responsibility of ''giving form and shape,'' of ''molding a masterpiece,'' of giving drama ''a contemporary point of view,'' and of ''serving the actor.''

What Aronson did not accept about Meyerhold was the director's post-1917 experimentation with a propagandist ''communal'' theatre—a theatre that not only stripped the stage to its essentials but, in Aronson's view, might also pander to the audience's lowest common denominator. Aronson was instead attracted to the work of another iconoclastic director, Alexander Tairov (1885–1950), who, in 1914, founded the Moscow Kamerny Theatre (i.e., intimate or chamber theatre). Tairov had no ideological program (''A propagandist theatre after a revolution is like mustard after a meal,'' he once declared). Although he shared many of Meyerhold's aesthetic convictions, Tairov believed in the supremacy of the performer. His actors were trained in singing, dancing, mime, and circus acrobatics, and, unlike Meyerhold's, were regarded as principal creators of a production, not merely puppets at the director's disposal.

''An actor is three-dimensional and has to be afforded the greatest freedom,'' Tairov wrote in his artistic credo, *Das entfesselte Theater (The Emancipated Theatre)*. He condemned not only naturalistic, three-dimensional theatre which gives ''the false impression'' of ''the actual reality of life'' but also the stylized theatre in which two-dimensional backdrops make ''a marionette out of the actor.'' To liberate the performer and ''give the theatre back its dynamic,'' Tairov decided to put the emphasis on the stage floor and minimize the scenic background. ''The stage floor has to be of broken surfaces'' with ''no symmetrical planes,'' because ''an even floor is expressionless.'' He also felt that each play, having its ''own rhythm,'' had to have its own ''scenic solution.'' These solutions ''don't recall any true-to-life illusions, but they are freely created forms which come out of the

1 Among the early Russian influences on Aronson was this musical comedy, *20000*, inspired by Sholom Aleichem and produced at the Jewish Kamerny Theatre in Moscow during the early 1920s, when Aronson's friend Marc Chagall worked there. A fiddler can be found on the roof.

2 The theatre of revolution: A commedia dell'arte *Turandot*, as directed by E. Vachtangov and designed by I. I. Nivinsky.

rhythm of the performance. From the point of view of reality, they seem fictitious. But they are true—true from the point of view of theatre-art—because they are in harmony with the reality of the material." In his book, Tairov summarizes his aesthetic philosophy with a fable to which Aronson also subscribed: "At a fair, a traveling conjuror wanted to imitate the grunting of a piglet, and he managed to do it so well that all the onlookers applauded loudly. Then a peasant offered to do it even better. He quickly hid a living piglet under his coat and pinched it. The piglet began to squeak, but the peasant was booed and whistled away by the crowd. . . . The live piglet squeaked well, but not artificially enough. Yes, there are two truths—the truth of life and the truth of art. Sometimes they meet, but most of the time it is so that the Truth of Life in art is untrue and that the Truth of Art in life has a false sound."

Tairov's principal designer was the Constructivist pioneer Alexandra Exter (1882–1949). Exter had been trained as a painter in Paris and was familiar with all the modernist currents in French art, starting with Impressionism and continuing through Futurism and Cubism; she was a friend of Picasso and Braque in the years just prior to the war. Upon returning to Russia from France, she went her own way—creating a Cubo-Futurist style that adapted the modernism of Parisian and Italian painters to the stage. Like other Russian artists of the time, she found the theatre an opportune arena for carrying out Constructivist experiments that were ideally suited to execution in architecture but were prohibitive to realize. Her first triumph with Tairov at the Kamerny was a hotly debated production of Annenski's *Famira Kifared*, which had its premiere in 1916.

Like Meyerhold, who was ultimately executed in the Stalinist purges, Exter became a non-person in the Soviet Union once the doctrine of socialist realism ended Russia's transitory period of artistic ferment. (She returned to France permanently late in 1923, dying forgotten and in poverty there a quarter-century later.) But, like Meyerhold, Exter is now recognized in the West as a major figure in the history of modern theatre. She was also a major force in Aronson's development. For at least two years, Aronson was a pupil in Exter's workshop in Kiev, and by 1919 he had become one of his teacher's principal aides. There he solidified his notions of theatrical design.

Exter taught modern painting, but prepared her pupils in a variety of areas, book illustration and theatrical design among them. She made her students work in various styles, such as Cubism and Fauvism, simultaneously—often on the same day. The lesson stayed with

Aronson later on: he would allude to "styles" as diverse as those of Klee, Hopper, Magritte, and Bacon in his designs, depending on the needs of the individual play. He also desired to emulate Exter's working relationship with the director, Tairov. Her collaboration with Tairov was not that of a craftsman executing a predetermined design pattern, but that of an active creator involved with the entire production process.

Aronson saw the process close up when he assisted Exter with the execution of the costumes and the stage models of her designs for Tairov's legendary *Romeo and Juliet* at the Kamerny in 1920. "For the first time in any theatre," the American designer Donald Oenslager later noted of that production, "the stage's total cubic volume was divided vertically into abstract playing areas that did not mean to create any life-like illusion of the Capulets' Great Hall or Juliet's tomb." The set also used mirrors to reflect the actors and to create the illusion of "a multiplicity of spatial planes." Audiences would find these devices no less startling when Aronson adapted them in designs he created on Broadway a half-century later.

In his first newspaper interviews in New York a decade after his tutelage with Exter, Aronson credited her with teaching him the primary purposes of a stage set: "It should . . . permit varied movement for the actor; present significant details characteristic of the mood of the play; dramatize the emotion of each scene; by its organic fusion of forms and color, be beautiful in its own right. A set must possess a compositional and synthetic beauty." Aronson further described the legacy of Constructivism—and that of directors like Meyerhold and Tairov who fostered its theatrical applications—in an essay he wrote for the New York Yiddish press in 1926: "In the naturalistic theatre, there was only one method of stage design; a set always had to be an exact copy of real life. Only on the basis of *external* signs, of differing combinations of details from real life, could one production be distinguished from another. Now, however, the intention is, in principle, to bring out the inner essence of each dramatic work. . . . Instead of one-dimensional painting, which had no organic connection with the stage, [Constructivists] constructed three-dimensional stage sets made up of several levels, platforms, stairs, and ladders, which allow the actor to move about freely and to employ diverse means of expressing his emotions effectively."

The decidedly urban aesthetic of Exter and other Russian theatrical innovators had a subsidiary effect on Aronson as well: they set him to dreaming of America. Although by 1921 he had moved permanently

3 Meyerhold's legendary production of *The Magnanimous Cuckold*, designed by L. S. Popova and seen by Aronson in Moscow in 1922.

4, 5 Costumes by Aronson's teacher Alexandra Exter for the Tairov production of *Romeo and Juliet* (1920), on which the young Boris worked as an assistant.

OPPOSITE

6, 7, 8 Aronson's design for an "Oriental Dance" performed by B. Agadati, New York, c. 1924.

to Moscow, in his words "the Mecca of the theatre world," Aronson was already suspicious of official Soviet government culture and its "rampant cultism." While new policy encouraged cultural diversity (including that of "ethnic minorities"), he suspected that "the Revolution would turn bourgeois, destroy creativity," and favor art that he called "home-sweet-home calendar art." Aronson began to draw fantasy sketches of a visionary city full of skyscrapers—a city whose indigenous, technological art truly expressed the masses who inhabited it. He knew such art could not exist in pre-industrial Moscow: When the Constructivist visionary Vladimir Tatlin dreamed up a plan to erect a steel structure taller than the then-tallest American skyscraper, the Woolworth Building, the plan was abandoned because Moscow's land was too marshy to support it. "At the time of the Revolution, Moscow barely had electricity," Aronson said. "The fascination of America lay in the concept of a new world—a technical civilization. The mechanical inventions of America represented romantic fantasy. It was Jack London, not Thoreau, who symbolized the American idea

—things, not thoughts. I wanted to go to this world, a place just opening up, to see what I could do on a larger, freer scale."

In 1922, Aronson departed post-revolutionary Russia for good, leaving behind, in his view, "masses of people all looking alike, scurrying about with briefcases under their arms, wearing lapel buttons proclaiming their partisanship." With false papers, he traveled to Poland, where a sympathetic uncle (noting that "the young man has something") gave him the financial wherewithal to join the great wave of emigration to Germany. Aronson settled, albeit briefly, in Berlin. There he studied and painted, participating in the first foreign exhibition of Soviet art, at the Van Diemen Gallery. The exhibit, which later went on to Amsterdam, marked the West's first exposure to the modernist explosion that had occurred in Russia during its isolation since the outbreak of war in 1914.

While in Berlin, Aronson also published two books. One of them, a treatise on "contemporary Jewish graphic art," was dedicated in part to proving that Jewish art didn't really exist. "When the Japanese

6

7

8

draws a cloud, it looks Japanese," he argued, because the Japanese has lived in the same place for thousands of years and has "a way of looking at a cloud." Jewish art, he felt, was not genuine because Jews are dispersed throughout the world and would produce art influenced by their adopted culture. His other book was an early critical study of Marc Chagall, a Moscow friend who had designed sets for the Jewish Kamerny Theatre. Of Chagall's work for the theatre in 1920–21, Aronson wrote, "[He] has synthesized the Harlequinade of the Jewish theatre and the grotesqueries of the Jewish ghetto. He has created a plastic pantomime in which his somersaults of fantasy attain an extraordinary acuity." (Four decades later, Aronson would refract Chagall's art through his own "plastic pantomime" in his designs for the Broadway musical *Fiddler on the Roof.*)

Aronson could not find a foothold in the Berlin theatre world. Fortunately, his books, which were successful and translated into several languages, provided a way out. "I had a very easy time to get a visa to come to America because of my being an author of books about art and I could very easily prove I was an artist. With thousands of inflated German marks (actually about 400 American dollars), I considered myself well-to-do and decided to go to America." In November 1923, he traveled to New York on the *Aquatania*, arriving with "awkward luggage—some drawings, two books, a pair of socks, a membership in a union of German artists, paintbrushes, crowded emotions, little money, and less English."

What Aronson didn't know upon arriving in New York was that the American arts, especially the theatre, were often as backward as American urban civilization was advanced. The relationship between artistic and technological progress in the United States was, if anything, the inverse of that in Russia. If New York's skyline expressed the same modernist spirit as Moscow's avant-garde artists, New York's theatre had more in common spiritually with the dowdy Moscow cityscape. Not only had the experiments of Meyerhold and Tairov yet to take root in the American theatre; even the psychologically realistic theatre of Stanislavsky was still waiting to be transplanted to

New York (a development that would occur during the Depression, under the auspices of the Group Theatre).

Because Aronson's thinking was thirty years ahead of the mainstream New York theatre, he had to wait for history to catch up with him. This is why, unlike many American theatre artists, Aronson found that his work became more and more fashionable the older he got. It was not until Brecht, an aesthetic descendant of Meyerhold, achieved belated popularity in New York after World War II that Meyerholdian ideas of total and epic theatre found acceptance on the commercial stage. It was not until those ideas were adapted to Broadway's most indigenous theatrical form, the musical, that Aronson, under the auspices of the directors Jerome Robbins and Harold Prince, would be a full collaborator in the creation of a production, as Exter had been with Tairov. But along the way to his mature realization as a scenic artist, Aronson achieved an equal measure of aesthetic victories and defeats. The victories came when sympathetic directors, not all of whom fully understood his ambitions, gave him a free hand to adapt his sophisticated ideas to (or enforce them on) their productions (especially if those productions aspired, however vaguely, to the experimental). The defeats usually occurred when Aronson had to design conventional sets for which he had little sympathy—or when he tried to impose avant-garde design ideas on plays which had no use for them. But many of Aronson's designs prior to the late 1950s and early 1960s occupy a fascinating middle ground: forced to compromise between the conventional demands of the New York theatre and the free-wheeling dictates of his own imagination, he frequently arrived at ingenious design solutions that both served the play at hand and fulfilled his own artistic convictions.

When Aronson initially arrived in New York, however, he was handed his first—and for almost forty years his last—opportunity to design sets with complete freedom, in the Russian avant-garde style. Needless to say, this opportunity did not occur on Broadway, or in the English-speaking theatre, or, at first, even in the front-line Lower East Side Yiddish theatre on which Aronson had set his initial career sights. Instead, Aronson secured work in the experimental Yiddish theatre— one might say Off Off Second Avenue—in the upper reaches of the Bronx. He received his first job a month after his arrival, as his money ran out, and found himself "doing shows about heaven and hell." His first designs, in 1923–25, were for plays by Ansky, Pinski, and Dymov in the Unser and Schildkraut theatres, as far uptown as 180th Street. They began to attract attention from far beyond the neighborhood. In

The New York Times Magazine, Kenneth Macgowan, a close theatrical associate of Eugene O'Neill, lauded Aronson's adventurous work. Macgowan wrote of having first seen what he described as "futurism" on stage at Tairov's Kamerny Theatre in Russia in 1914, but, he added, "in America it remained for the Bronx to demonstrate foreground and background and costumes all shaped and distorted into a visual dramatization of futurist theory. There in what is now Rudolph Schildkraut's Theatre, an artist from Moscow, B. Aronson, supplied extraordinary decorations for stage and actors."

As Aronson had hoped, his striking Bronx designs led to his employment by the foremost downtown Yiddish theatre impresario, Maurice Schwartz. From 1925 until 1929, Aronson worked regularly for Schwartz—and with the same boldness that marked his previous designs. It was Aronson's particular good fortune to design the opening extravaganza of Schwartz's new Yiddish Art Theatre. The show was a musical, *The Tenth Commandment* (1926), and it contained some of Aronson's most elaborate flights into Constructivism, symbolism, and whimsical fantasy. Schwartz's productions were reviewed by the major newspapers, and, in Horatio Alger fashion, *The Tenth Commandment* helped bring the young immigrant artist to the attention of many of the most powerful critics and commentators of the New York theatre.

They soon took the remarkable step of organizing an exhibition of Aronson's Yiddish-theatre designs in midtown, at the Anderson Galleries on Park Avenue at 59th Street. A press release heralded the show, which ran for two weeks in December 1927, as "a one man theatre arts exhibit, unique enough even for blasé metropolitan first-nighters." The exhibition contained twenty-five miniature Aronson set models, "lit with 6-inch spotlights, each with its own pedestal, own proscenium arch and drop curtain." Nine productions, designed over Aronson's four-year-old American career, were represented; a second gallery room contained one hundred paintings of costumes which Aronson had designed for those productions, as well as woodcuts, illustrations for children's books, pen-and-ink drawings, and photographs showing how the designs were realized on stage. The exhibition's sponsors were an illustrious crowd: Kenneth Macgowan; Edith J. R. Isaacs and John Mason Brown of *Theatre Arts Monthly*; J. Brooks Atkinson, drama critic of *The New York Times*; the critic Sheldon Cheney; Maurice Schwartz; and the designer Cleon Throckmorton (whom the release described as "enthusiastic about Aronson's work even though it is different from his own").

9

10

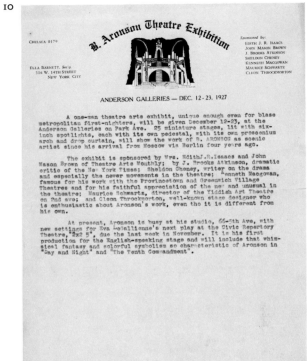

11

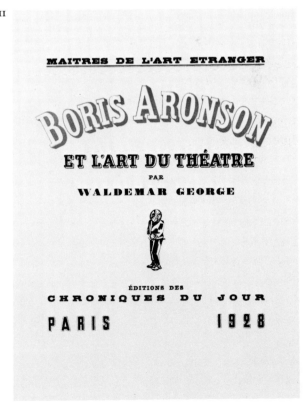

9 Aronson's first design for the English-language theatre: Gustav Wied's $2 \times 2 = 5$, for Eva Le Gallienne's Civic Repertory Theatre (1927).

10 A press release announcing the Anderson Galleries exhibition of Aronson's work, New York, 1927.

11 The frontispiece of Waldemar George's monograph heralding Aronson, published in Paris in 1928.

The exhibition catalogue contained statements of support for Aronson's work, most of which expressed dazzlement at the exotic, striking vision that Aronson had brought from revolutionary Russia to New York. Cheney wrote that the designer "goes beyond what is ordinarily understood as decoration. He doesn't mistake realistic and journalistic plays as the sum of all playwriting." Schwartz described *The Tenth Commandment* as "one of the finest productions conceived in America within the last 10 years." Aronson, he wrote, "gives his own conception to the productions he designs. He is entirely theatre—one might even say, he breathes theatre." In the catalogue's introductory essay, titled "Announcing Aronson," Brown wrote that the designer "has seen behind the ugliness of those gaunt steel ribs which pierce Manhattan's ever-changing skyline and has understood the strength and restlessness and power that they represent. He has been able to see them as symbols of the age and to use them for their full symbolic content in the theatre." Edith Isaacs added: "We have watched [Aronson] work his way from the outskirts of the city nearer and nearer to its heart, and feel that the theatre has gained by his coming."

Unrelated to the exhibition—but perhaps just as important to the young Aronson's growing reputation—was another celebration of his Yiddish-theatre designs, a book published in Paris in 1928. Written by Waldemar George, the French art critic, this monograph combined a substantial critical essay about Aronson's designs with sumptuous color plates of the Bronx and Second Avenue sets. George decried the "immobile" scenic art of the nineteenth century, an era of naturalism during which "real furniture replaced painted furniture," and chided Stanislavsky's "slice of life" theatre for "losing itself in a thousand details." The critic placed Aronson in the rebellious new wave of Craig, Max Reinhardt, and Meyerhold, who saw sets as "machines for playing" and who returned the theatre to "its natural voice" by borrowing "dynamic and optical elements" from the circus and music hall.

George was a sympathetic reader of both Aronson's intentions and his inspirations. At a time when American directors thought that ideal sets were fast and noiseless, changing in darkness out of view, Aronson believed that the machinery of sets should be exposed to the audience; otherwise, "the fun and make-believe elements of theatre were lost" and "the best part of the show was done for the benefit of the stagehands only." Aronson's belief in the full disclosure of theatrical magic came in part from his Moscow training: modernist art, whether in the form of Cubist paintings or Constructivist sets, re-volted against decorative romantic art by exposing the machinery of the creative method. But Aronson's belief in exposed theatrical machinery was strengthened by his practical observations of vaudeville and the circus, both of which he regarded as models of total theatre. Aronson frequently traveled with the circus to observe and sketch its spectacle. He was a great admirer of Charles Chaplin, who, like the performer in Tairov's favorite illustrative fable, had "a sublime ability to perform a trick and then tip the audience off to the fact that it is a trick, although a right smart trick and well done." To Aronson, this was "not charlatanism, but the glamorous illusion of the theatre." He thought that "designs should carry an illusion of the real thing, but not be the real thing itself." He called for theatre artists to "be honest and admit our tricks—but let us make them good tricks, excellent and professional."

In his essay about Aronson, Waldemar George also applauded the designer for his genuine "humility"—his refusal to see scenery "as an end in itself." Worrying that the theatre must compete with the new art of cinema but cannot become "a uniquely visual spectacle," the French critic concluded that designers like Aronson could not fulfill their mission until they found modernist collaborators who might be the theatre's equivalents of "Rimbaud, Proust, Picasso and Satie."

George's ruminations made their way to the United States and prompted a prescient—and sharply equivocal—essay by the designer Lee Simonson in *The Nation*. Noting that "pictorial methods enter the theatre ten or fifteen years after painters have invented them," Simonson argued that, unlike Cubism or Futurism, Constructivism was the only modernist art style that could address the "separate aesthetic problem" of the stage. In contrast to other anti-realist art movements, Constructivism recognized that "the fundamental values of the stage picture are architectonic, framing and limiting space through which human beings move, and that the basis of every stage picture is structural." Simonson acknowledged, too, that Tairov's and Meyerhold's theatrical use of Constructivism expressed "the new structure of society about them."

But Simonson also questioned the value of such techniques to the existing American theatre, and, in doing so, pinpointed Aronson's dilemma in his adopted culture—one unlikely to produce the Proust-and-Satie-like theatre artists that Waldemar George had called for. "Despite Aronson's technical proficiency, his intelligence and his ingenuity," Simonson wrote, his design style "remains an exotic and transplanted thing. We do not breed the Constructivist director as yet because we so rarely need him, nor are symbolic settings often relevant to the work of our most creative playwrights. [These playwrights] are, at present, with the exception of O'Neill, debunking the American scene as realists, substituting first-hand observation for our stock of inherited theatrical clichés and sentimentalities, and winning audiences to accept their findings, increasingly cynical and skeptical, as to what we are really like. As a nation, we are getting onto ourselves in the theatre. The greatest progress in that direction is made by such popular plays as *What Price Glory?*, *The Silver Cord*, *Holiday* or *The Front Page*. The process is not yet completed, as it was in Europe 20 years ago. Once we know ourselves, creative American playwrights will begin to ask what we can make of ourselves, will search for a synthesis of American life, and struggle to find symbols for it. In the meanwhile, I hope Aronson will be able to divest himself sufficiently of his Russian dogmas so that his undoubted talents can be more readily used to express the current realities of the American stage."

With extraordinary acuity, Simonson had diagnosed Aronson's predicament in America (even as he correctly predicted the course American theatrical history would take and how that history would ultimately converge with Aronson's career). For the young Russian designer in 1920s New York, the questions were clear: How could he apply his avant-garde ideas to the realistic New York theatre? How could he, in any case, use Constructivism to abstract an American landscape that he didn't even know? Aronson's first English-speaking assignment begged the issue, for, like his Yiddish-theatre work, it was an experimental play: Gustav Wied's $2 \times 2 = 5$, for Eva Le Gallienne's Civic Repertory Theatre, only a short distance away from Maurice Schwartz's downtown playhouse. Aronson had applied for the job as soon as he saw a sign announcing the play's eccentric title in front of the theatre at Sixth Avenue and 14th Street; he was preparing the sets at his studio at 66 Fifth Avenue as the Anderson Galleries exhibit opened in 1927. Once again, a brand of European modernism was called for. "The play was about a home where the husband and wife had completely different opinions about life. I designed two sections, which are completely different, in the same house. The wife liked everything modern; the husband liked everything old-fashioned. They had correspondingly different habits. Neither his nor her half bore any relation to the other. It turned out to be a very funny play, but, more than that, born out of the necessity of the play, I found a quality in my work that today would be called surrealism."

"If it had been $2 \times 2 = 4$," said Aronson later, "they never would have given it to me." That one assignment notwithstanding, he knew he had to break into a truly American mode if he was ever to avoid ghettoization in the Yiddish theatre. "The emigration of European Jews was slowing down. The younger generations started to assimilate, and all the ethnic theatres were affected by that reality. Maurice Schwartz used to appeal to the audience—sometimes in the middle of a show—to sponsor his theatre. I was longing to work in the English-speaking theatre. I was on a much higher level than the Yiddish theatre of operetta and melodrama." Determined to make his name beyond the Lower East Side, Aronson decided to quit the Yiddish theatre entirely, even though he had no immediate job prospects elsewhere.

He knew this meant that he would have to master the reality of the new world around him, but he found the buzzing city so exciting that the task seemed not at all odious: "It was a very great discovery and novelty for me to see a Bronx apartment or a home in Ozone Heights or a bar on Third Avenue or even the architecture of the kind of ugliness Staten Island is famous for. Those real things were very fantastic to me." And, to Aronson, such homely Americana had their own indigenous aesthetic value; he saw them from a perspective that, like some of his early American designs, prefigured artists from Stuart Davis to Andy Warhol. As he wrote in a flier for *America 1930*, a book commissioned from him by Waldemar George's Paris publisher (but never written): "The American rhythm is expressed in the forms which are the daily visual experience of every American. These forms have utilitarian motives: to attract, to sell, to please. But as they are the experience of America, they are also the expression of America. Hence they may be called the American art: indigenous and lively rather than borrowed and effete." He also found an inherent plastic theatricality in this environment: "The American idea in my mind at that time was not connected with easel painting or sculpture, but with a new medium combining invention and science. The peak of my ambition when I arrived in New York was to design one of the huge electric signs on Times Square for Wrigley's Chewing Gum. I was fascinated by the idea of using electric bulbs as one would use tubes of paint."

Yet even as Aronson set out to master the New York reality, he knew that someday he would have to return to his original goal as a designer—the Exter ideal of remaking reality in personal terms. As he observed much later, "My development in the States was very, very

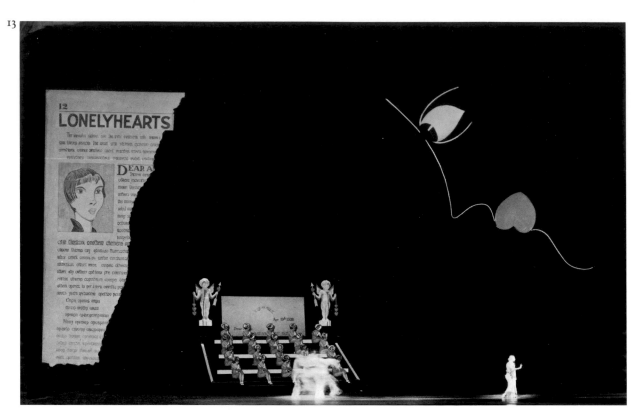

12, 13   In an Aronson design for a Radio City Music Hall stage show, as sketched (12) and executed (13), the book jacket of Nathanael West's 1933 novel *Miss Lonelyhearts* served as a backdrop, chorus girls as typewriter keys. The original jacket for West's novel had also been designed by Aronson.

14   For Robert Rossen's *The Body Beautiful* (1935), Aronson designed the first of his many backstage sets. This sketch shows just one of several sets in a production that required two turntables for scenic moves.

slow. The whole story of my development was from familiarizing myself with the American scene and, after almost forty years, getting to know it to the point where I wasn't in any way satisfied with just reproducing it, but could give the essence of it. As I discovered the reality of the American scene, my work progressed from literal representation, with illustration and documentation of a certain locale, to a grasping for *mood* and *essence.* My development therefore progressed from naturalism to expressionism and finally to an abstract economical ordering of space. There remains the perseverance toward *self,* the difficulty of being recognized for yourself in an environment which constantly challenges and does not allow you to progress methodically, step by step.''

That Aronson was able to stay doggedly on his forty-year path of development was a testament to his self-possession as an artist: "I never followed the American idea of age. I started at 180th Street and slowly crawled from one rung on the ladder to the next until I got to the Metropolitan Opera. It is not the American way. In America, you are a genius at eighteen and finished at thirty. To me, each experience is a rejuvenation." Aronson was also convinced that when the time came for him to remake American reality according to his own "self," there would be an audience for his work. Part of this conviction, he felt, was strengthened by an international exhibition of theatre art that he saw in the Steinway Building in 1926: "The Russian models and sketches were of sets with escalators, revolving stages, mechanical gadgets, elevators. I looked through the twelfth-floor window and saw a view of the city which was identical with the Russian stage sets. In Moscow, with its horses and buggies and snowy streets, escalators and elevators were the height of romantic fantasy—that which was commonplace reality in New York. American designers like Robert Edmond Jones, on the other hand, were doing romantic realism. Jones wasn't interested in simply repeating his own milieu. This was a very great lesson to me, because in Moscow, where you had a very romantic atmosphere in reality, all those escalators meant something fantastic. Escalators in New York are not a novelty. And that's why I believe audiences are much more interested in something which represents an imaginative approach to life than in literal realism." Still, it was not until forty years later, when he designed the Broadway musical *Company* in 1970, that Aronson was finally able to interpret New York's reality, its elevators and skyscrapers, in the non-realistic, Constructivist style that had been dominant in the Russian avant-garde theatre of his youth.

Though Aronson apparently had to scrape about for a couple of years, work in the English-speaking theatre soon came his way, Broadway assignments included. His early benefactors were unlikely ones —Courtney Burr, the patrician producer, and George Abbott, a director whose snappy, realistic style epitomized Broadway at its most slick and all-American. Burr gave the designer his first Broadway job, a lavish 1932 musical, *Walk a Little Faster.* Built on vaudeville turns (featuring Beatrice Lillie and the clowning team of Bobby Clark and Paul McCullough), the show was a precursor of later experimental, vaudeville-oriented musicals designed by Aronson, *Love Life* (1948) and *Follies* (1971). Such was the designer's contribution to *Walk a Little Faster* that he received the credit, unusual at the time, of having "conceived and designed" the production. Burr also produced the shows Aronson worked on next—although the producer had no connection with the most notable of the four Aronson-Abbott collaborations of 1934–35, the hit farce *Three Men on a Horse.*

It was also in 1935 that Aronson began a short-lived association with Radio City Music Hall and a lasting one with the Group Theatre —two theatrical organizations that could not be more disparate. At the movie palace, Aronson was hired as one of three art directors for the stage show which preceded each film. While he worked on many design projects—including an elaborate fan that anticipated a design motif for *Follies* thirty-five years later—they surfaced on stage only in the Easter show (starring Jan Peerce) that played in tandem with the film *Cardinal Richelieu* (starring George Arliss). They were impressive enough to inspire the critic Cecilia Ager to write that Aronson "interprets the ideas assigned him with taste, deftness and the strength of a true artist." But the designer found himself in immovable conflict with Radio City's idea of theatre: "My basic inclination was to make things smaller so that the set would be more related to people and to happenings. The tendency of the Music Hall is to enlarge, to make things big, and bigger than anything anybody else has to show." Aronson was amused to visit the Music Hall's rival, the Roxy, and find even more elaborate overkill: "two hundred girls in startling, colorful costumes, distributed on a dozen moving platforms, a riot of movement and display—all this marvelous technique applied to the minor problem [of] saying good night to the audience!"

Aronson was brought into the Group, whose principal designer was Mordecai Gorelik, by Harold Clurman, the director who co-directed the pioneering ensemble with Lee Strasberg and Cheryl Crawford. It was the beginning of a lifelong friendship and artistic collaboration; Aronson worked with Clurman more than with any other director; it was through Clurman that he subsequently worked on plays by Arthur Miller, Tennessee Williams, and William Inge in the 1950s and 1960s. Clurman had first heard of Aronson's designs in the late 1920s, when his directing teacher, Richard Boleslavsky, told him of *The Tenth Commandment.* Aronson's first assignments for the Group were Clifford Odets' back-to-back family plays, *Awake and Sing* and *Paradise Lost* (both directed by Clurman in 1935).

Aronson had his reservations about the Group. Its leaders regarded Stanislavsky's realism, which they introduced to New York in Americanized form, as innovative—whereas, for Aronson, Stanislavsky represented the old-fashioned theatre he had revolted against as a young man in Moscow: "I was never wholly dedicated to the Group Theatre. They were conscious of what they wanted to do, but it wasn't theatrical enough for me. The wonderful achievements of the Stanislavsky theatre were in the performance of the plays. Very little attention was given to scenery as a work of art. I don't think they would have allowed a great artist to design scenery for a Chekhov play. In the Tairov theatre, it was just the other way around. The physical productions were fascinating. So I was more interested in the more experimental Mercury Theatre [for whom Aronson never worked], headed by Orson Welles and John Houseman, simply because this type of theatre is closer to my way of thinking, upbringing, and inclination."

Among the other lifelong associates Aronson met at the Group were Odets and Elia Kazan. The designer's relationship with both men was close, if at times tumultuous. Kazan, whose association with Aronson spanned from the Group Theatre through a collaboration on the landmark set for Archibald MacLeish's *J.B.* (1958), thought the designer "was a pure artist, like a child in a way." Odets wrote of Aronson in his diaries: "[He] is always the artist, always the bohemian, but in the best and true sense of the word." When Aronson helped Odets arrange the furniture in a new apartment, the designer inadvertently taught the writer a lesson about stage design. "I was surprised to find how one shape or object determines and conditions that of another object," wrote Odets. "Everything, it is plain to see, exists only in a context!" For his part, Aronson said of the playwright, "There was no other author in my life with whom I had such an intimate relationship —on so many levels, not just as a designer." At one point, the two men considered the idea of working together on a play from the beginning of the writing onward. But the experiment, a long-cherished dream of Aronson's, was never carried out. While the men continued

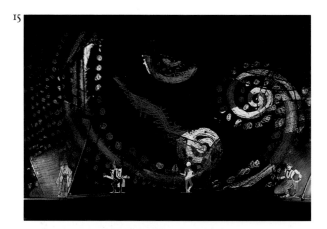

15, 16   For William Saroyan's "ballet-play" *The Great American Goof* for Ballet Theatre (1940), Aronson conducted unusual experiments with scenic projections—as seen here in model form.

17, 18   For Clifford Odets' *Clash by Night* (1941), Aronson provided the odd angles and perspectives characteristic of his work during the period. Tallulah Bankhead, who starred in the play, jokingly referred to the sightlines of the sets—of a Coney Island dance-hall veranda (17) and a projection booth, (18) among others—as "un-American."

19   Aronson's fascination with the circus surfaced in this design for *Miss Underground* (1943), a show intended for the Cristianis, fabled circus performers. The project, which also involved the composer Vernon Duke, the lyricist Lorenz Hart, and the choreographer George Balanchine, was never produced.

20   Jerome Robbins' ballet *Ballade* for New York City Ballet (1952).

21   Arthur Miller's *A View from the Bridge* (1955).

22   The landmark set for Archibald MacLeish's *J.B.*, directed by Elia Kazan (1958).

23

24

23 A commercial breakthrough: Tevye's house, the basic set for *Fiddler on the Roof*, staged by Jerome Robbins (1964).

24 The Prince era begins: *Cabaret* (1966).

25   A sketch for *Company* (1970).

26   The model for the gutted theatre of *Follies* (1971).

27   Commodore Perry's ship arrives in Japan in the model for *Pacific Overtures*, Aronson's last Broadway production (1976).

their creative partnership as late as *The Country Girl* in 1950, Aronson wrote to Odets in the late 1940s, "Of all the friends I ever had, my friendship with you is most uneven." Some of that unevenness was prompted by Odets' solicitation of Aronson's opinion of the playwright's own venture into the visual arts, as a painter. Never one to suppress his true feelings for tact's sake, Aronson upset Odets by writing to him that "it is absolutely impossible to look at your pictures without being conscious that this is the work of a very famous playwright. . . . They have a quality of very personal valentines—or complicated and expert doodles. . . . I am convinced that this is a phase of your activities which five years from now you will consider only as an interesting experiment which you just had to go through." The letter ended with Aronson's admonition that Odets, then on a writing tailspin, "sit down and write."

As Aronson's connection with the Group led to his long-term associations with Clurman, Kazan, and Odets, so his parallel work in the commercial theatre with Abbott during the mid-1930s accounted for much of the rest of his subsequent career. Aronson never did another Abbott show after the Depression, but he did much of his most important work for Abbott protégés. They included Garson Kanin, who was Abbott's stage manager for *Three Men on a Horse* and later the director of Aronson-designed plays, most notably *The Diary of Anne Frank* (1955); Jerome Robbins, who choreographed several postwar Abbott musicals and enlisted Aronson as the designer for *Fiddler on the Roof*, which turned out to be the last and most successful Robbins musical; and Harold Prince, who co-produced many Abbott musicals in the 1950s, later produced *Fiddler*, and then used Aronson as the designer on the musicals he directed himself, from *Cabaret* (1966) through Aronson's final Broadway show, *Pacific Overtures* (1976).

Once Aronson was aboard what he called "the Broadway merry-go-round," he worked with other important directors and choreographers as well—including Max Reinhardt (*The Merchant of Yonkers*, 1938), George Balanchine (*Cabin in the Sky*, 1940), and Peter Hall (*The Rope Dancers*, 1957; the Stratford-on-Avon *Coriolanus* of 1959). But even though the decade of the thirties ended with Aronson doing one of his most influential sets, for Clurman's Group Theatre production of Irwin Shaw's *The Gentle People* (1939), his career was in limbo during much of the forties and fifties. Many of Kazan's most important productions, including *A Streetcar Named Desire* and *Death of a Salesman*, went to Jo Mielziner, the Robert Edmond Jones successor who was the most highly regarded and prolific designer of the era.

Aronson increasingly was thought of as a turgid, Old World designer. He designed many heavy, realistic sets that were far removed from his own ambitions as an artist. He did not design conventional box sets, however: his characteristic sets of this time were oddly angled and contained partial obstructions, prompting Tallulah Bankhead, who inhabited some of them (in *Clash by Night*, 1941), to call Aronson's sightlines "un-American." More than a few of these plays took place in bars, kitchens, and hotel rooms; productions requiring delicacy, as well as musicals, went to Mielziner and to another prominent postwar designer, Oliver Smith. An admirer and casual acquaintance of Aronson's, Smith would run into his colleague in the theatre district and find him disconsolate over his inability to snare any of the big musicals. "Boris was a gigantic talent who was really poor economically," Smith remembered. "He had a sour view of the theatre because he was not really appreciated."

The discrepancy between Aronson's style and the then-reigning style of advanced American set design was formulated by Harold Clurman years later in an essay comparing Aronson's work with the legendary and, for its time, innovative output of Jones (who happened to be the American designer Aronson most admired). Clurman wrote that Jones' artistry was distinguished by "its ineffable purity, its pristine, fragrant asceticism, its traditional sense of balance, tact and lack of stress—all reminiscent of an earlier day in our history." Aronson's touch, by contrast, was "turbulently dramatic, [setting] before us the clash of elements in contemporary society, both the comedy and the excitement of such contrasts." Others, too, would later divide American theatrical design according to polarities loosely represented by Jones and Aronson. Oliver Smith, who first saw Aronson's work as a college student in the 1930s, found that "the strong, expressionistic composition and forced perspective made you sit up and take notice" in a way far removed from "the polite forms that Jones preferred and Mielziner emulated." To Robert Mitchell, a designer who worked as an assistant to both Aronson and Mielziner in the sixties and seventies, "Jones and Mielziner emphasized light and shade [while] Aronson works with the figure and the field, with foreground and background."

Aronson felt, not without reason, that he was artistically out of sync with the Broadway theatre of this time. "Life is more exciting than our theatre," he said. "It should be the other way around." He loved to tell the story, perhaps apocryphal, of a leading Jewish actor from Russia who visited New York: "He had a limited knowledge of English, and the first play he saw was *Life with Father*. Then he saw many other plays on Broadway. I met him and was very eager to know of his reaction to the Broadway theatre at that time. His answer was that he thought he was constantly seeing *Life with Father.* Every production was *Life with Father,* or mother—or the uncles. The actor thought, because he did not understand the language too well, that every play was a continuous variation on *Life with Father.*" To Aronson, the theatre had become standardized. "There was a time when the living room was characteristic for dramatic happenings; the great part of life was spent there. Today, it's obvious, if you trace your activities over one day, that the living room plays a small part. The industrialization of modern living has changed the content of life and the physical environment. But in the theatre we still find ourselves in the same living room. The stage set of the present-day drama is symmetrical, when our everyday existence is asymmetrical."

Aronson was more interested in epic plays requiring scenery that was not only asymmetrical but full of obstacles, requiring the audience to look in several directions at once. He felt that living-room plays, "plays about relatives," were the province of radio and television—that the theatre should do something "much bigger." While he waited for those epic plays to arrive, he had many jobs, but he didn't have the multiple, concurrent assignments that allowed then-underpaid designers to flourish financially. In 1945, he told an interviewer that he considered himself—or any designer—lucky to earn "a net of $2500 a year."

"I've done so many kitchens, I don't know how to do them anymore unless it's James Joyce's kitchen," Aronson said, in describing his many routine assignments of the period. Even so, he took pride in turning down some jobs: "When you are not well-to-do, when you really have to make a living in order to exist, your greatest achievement is the smash-hit shows you refuse to do." One example was *A Majority of One,* a Gertrude Berg "relative play" of the 1950s in which, in Aronson's dismissive view, "the whole Jewish problem is solved because she could make gefilte fish for a Japanese fellow."

Ming Cho Lee, later a prominent designer, apprenticed with Aronson in 1959–60 during "his low period—not creatively, but in terms of success, where he stood among the theatre community." According to Lee, Aronson's obsessiveness and iconoclastic manner of designing "were so far ahead of what other people were doing that they didn't know what he was doing. What was expected of a designer on Broadway at that time—the method of designing—was all very clear. Indeed, there was something a little bit deadly about the clear-cut steps

involved. First you did a sketch, then a floor plan, then you have a set and are out of town. Boris didn't work by this well-defined routine. While other designers made designing for the theatre like being in a department store, Boris would say forget all those things—just go with it. He had a very personal reaction to a play; he would try experimental things that, if you're being strictly efficient, did not seem to have anything to do with the next step of building a set. He was not well organized. Work piled up; it created a certain tension in the studio. Every morning, he'd have a new thing coming out of his pocket. My best introduction to working for him was one morning when he insisted we go the Jewish Museum, by bus in pouring rain, to see all the Torahs. He thought the menorahs there were like Giacometti sculptures, and soon he was creating a similar look by melting down crayons and letting them run—I had never thought of that."

"At the end of the day," said J. J. Moore, an Aronson assistant in the 1970s who later became a film production designer, "we'd always feel we'd done a lot of work—little knowing that when we came in the next morning it would all be thrown out, that something had happened overnight after we left when all those great things we thought we had done had suddenly dissolved. You'd see all your dreams slide down the drain, and then start all over again. It was a marvelous and exasperating process. The end result was the important thing. You found out how delicate the creative process is, and the agonies you have to go through, because there's no easy way of doing it. You were forced to use yourself in a way that you didn't expect you could. You were made to examine every little intricate part of a project, to the point that you got the best out of it that you could ever get out of it. You really exhausted all the possibilities. You were always challenged to sweat a problem out, for a very good solution might not be the best solution. At the end, you really felt you had been a contributor. And with each new show you felt you were starting from square one."

"In the late fifties," said Lee, "all-white beaverboard models of sets were in vogue—as if to prove that designing for the theatre is not really playing doll's house. With Boris, I realized how incomplete an experience that really is; it presupposes a designer knows what he really wants. Working with Boris, you never knew what you wanted until you saw it—and without painting it, how do you know? So he painted his set models, which were built out of gray shirt cardboard. But first he'd do many rough expressive sketches that would lead to the model. Often, at that time, directors would commit themselves to a set sketch without bothering with a model, if the sketch was beautiful. We didn't do such 'presentations'—Boris wouldn't say that word; his sets were always 'in work.' Even when the set was in the shop [being built], he was always there, working. He'd do the gorgeous sketch afterwards for exhibition.

"With Boris' sets, there was a person behind it that other sets didn't have—a personal commitment. He did have a characteristic [artistic] handwriting—everything he did had a Boris Aronson integrity. That was truly shocking to me. Without Boris, I don't think I would have a sense about the range and possibility of theatre expression. I learned that, in theatrical collaboration, a director must talk emotionally about the work—not the design of it—and *that* is what you reflect in your design."

Robert Mitchell, who worked simultaneously for Aronson and Jo Mielziner, was startled by the differing approaches followed by the two major designers: "Mielziner was well organized, like a bank. He tended to suppress contradictions in design, while Boris reveled in them. Mielziner was the son of a painter [Leo Mielziner] and felt a connection with the brush; he did beautifully painted renderings of his sets, not models. The brushes were nicely organized in jars, their points closed. Boris stuck his brushes in jars with glue in the bottom; you couldn't find one completely perfect brush in the house. He was frightened of facility, hated anything to be too easy. Where Jo would do a perfect English watercolor, Boris took pleasure in seeing what you could do with an old brush.

"Jo's renderings were illustrations of what sets would look like on stage; they emphasized lighting, and you knew it was a theatre experience. Boris' sketches were less involved—they expressed a reaction, required an interpretation, and you couldn't necessarily see the proscenium; his sketches were closer to painting, the immediate expression of experience. Jo's renderings were always in scale, worked out with a ruler. Boris had no particular respect for rulers in the early design stages; only later would he be concerned whether things fit. But Boris was fascinated with the psychology of scale. He felt that the sense of scale in the theatre can be totally perverted by one prop or one real thing. He felt that psychology had nothing to do with rulers. Somehow, one actor placed on a stage can dominate a whole set or fade into the woodwork.

"Jo said, of all the shows he did, he only enjoyed ten percent of them—and he took on everything. Boris only took on projects that fascinated him—he was an enthusiast. To Boris, life and theatre were inseparable; Boris made me look at the theatre as total experience, not as an expression of the literate intelligence. You always had the feeling that a conversation with him was never at an end—he could never sum up anything in beautiful, well-chosen phrases. Life was an endless dialogue—he was eternally talking about something. This was not the American way—to talk and talk until there was nothing more to talk about and then start designing. When I was at Nolan Studios [a scenery-building shop], they added ten percent to the set budget for Boris' experimentation. He'd bring ten different sketches and samples there and wanted them to use a little bit from each one."

Mitchell and J. J. Moore had to deal with the practical considerations—the hashing out of inches and feet—that Aronson tended to ignore along the way. No matter what size the set was, according to Moore, "it was always bigger than the theatre. At Feller's [another scenery shop], we used to threaten to draw all the drawings of the theatres a foot smaller all the way around before we ever allowed Boris to have a set of the drawings." Aronson was demanding of the shop's painters as well. "He wanted the artist to perfect a sketch," said Matthieu Slachmuylder, a studio "chargeman" who supervised and assigned scenic painters. "To Aronson, nothing was unimportant. No matter how simple he told us a show was going to be, we knew it was going to be difficult. After a show was over, we were very tired of him, but the results were always excellent. He would always fight for his show in the shop." John Keck, another scenic painter, remembered that "when you were painting for Boris, you had to suffer a little bit and scrape around with the colors and do things that Boris did when he was doing the sketch."

The directors and playwrights associated with Aronson saw him in much the way his studio associates did. To Kazan, Aronson was "the most original guy I ever met [in an] increasingly homogenized culture. He never said what I thought he was going to say. He was the king of the unexpected. Contradictions did not bewilder him; he embraced them." The director found that he turned to Mielziner to solve "the complexity of mechanical problems," to Aronson for "subtle or deep mood." And he found, too, that endless dialogue was a major aspect of his collaborations with Aronson. "Other designers would ask me where to put the chairs in the set. Boris could talk my language—I didn't have to talk specifically, but spontaneously. Once, we crossed the continent to Hollywood by car, and he talked three thousand miles straight."

28   Aronson in Russia, c. 1917.

29   Aronson, lower left, at an artists' party, Berlin, 1923.

30   Aronson in America, mid-1920s. His two
published books are proudly displayed on his desk.

Arthur Miller felt that "every play was a new adventure for Boris. He had no ready solutions. He floundered for months, and needed guidance from the director and author to know where he was. But once he knew! He'd come up with the strongest angles. Most other set designers want the work done for them." Miller also felt that Aronson was a natural match for Harold Clurman, whose approach to direction paralleled Aronson's abstract, indirect approach to design. "Clurman could tell color, but not structure—either in a script or a set." One of the last plays that Miller and Aronson did together, *The Price* (1968), contained a character, an elderly Jewish furniture dealer, whose discursive philosophical diction was modeled on Aronson's.

Besides employing Aronson regularly, Clurman also wrote about him often in his drama criticism. In one such appreciation, written just before Aronson's career reached its celebrated final stage, Clurman expressed dismay that his friend—"who more unequivocally deserves the title of master visual artist of the stage [than any designer] since [Robert Edmond] Jones"—should have "received scant attention except from fellow craftsmen in the theatre." He continued: "One reason for the comparative public neglect of Aronson's work may be ascribed to the fact that it has no immediately identifiable mechanical or aesthetic trademark. Most designers' appeal lies in their settings' prettiness: a candy box or calendar picture sweetness. They remind one of travel ads intended to cajole us with the prospect of a dreamy trip. Aronson's sets rarely reach for glamour. They are not fashionable." Like Aronson, Clurman was suspicious of sets that are greeted by audience applause when the curtain rises: "The applause is meaningless. One cannot determine the value of a set at first glance. One must judge it in the light of the action which it houses." To Clurman, Aronson was not a mere decorator, making "pleasing arrangements of fabrics, furniture and carpentry," but an artist "who adds to a play's value as a form of expression."

The end of Aronson's career drought—and the beginning of his belated rise to the height of fashionability—began with *Fiddler on the Roof* in 1964. Whatever its other merits, *Fiddler* was also, in Broadway terms, the most potent type of career boost any theatre artist could receive—a musical destined to have one of the longest runs in the history of the American theatre. Aronson had been involved with only one previous successful musical—*Cabin in the Sky*, a quarter-century earlier—and had never been connected with any production remotely as commercially successful. But if *Fiddler* increased the demand for his services, the show was a watershed in his career mostly because it marked the beginning of his association with Harold Prince, *Fiddler*'s producer. Although Prince had not originally endorsed the decision of director-choreographer Jerome Robbins that Aronson should design *Fiddler*, he soon became an Aronson convert. Prince then hired Aronson to design a succession of musicals that he directed himself, four of which were collaborations with the fast-maturing composer-lyricist Stephen Sondheim.

Prince thought that Aronson's "strength was also his weakness—that crazy tenacity and impatience with compromise and second-rateness. That was the big difference between Boris and me. He was good for me, and I was good for him. He would not practically compromise if left to his own devices, and I would. Therefore, with me, he did more shows than he'd have done if the decision had just been his. At the same time, he could poison me—he would make me no longer accept [the production compromises] that I'd planned to accept. He could make me pick the scab off when I'd been quite content to leave it there and go on with life."

With Prince, Aronson was not only, at last, a complete partner in the creation of a show; he was also, most of the time, given the license to execute in full the ideas that he had first developed in Moscow over four decades earlier. As in the Meyerhold-Tairov theatre, scenery would be moved in view of the audience, by actors and stagehands; the set became a total environment for a show—a "limbo" area—that would contain, in full view, all the elements that might come together to define a musical's multiplicity of locales.

The process of creating such sets was complex—in Prince's view, "exciting and occasionally exasperating." As was also the case in the director's collaboration with Sondheim, the process would begin with endless talk—as much as two years' worth, after the idea for a musical had been hatched. Prince found that he was encouraged by Aronson not to edit his thoughts—to "say damn foolish things," to "free-associate." Often a "two- or three-word phrase could trigger something useful in the end." Aronson would deal "with all the senses before dealing with sight—sound, smell, feel." The shows were designed by finding their "rhythm" and "motor": the agitated and neurotic pace of *Company*, the Eastern slowness of *Pacific Overtures*.

In an essay written for a catalogue accompanying a posthumous exhibit of Aronson's designs at the Library of the Performing Arts at Lincoln Center in 1981, Prince explained further: "[We talked about] characters, period, philosophy, the play in relation to its times, to these times. How were the politics of the time reflected in art? The mores? What changes did the time reflect of earlier times and how were they to influence the future? The research is endless. The usual photographs, obscure treatises, and conversations with experts, with fanatics. Boris is comfortable with fanatics. He is one. He is also domineering. And selfish. Impatient. Even monomaniacal. And . . . persistently entertaining. . . . It is likely no author has engaged my mind, lit a fuse which ignites my imagination, tempted me to inch ahead more than Boris.

"Now, what exactly is the process once the *talking* is over? First having drained you, he leaves you exhausted wondering how in hell you'll ever get all that subtext onto the stage. (You don't; you needn't —but you don't entirely accept that *yet*, and later what confidence that has given you. Nothing shakes the foundations you've built under the work. I think this must be somewhat like Stanislavski's eight-month rehearsals. I couldn't begin to fill eight months with rehearsals, but the eight months Boris and the other authors and I have put in leave us with the same knowledge, security, that must have underpinned those Moscow productions.)

"The process? Leaving you drained, he begins to design, in seclusion. You do not hear from him for weeks, months. No tempting choices of concepts, no presentations of front curtains, no swatches of color. No rudimentary scheme from which the production could evolve—*if* you approved. No. When he is ready, he shows you the entire production and it works. It contains its motor, a rhythm peculiar to *that* play that will help the staging to be inevitable; consistent, the work of collaborators. Added to that, each design has a surprise. I have watched Boris withhold his surprise until the end. As if to say, we did all of this together, but this next . . . this is all mine." These "surprises" were among Aronson's proudest and most acclaimed achievements, often encapsulating the entire thrust or mood of a production: a trapezoid-shaped mirror that reflected the audience in *Cabaret*; concealed elevators in the Manhattanscape of *Company*; a flowery "fan" that dropped to transform a gutted theatre into a vaudeville palace in *Follies.*

Aronson left his design ideas so open-ended that Prince would go to rehearsal not knowing where every scene could be done within the set; he was satisfied as long as Aronson assured him that everything in the script could be staged within the set. When the rehearsals arrived, Aronson attended them with an alacrity that Prince had never previously encountered from a designer.

During final rehearsals out of town, Aronson sat most often with the lighting designer or stood in the back and kibitzed with the show's other creators. As Stephen Sondheim described it, "The tone of the conversation was that of the two smartest kids in class. Here was a man who is a course in the history of twentieth-century theatre, and we were making sly remarks about everything in the show, just this side of bitchiness, and then following it up with intellectual stuff about art and theatre, the philosophy of life." Sondheim's involvement in the design of his musicals was minimal, but he was struck by Aronson's insistence on listening to the songs he had written for design clues: "I was always surprised that he would get so much from music, because it's such an abstract art, but he claimed it helped a lot. He was not someone who jumped up and down when you played him something, but he was always supportive. Boris, being a creative artist, understood what being a creative artist means."

Michael Bennett, the director and choreographer who collaborated with Prince on the staging of *Company* and *Follies*, stood in the back of the house with Aronson, discussing every aspect of the production in progress. Bennett was astonished that Aronson "didn't do three projects at once," as many designers did, but instead "watched every line change every night." Bennett soon broke out on his own as a director-choreographer, going from *Follies* to *A Chorus Line*, and he credits his introduction to the notion of forming fully collaborative design teams to the example, new to him, set by Aronson. Bennett had never before seen a designer who was "a real collaborator," who talked about a show's "essences" instead of about "scenery, technical stuff and execution." The veteran lighting designer Tharon Musser— who first worked with Aronson in the 1950s, later worked on all the Prince-Sondheim-Aronson musicals beginning with *Follies*, and has since been an integral contributor to the innovative production designs of Bennett's musicals—felt that she learned more from Aronson than from any other set designer in her long career: "His design concepts were so strong that if someone went against them, the show would be ruined."

As a result of the critical and commercial success that generally attended the Prince musicals, Aronson at last received full Broadway lionization. He won Tony Awards for most of these shows, was a frequent interview subject in newspapers and magazines, and was offered many more projects than he could or wanted to design. Yet the recognition, if anything, only solidified his cynicism about the commercial theatre—and his disappointment with the American theatre in general.

31

31 Arthur Miller's *A Memory of Two Mondays* (1955).
Aronson instructs a painter at a scenic studio while
his five-year-old son Marc watches.

32 Aronson and Lisa Jalowetz at work in 1945, the
year of their marriage. They worked together
beginning in 1943.

33   Aronson, right, confers with the director, Harold Prince, at the Colonial Theatre in Boston during the technical run-through of the musical *Follies* in 1971.

34   At a lighting rehearsal for *A Gift of Time* (1962) at the Ethel Barrymore Theatre, New York. Garson Kanin, the director, leans forward in front of the stage; Aronson confers with the lighting designer, Jean Rosenthal, mid-auditorium.

"The term 'theatre designer' never described him," said Robert Mitchell. "He was a philosopher and a generalist. He was cosmopolitan. Though assimilated and highly sophisticated about what it meant to live in America, he never left Russia in a sense. He was rooted here and not rooted here—a series of contradictions. He loved to upset people by not conforming.

"He was always running counter to the American way of doing theatre—especially show business, where everyone is supposed to be a specialist. He spent his whole life trying to define concepts about how to do theatre. When he was offered one big musical, which he declined, a producer was offended that Boris had some ideas about the material itself."

Both in public and in private, Aronson was unfailingly candid about his views of the theatre world around him. Always known as a curmudgeon—Sondheim found him the embodiment of "that old joke about Russian gloom"—he was an intimidatingly crusty presence; a journalist once wrote that "above his high forehead a frizzy shock of hair always seems pulled upward by some electromagnetic force." Aronson thought nothing of snubbing illustrious Broadway producers whom he regarded as schlockmeisters; he openly referred to the producers of a revival of one of his musicals as "fascists." He marveled publicly that Broadway's first new theatre in decades, the Uris (now the Gershwin), could look "like a department store, while Bloomingdale's looks like theatre."

To Oliver Smith, Aronson was "a man of incredible complexities . . . very dour, with a wicked sense of humor and a very Oriental quality. . . . He was a fighter. Nothing could terrify him. He wouldn't work on a show if he disliked the director; he was an example of a designer who held his directors captive. The minute you looked at an Aronson set, you could see that it was very opinionated. He did what he wanted to do—it was very rare that he made concessions that deviated from his philosophical approach to the material. He was not beloved by the theatrical establishment; they were frightened of him. They thought of him not as an artist, but as being arty. That was their stupidity. Most producers are frightened by really powerful artists because they think they are uncontrollable—which they are."

In interviews late in his life, Aronson confessed to having the "lowest possible opinion of Broadway audiences." He told Garson Kanin, "I used to think if you could assassinate [the producers] Billy Rose or Kermit Bloomgarden, it would help [cure the ills of the Broadway theatre]. Now I see there are a thousand people you would have to

do it to." On another occasion, he remarked that "the Broadway theatre is living on a pension," its potential vitality vitiated by "the cult of the precious, the malignant influence of the dealer, the real-estate operator and merchandising practices." Yet Aronson never quite abandoned all hope. "The very impermanence of theatre makes for its vitality," he often said. "Despite everything, Broadway remains vital —it lacks only continuity because it is constantly awaiting a fresh spark to set it off again."

In his harsher statements, Aronson was saying what any perceptive critic of the American theatre knew: that there were few new plays in the commercial theatre expressing the dynamic society of their time. It was a sharp contrast to the avant-garde theatre Aronson saw in Russia and in the adventurous Yiddish theatre of his early days in New York. Even at his most successful on Broadway, he clung to the conviction that the theatre had only deteriorated in the half-century since his apprenticeship. Though he worked in the Bronx "under impossible conditions, as far as money and craftsmanship were concerned," he fondly remembered that those conditions allowed experimentation. "When I came here in 1923, I worked in the Bronx at 180th Street and did my most experimental work—which I haven't topped yet," he said. "It should, of course, be the other way around— that you do your finest work when you mature, that excitement and discovery grows and grows—but that is not so in the theatre of today. I feel we live in a time of tremendous happenings. Yet our theatre doesn't in any way represent twentieth-century man the way Chekhov represented his time.

"There's enough going on to write about; it's just a matter of seeing it. I flew to Europe and there was some difficulty on the plane; they had to stop in Ireland, and I looked at the pilot as a great man who had the destiny of all those people in his hands. When we stopped in Ireland, he went to some eating place there, and I was watching him. I said to myself, 'What is this man going to say, or ask for?' And he got a sandwich, and he wanted some mustard, and I said to myself, 'Here's this great man, and it winds up that all he wants is a little mustard.' That's the dilemma of our time, the combination of these two elements—the human element of the man wanting something very simple like mustard and yet, still, here he is, flying God-like all over the world, with the destiny of hundreds of people in his hands. And the trouble with a lot of our playwrights is that they only write about the mustard. I think it's a great time—a Renaissance—but I don't see it reflected in our theatre."

He continued to find solace and rejuvenation in his adjunct career as a painter: "The painting feeds me as a designer, not the other way around," he explained. In Robert Mitchell's observation, Aronson's painting experiments paralleled his scenic work—from his Cubist exploration of figure-field relationships (in the 1930s) to his abstractions and experiments with light diffraction (the 1940s) to the attempts to combine sculpture and painting (the 1950s). One was "always aware of the painterliness of Aronson sets," said Oliver Smith. "While most designers do pastiches, he was an original painter. . . . He was one of the first to encourage white lighting in the theatre, anticipating contemporary lighting, because he didn't want colored lights superimposed on his palette." The scenic painter John Keck recalled that in the 1950s "people would say that Boris's colors were all gray and brown, but they weren't. If it was gray, it was a little green and a little orange on top of that, a little purple scrubbed around that. This 'underpainting' was innovative for the time."

During his later years, Aronson also designed Holy Arks for synagogues—in Washington, D.C., and Sands Point, Long Island—even though he had not been in a synagogue in decades; he wanted "to do something they couldn't tear down afterward." Though not in good health, he agreed to lecture to Ming Cho Lee's design students at the Yale School of Drama after *A Little Night Music* had opened in 1973. Fearful that his talk would not go over with the young students, he asked Lee to visit him to hear a dry run of the lecture—which, in characteristically obsessive fashion, lasted five and a half hours. At the end of the visit, Lee was "exhausted but so excited" that he went home and, "high and unable to sleep," worked until two in the morning. Aronson was so exhausted by his rehearsal that he had to postpone the Yale visit until a year later—when, in Lee's words, he was "a great hit."

For all Aronson's expressions of disgruntlement, he looked back on his career with pride. "Variety has marked my career," he said. "The very obstacles of the Broadway situation contribute to innovation—if one successfully resists the temptation to repeat oneself, to accept the formula way out. When I solve a [design] problem, my individual imprint is part of the solution. But once I have succeeded with it, I don't make a formula out of the solution. This is what I call 'rejuvenation,' and it applies to each assignment. You have to be reborn each time. The minute you have a feeling you know how to do it, you should stop right there." But Aronson never had that feeling.

Kazan, for one, had always discounted Aronson's pessimism.

"Like Miller," he said, "Boris would always write his own notices before they came out. He was crazy for his place in the sun. And, in the end, he left a mark—he did fulfill himself." Robert Mitchell remarked that "Boris lived just long enough to see America turn into one of his paintings—a kind of celebration of disjunction somehow unified in the ambiguous space of collage."

Aronson's last design was for Mikhail Baryshnikov's new version of *The Nutcracker* for American Ballet Theatre in 1976. In an interview at the time, he said, "There is only one thrill which is irreplaceable. And that's when I see my design for the first time [on stage] and it works. Everything, which up to this point was instinctive, works when the actors look like they were born on the stage. Until that moment, I can't guarantee that it will. But when it does—that feeling is worth a million to me. Because I had a dream—as the famous man said—and the dream came true."

35 An assemblage—characteristically combining paint, plastics, and other collage elements—made by Aronson in the last year of his life, 1979.

YIDDISH THEATRE

There is, in actuality, no such thing as a stage designer. Anyone who successfully designs for the theatre is also a painter, sculptor, architect, or engineer. In rare instances, he is all of these. It is simply not possible to be only a scenic designer. All of an artist's sensibilities and talents come into play in whatever he undertakes. Basically, you have a certain fundamental thing which makes you an artist. And then you apply it. You can learn the crafts of the theatre, but don't bother studying theatre design in a school. The best way is to work, to get a job in the field. The rest is unknown. Art is a mystery, the glory of man. It cannot be contained in a how-to manual.

Although the creative and career dividends ultimately proved immense, Aronson originally went to work for the Yiddish theatre out of strict necessity: "It wasn't a matter of choosing—just a matter of reality, because when I arrived in New York I did not speak one word of English. On the boat [to America], I listened to people talking, and I was very conscious of the word 'please,' and I heard people repeat it very often. I asked someone what does 'please' mean and was told that it meant the same as *pajolista* in Russian or *bitte* in German. 'Please' sounded to me like something very solid and seemed to have nothing to do with politeness. It was too abrupt and harsh; I could not associate the word with the same meaning in the other languages I knew. I had entered a world with a language I knew I would never master. So, I naturally wound up in the Yiddish theatre.

"Out of seventeen Yiddish theatres in New York, I ended up in a tiny theatre in the Bronx, Unser [Our] Theatre. It was originated by the Society for the Promotion of Jewish Dramatic Literature. The advanced Jewish writers—like David Pinski, Perez Hirshbein, S. Ansky —were associated with this institution; my first play there was Ansky's *Day and Night*. No one [at Unser Theatre] knew for sure if

they would be paid or not, but they had an adventurous spirit and were concerned with the experimental. I happened to arrive at the right time—they were willing to do unusual things. But, like the Moscow avant-garde theatres of Tairov and Meyerhold, Unser Theatre was not representative of the average Yiddish theatre.

"The typical Yiddish theatre had two formulas—one for drama, one for musicals. Both were meant to satisfy the customers. A 'drama' went like this: In Act I, Jennie Goldstein (who is fifty years old if she is a day, and built heavy) appears as a sixteen-year-old girl. She is naïve and innocent. In Act II, she meets a gangster, although naturally she never suspects he is a gangster. It is love at first sight. By Act III, she has 'a fruit under her heart,' which means she is pregnant. In the fourth act, she has aged tremendously—she looks eighty—and toils the streets, white-haired, forgotten, bewildered, lost. Then, one day, she accidentally on purpose bumps into a stranger who turns out to be, of all people, her son! By the fifth act, she is younger, completely rejuvenated, with a husband and a house on Riverside Drive, and is going to be happy ever after.

"The musicals were partly tragic, partly comic. A 'musical' began

1, 2   Aronson's design of a mural for the auditorium of the experimental Yiddish Unser Theatre in the Bronx (1), and a photograph of a detail of the mural as realized in the playhouse (2).

OPPOSITE

3, 4, 5   Aronson's first American designs, introducing Constructivism to unsuspecting Yiddish audiences, for Unser Theatre's production of Ansky's *Day and Night* (1924).

in the Old Country, in a Russian village (or Polish, or Romanian, or wherever it begins), with a Jewish family. That's the first half. In the second, the family arrives in the *New* Country. Everything changes; they become prosperous. No matter what musical you saw, it was always the same thing. My most vivid recollection of the Jewish musicals is of the chorus of 'boys' and 'girls'—a more grotesque collection of oddly formed figures has yet to be found. The composite age of the ensemble must have been somewhere between two thousand and three thousand years. Never did such haphazardly applied baby-face makeup on old, wrinkled features produce a more permanent catastrophe. The youngest girl was between seventy and eighty years, and Daumier could not create anything more remarkable, more grotesque. The boys kept a respectful distance from the girls; and the girls looked festive, as though they had just eaten. Regardless of which musical they appeared in, the boys had two parts to play: In the first act, they were chimney sweeps in a village—droll-faced, with sackcloth and ashes, with black high hats for some mysterious reason, sooty faces, and big brooms in their hands. They looked like commedia dell'arte witches with goose pimples. In the second act, they became guests on Riverside Drive, ready for a hearty repast."

What fascinated Aronson about the Yiddish theatre was the mixture of charlatanism and glamour. He used to join the actors when they congregated at their famous Lower East Side hangout, the Café Royale, to gossip and tell stories: "There was one tale about a minor writer who specialized in unpopular, artistic plays. One day he said, 'Enough is enough. I'm going to write commercial stuff and make some real money instead of doing this arty business. This time, no fine points of writing, no characters, no dialect. No art—just money.' He worked on it for some time, and when he had finished, he read it through. 'So,' he said, 'I've failed again. It is a work of art.' " In 1942, Aronson joined Elia Kazan and the writer Hy Kraft to re-create the by then vanished Café Royale in the fictionalized form of the Broadway comedy *Café Crown*.

While still uptown at Unser Theatre, Aronson designed nonformula plays, largely of an allegorical and mystical bent. "My work with the Yiddish theatre was a residue of my Russian experience," he explained. He also painted an elaborate mural, with eighteen figures, for the auditorium. Then Unser Theatre folded—"like many a noble experiment before and since"—and was taken over by Rudolph Schildkraut, who had come to the United States from Germany, where he had been a reigning stage star. Schildkraut, too, employed Aronson, most notably for *The Bronx Express* (1925).

Not long after that, Aronson found his way to "the Mecca of the Yiddish stage"—Maurice Schwartz's Yiddish Art Theatre on Second Avenue. "Schwartz was extremely ambitious," as Aronson later remembered. "He presented plays by Gorky and Andreyev and the most famous European playwrights, often personally translating them into Yiddish. As a performer, he could play tricky and conniving characters excellently, with a certain kind of humorous quality mixed in, working in nuances and double meanings. But, like all people who are trying to work against what comes naturally, his ambition was always to play big parts: historical giants, high-society people, kings, and dukes. The height of aristocracy as he conceived it was a regal costume with a silk handkerchief tucked in his sleeve. He was so hammy when he did this type of part it was absolutely unbelievable. It was just impossible to watch him. His speech would change as though he had wet cotton in his mouth.

"When he opened his new theatre on Second Avenue at 12th Street, it was called a million-dollar operation. It was ornamented with a Star of David on the ceiling which took an entire congregation of Italian workers months to plaster. It was elaborate and aroused great amounts of talk and speculation. But when the building was completed, the discovery was made that the star was visible mainly to the actors and stagehands."

THE BRONX EXPRESS   (1925)

Ossip Dymov's comedy was Aronson's first production for Rudolph Schildkraut, after Unser Theatre folded, and his first Jewish-American play. "Schildkraut starred as a tired buttonmaker who goes home after working all day and falls asleep in the subway. He dreams he visits the

6   Heaven and hell were frequent settings for the allegorical plays Aronson designed in the Yiddish theatre. This design, "a concert hall in the skies of hell," was for *Angels on Earth*, as produced by Maurice Schwartz at the Yiddish Art Theatre in 1929.

7, 8, 9, 10   David Pinski's four-act tragicomedy *The
Final Balance* (1925) was Aronson's second production
for Unser Theatre. The first three sets—for Acts I,
II, and III—all represent the same room in a flour
merchant's home. As the merchant prospers, his home
grows more pretentious—with arches added for
Act II and modern furniture added for Act III. The set
for Act IV, representing a street in the city, contains,
at top, a pulsating electric sign with a Stuart Davis–
like abstraction of an advertising logo (10).

places [evoked by the products] on the subway car's advertising cards. The play follows him through his dreams: in Florida at the home of Pluto Water, at the apartment of Murad Cigarettes, and so forth. He meets all these people, and the nature of the dream made it possible to do very stylized things in the settings. My idea was that when somebody falls asleep there is always a chance to awaken temporarily, and what happens is that when one awakens, one finds oneself in the same locale where one started to dream. So I had the subway disappear when the buttonmaker is dreaming, but when he finds himself in the Pluto home in Florida, the ceiling of the subway is still there. In each set, I left the hanging straps, so that in the middle of a dream the hero might wake up and grab one—like an aside. But also, while he is in any of those fantasy places, as in Florida, he could put his foot outside of the proscenium and shiver and say, 'Oh, cold,' as if it were the water.

"When I presented Schildkraut with a sketch of his costume as the buttonmaker, he looked at it, admired it greatly, and said that he would take it home, frame it, and put it on his mantelpiece—but that he could never wear it. The costume was too complete as an indication of the character, leaving him nothing to do but model it back and front. 'I must create the character myself,' said Schildkraut, who never wore stage makeup. This was my first lesson in how the designer must consider the actor. When I saw him perform, I could see how right he was—a great actor needs very little help from the outside."

A critic for the *Sun* said that in *The Bronx Express* Aronson gave his settings "a symbolism so patent to even a Bronx audience that no stagehand was required to come out and explain that the next three acts were only a dream. The dream was evident in every scene—the subway ceiling, its flickering lights, its roar were constantly brought forth, whether the scene was in the Palace of Mr. Pluto Water or on the Boardwalk of Atlantic City or in his own Bronx flat. The old buttonmaker even used the subway *Sun*, in the dream that is, as a towel to wipe his hands before the evening meal."

But the Yiddish press was troubled by Aronson's work and by his program credit as co-director of the production. "He's too aggressive, he meddles too much in the directorial aspect, his scenery 'directs' the actors," wrote one critic, who was seconded by, among others, the influential writer Abraham Cahan. It was the first time scenery had so influenced a Yiddish-theatre production, and Aronson was upbraided for overstepping the bounds of the scenic artist and for his "flaming creative temperament."

OPPOSITE

11, 12 *The Bronx Express* (1925): The subway, with its advertising cards, that carries the tired buttonmaker home from work (11). Costumed by Aronson for a dream sequence in which the people in the subway's advertisements come to life. The "Uptown/Downtown" sign preserves a touch of the subway in the Bronx apartment setting (12).

13 When the buttonmaker dreams of a beach-resort boardwalk, the ceiling of the subway where he is dreaming remains intact.

14   Aronson's employment contract, in Yiddish, to design *The Bronx Express* for the Schildkraut Theatre. The costs of constructing the sets and costumes were to be paid out of the designer's fee. The contract reads: "Schildkraut Theatre—Manager. This is to verify an agreement made between Schildkraut Theatre and Boris Aronson. BA herewith dutifully accepts to paint and execute the decor of 'B.E.' for which the S. Theatre is willing to pay BA $350.—for the work. And $25 a week if the play will play more than 4 weeks. He is to supply sketches for 'B.E.' and then execute all the scenery and costumes for said sum. The S. Theatre pays B.A. $100.—at the beginning of the work and the remaining $250. in part until the opening of the play."

This lavish musical adaptation of Abraham Goldfaden's play was Maurice Schwartz's choice to open his new Yiddish Art Theatre. Aronson had to move next door to Schwartz in Sea Gate, a private and exclusive extension of Coney Island, so that the impresario could supervise his work.

Aronson recounted: "I was very anxious to show him the first Constructivist model for one of the sets. It had a very simplified shape, very architectural and geometrical, stripped of all detailing. It was supposed to represent a structure of many levels; abstract to the point where the shape of the wood in its natural forms was stressed without any added gingerbread or any kind of decoration—a functional thing of many levels and stripped of any kind of schmaltz. So, finally, Schwartz arrived with his wife to take a look. For fifteen minutes, he was silent. It was the most difficult fifteen minutes I ever experienced in my life, waiting for a great man to pass judgment on one of the most ambitious things I had done in my career so far. I was on pins and needles. Finally, he turned to his wife and, pointing to the model, told her, 'You have to admit that I am a great man.' I knew I was in. But I must say that, for all his idiosyncrasies, after he acknowledged his greatness, he said, 'I like it very much.' But he added, 'The edges are too sharp and hard. Could you grow some moss on them to soften them a bit?' That was my first exposure to the need to tame the Constructivism in my work."

Schwartz directed the show and played eight roles, one of them female. There were twenty-five scene changes and 360 costumes, not to mention a Charleston-flavored ballet in heaven, choreographed by Michel Fokine. When Otto Kahn, Schwartz's millionaire sponsor, left on the opening night at 2:30 a.m., the first act had yet to end.

In *Theatre Arts Monthly*, the critic John Mason Brown described *The Tenth Commandment* as "a long-winded and rather discursive play, built around the 'shalt not' of the tenth commandment, and employing good and evil angels to lead its heroes through temptations on earth until they finally find themselves in heaven or hell. . . . But the helter-skelter of the method, its mad excesses, its tender quiet moments, and its gay seconds of complete confusion, suit it admirably to the particular kind of production it receives at the hands of M. Schwartz and his actors. These players are masters of a strident stylization, and can give to this Yiddish *Faust* something of the gusto that such a director as Jessner can give to Goethe's. Yet the stylization

15

15, 16   Sketches for the little house in the woods (15) that opened up to reveal its interior (16) early in *The Tenth Commandment* (1926), the opening production of Maurice Schwartz's new Yiddish Art Theatre on Second Avenue. Both in design and in technique, the house anticipates Tevye's home as designed by Aronson for *Fiddler on the Roof* in 1964.

17

17   Actors inside the house, as seen in the production.

16

18

18   Aronson's sketches for male chorus costumes.

has nothing in common with the shadowy unreality of the Habima's playing of *The Dybbuk.* Instead, it has a vast energy, a blatant, exciting kind of underscoring that is more familiar to Berlin than Broadway. Its writhing devils under green lights, its trapdoors, its constant use of actors rushing over many perilous levels and its costumed stagehands, shifting scenery in full view of the audience, give it that vivid, deep-dyed . . . theatricality, in which the German theater abounds, and which is sadly missing in our quiet, everyday theater of parlors and kitchens. Though the playing at the Yiddish Art Theatre lacks the finish to achieve the full style of the direction, the production takes on a special interest because of its scenic features. . . . The settings and costumes are the bravest experiments in scenic design that the present season has disclosed. [Aronson's] endless costumes are thoroughly thought out in terms of individual detail as well as being tonal factors in the large ensembles. By employing not one, but many constructivist settings, which range from heaven to hell, he conditions the style of the entire production, and brings a welcome vigor and originality to our theatre."

To design this elaborate show, Aronson used Constructivism in the early scenes, symbolism at the end. The action opens in a little house in the woods; then the house's roof and sides open up to allow the action to continue inside. The show's most famous set was a vision of hell. According to the play, hell occurred in one's brain—hell being, in Aronson's view, "the flame of work and passion, labor and drudgery." He designed it in the shape of a huge human profile and made it a fiery red crucible with steep ladders, evocative of an Essex Street sweatshop factory on a hot summer day. "A fire escape was constructed as a symbol of emergency and trouble, practical for action and emotion. Twenty actors gave the effect of a hundred by sliding down the fire pole, returning up the staircase, and sliding down again, thereby each appearing as several people." Heaven, by contrast, was conceived as a theater, "like the Metropolitan Opera, where each family had its own private box." John Mason Brown also applauded Aronson's castle scene, "with its two-story staircase, turrets, flying buttresses and balustrades, [which] gave [the] opportunity for the playing of mass scenes and hysteric terror on many levels—[an effect] new to Broadway as well as to Second Avenue." As another critic noted, "In this lavishly colorful and ravishingly artistic production, the play's not the thing."

19 Maurice Schwartz in one of his eight roles— as a woman—with co-star Joseph Buloff.

20 Design for Buloff's costume.

21 Design for Schwartz's costume.

22   The model for "hell," conceived as a sweatshop set in a man's brain.

23

23 Hell as seen on stage.

OPPOSITE

24, 25, 26, 27   Production photographs of heavenly way-stations, and Heaven designed as boxes at the Met (27) .

28

28, 29   The model for the main castle set with its perilous playing areas (28), and the castle in action, with actors providing "mass hysteria." (29)

29

30

31

30, 31, 32 Production photographs of the novel
revolving sets for the Yiddish Art Theatre's
production of Sholom Aleichem's *Stempenyu, the
Fiddler* (1929). "With all Schwartz's limitations and
lack of finesse," said Aronson, "he had a wonderful
sense of the theater and let me do what I wanted to
do—I had many big chances with him. Every once in
a while, he did the most remarkable theatrical things.
His adaptation of Sholom Aleichem's *Stempenyu,
the Fiddler* was the kind of play that he did very well,
because it was a combination of sentimentality mixed
with genuine humor and pathos; the style of acting
and direction and design was of a piece. Never
before or after did he achieve anything that had such
a oneness about it. In most of his other shows, the
scenery was too strong, or the direction was too
weak, or the play was the kind that didn't need his
interpretation, or the actors were all pushing in
different directions. Harold Clurman was highly
affected by *Stempenyu, the Fiddler*. All the best actors
were in it, including Schwartz and Celia Adler."
The set was novel for the Yiddish theatre because the
curtain was not lowered during the performance for
the many changes of scene. Instead, a revolving stage
with scenery painted on two sides rotated before the
audience to reveal, variously, a Russian town and
the interior of a house.

32

BROADWAY BREAKTHROUGH

I believe in clumsiness. By "clumsiness" I don't mean amateurishness, or a lack of knowledge, or a helpless search for accidental answers to questions. I mean that condition of not having a ready answer for a problem because the problem will not lend itself to an easy solution. If the solution to a problem appears instantly, it's usually a solution which has already been used. Solutions come by instinct and by groping and searching for something fresh. When everyone knows "how to do it," when there are great similarities in the way design problems are solved, then "clumsiness" is lost.

WALK A LITTLE FASTER (1932)

Walk a Little Faster, a lavish revue, was Aronson's first Broadway show and his first musical in English; it also showed off the still uncelebrated talents of its composer, Vernon Duke (Vladimir Dukelsky), and lyricist, E. Y. ("Yip") Harburg. S. J. Perelman wrote the sketches, tailoring them to the talents of the stars, Beatrice Lillie and the comedy team of Bobby Clark and Paul McCullough. The producer was Courtney Burr, a patrician Broadway veteran who had pursued Aronson after hearing about him from Robert Benchley.

As Burr and Aronson began working on *Walk a Little Faster*, the production's budget had yet to be completely raised. (Eventually, two of the producer's friends, Vincent Astor and Jock Whitney, came to the rescue.) From the beginning, Vernon Duke was struck by Aronson's personality and flair. The composer visited the designer "in his dingy Central Park West studio" and found that Aronson "looked as if he had just stepped from an Assyrian frieze and wore twentieth-century coat and trousers under protest." Duke felt that Aronson was "performing miracles of revolutionary stagecraft"; he and the revue's other authors "sat for hours, hypnotized by Boris' excited guttural explanations and the beautifully made little models of sets."

For Aronson, it was a novelty to work with such Broadway swells: "Burr was a man of great charm, a member of the *Social Register*. His Park Avenue apartment, where I met Dorothy Parker and Robert Benchley, had a fully equipped bar always within arm's reach. He had a parrot who said 'Darling.' "

Aronson built his design for *Walk* around the "concept" of New York: "My design was based on the extremes and incongruities of the city. For example, the fact that New York is seen vertically—looking way up at the skyscrapers, or looking way down into the subway grates. These environments have a reality which is completely removed from the European environment. [For the first time] my design wasn't built on memories of Russia.

"I was fascinated with the kind of incongruities I saw on Broadway. In one of the many big production numbers, I used those puppets which they sold on the street at that time, jumping figures made out of paper which keep on doing the Charleston and so on. I would walk into a nightclub and I would see performers—huge black men in double-breasted suits, over six feet tall, and very conscious of their looks, with ties, handkerchiefs, and a tremendous footage of goods

1   The show curtain for *Walk a Little Faster* (1932),
on which a contemporary girl looks at old-fashioned
lovers through opera glasses from her box. To
Aronson, it indicated "the contrast between the old
and the new, which is the tale of the whole revue."

covering them. Then, in very tiny, delicate voices, they would sing about something so romantic. There was such incongruity between the looks of the men and what they had to say. They looked grotesque and very, very big, full of power—but then they would sing a song about 'I didn't say yes, and I didn't say no,' and it was all so tiny and sweet, the complete opposite of Ethel Waters' delivery and power. They influenced me. I was trying to create that kind of incongruity, that kind of a mixture, that lack of pure style. I was trying to make an American style out of that lack of style. I was very ambitious and I was full of so many ideas that I would not be surprised if I overdid it.

"I used all kinds of gadgets in the show, all based on observation. I hadn't yet mastered the city enough, but I had ideas that were close to surrealism—I used zippers for a curtain and a camera lens shutter to iris in on intimate scenes. I used the mechanical pianola. The revolving [elements in the design] were all based on those machines that make chocolate in store windows, where the goo keeps revolving and moving. I felt that all these gadgets were characteristic of something which I experienced and which was around me. I had buildings which were small in the beginning and then, right in front of the audience, popped up to become huge skyscrapers. I kept trying to find a style in the inconsistent, disconnected things which are most characteristic of a city where there are so many architectural styles of different periods."

But one scene took place away from New York, in an English drawing room. "Miss Lillie, who had sized me up pretty well by that time, thought that a designer with an Anglo-Saxon background like Cecil Beaton ought to design this one scene. The producer insisted on having me try it first. I designed it using images from British sport prints—English hunting scenes where they have hunters in red caps. I divided the whole set by using a mantelpiece, but by using actual props of running dogs [in front of the wallpaper landscape], it turned out to be a collage (not a fashionable word at that time). Bea Lillie finally said that the set *almost* looked British, and was satisfied with it."

When the show reached Boston for its pre-Broadway tryout, the opening night proved a scenic catastrophe. Vernon Duke described it as "one of the roughest [opening nights] in history. Two or three of the more massive settings were not shown because of first-night handicaps backstage: two or three of the less agile stagehands unintentionally appeared with the actors, and some of the actors didn't appear at all, unable to find their way to the stage. To paraphrase the report of an eyewitness, it was a splendid performance, contributed by both the invisible actors and the visible stage crew, but the show easily rose above such trifles. The wonderful Boston audience . . . ate it all up good-naturedly, overlooking such items as the crash of a drop and its removal from the scene *for good*." By the time *Walk a Little Faster* opened at the St. James Theatre on Broadway, its rough edges had been smoothed out—only to reveal, as Duke put it, "a certain would-be recherché self-consciousness, a striving for originality at all costs." The revue received fair notices, then petered out after an unprofitable four-month run. Its one enduring feature, the song "April in Paris," did not find public favor until well after the show had closed. On opening night, the singer, Evelyn Hoey, had laryngitis and delivered the ballad in a hoarse whisper. Though Aronson had designed, in Duke's view, a "lovely" set for "April in Paris"—a Left Bank café behind a transparent gauze curtain—it alone wasn't enough "to put the song over."

2 "The Highway of Life," an Aronson collage illustration of the early 1930s, reflecting his aesthetic ideas of "vaudeville."

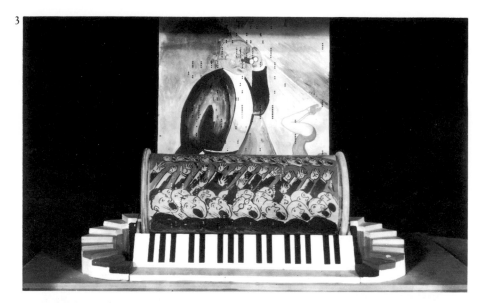

3, 4, 5   The model (3) and on-stage realization of one gadget-inspired set in *Walk a Little Faster* (1932). Aronson designed a huge piano roll, painted on both sides. The painted images formed different combinations to create a succession of varied pictures (4). As the song ended, the chorus was discovered inside, with chorus girls forming the piano case to accompany the music roll (5).

6, 7   Models of a lens-shutter set whose iris focused on intimate scenes.

8

8, 9   The set inspired by Aronson's observations of dancing puppets sold on Broadway and black nightclub performers—for the Act I finale, a production number called "Saturday Night." The set was to illustrate a cross-section of Broadway nightlife, set to a jazz theme. Behind the three musicians were three tiny puppets who at first were ornamental but later responded to the excitement and noise by jiggling about. Beams of light and adjustable black curtains were used to pinpoint the chorus dancers' feet and arms within the darkened stage.

10, 11   Another gadget design: a show curtain made of gigantic zippers.

10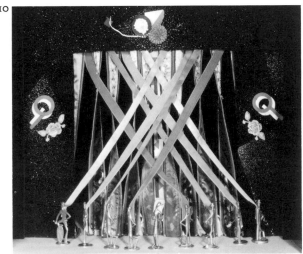

9

11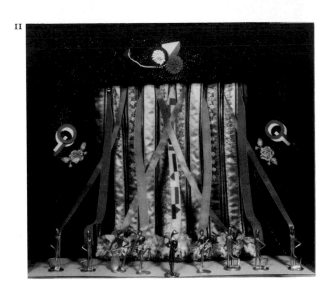

12   The romantic set for the one Duke-Harburg standard in the revue, "April in Paris." The dean of Boston critics, H. T. Parker of the *Boston Evening Transcript*, likened the set to "a white-walled street in the manner of Utrillo," but both the set and the song went unremarked at the Broadway opening a few weeks later.

13   A set for the song "Manhattan's the Loneliest Isle Without You," which was eventually dropped from the score. "My first reaction to New York was the insignificance in scale of the human body against the city," said Aronson. "The background was a huge bridge and towering building—the human being is infinitesimal and lost."

THE GROUP THEATRE

Often an author says everything he has to say in the text without being very clear as to where it takes place. As I first read the play, my mind begins to pulsate. I begin to make sketches. I make many sketches before I am satisfied, often coming back to the instinctive propulsion of the first sketch. I may make many more sketches after I have talked to the director, and even more as the play rehearses and unexpected problems arise. The sketch need not be a piece of art in itself, but represents one step in solving the problem of the stage set. This is often misunderstood by the producer or director.

Although he was in favor of the Group Theatre's championship of new American plays that reflected the life of their time, Aronson was never a complete devotee of the Depression's most famous and influential theatrical ensemble. "There was too much holiness in the Group," he felt. "Stanislavsky's methods belong to Russia at a certain period in history, not to New York decades later." Nonetheless, Aronson designed four Group Theatre productions, even as he kept his distance from the company's intense internal politics and fratricidal aesthetic wars. The first two assignments were Clifford Odets' family dramas, *Awake and Sing* and *Paradise Lost.*

AWAKE AND SING (1935)

Aronson had been impressed by Odets' famous debut play, *Waiting for Lefty*—a theatrically adventurous political piece that had the style and force of a union strike rally. "What was so remarkable about *Lefty*," Aronson said, "was that the form was extremely contemporary and alive and new. [The form] wasn't a complete invention, but it was

fresh, and it came out of the *meaning*. It was almost inevitable that you would have to stage it that way. It wasn't a fashionable thing to do, so I felt very sympathetic."

Odets offered Aronson *Awake and Sing* the first time the two met. This play also dealt with the economic inequities and hardships of the Depression, but it did so by presenting a realistic dramatization of a Bronx household. For Aronson, the work was a novelty, "because I actually wasn't acquainted with Jewish-American life. I didn't know the characteristics of this kind of environment and its people." Jules (later John) Garfield, who was cast as the play's protagonist, solved the problem by taking Aronson to visit his parents and relatives in the Bronx. For the designer, this excursion was like a visit to a "foreign country." The trip was helpful because "Julie's family could easily be the same family in the play—the same types, the looks of the place, the people, the conversation. His home had fingerprints by which the characters expressed themselves; as a designer, I always know that people move into a home and within hours the place begins to reflect their characteristics. I felt the heaviness of the furniture and the whole set-up. The house was overstuffed with things, and it was different and novel to me."

1, 2   Clifford Odets' *Awake and Sing* as produced by the Group Theatre (1935). Elia Kazan: "The set had qualities that a painting has—a glow that caught the mood of a remembered apartment, not just an apartment. It had to do with subtle blending of colors. It was the shabbiest of locales, but, like a painter, Aronson placed one color next to another—delicate roses and blues—so they all went together in a way that was magical." Jules Garfield, Morris Carnovsky, Art Smith, Luther Adler, Stella Adler, Sanford Meisner, J. E. Bromberg (1). Garfield, Carnovsky, S. Adler, L. Adler, Meisner, Smith, and Bromberg (2).

To Aronson, "the most fascinating thing about *Awake and Sing* was the play and the acting, and the set was just a set. When I first read it, there was talk that it does not represent specifically a Jewish family in the Bronx, that it has something to do with the middle class as a whole, and so on. Now, you can say this about almost every play; you can say that about Chekhov's plays or any play that has to do with humanity; if the play's well written, it's not just about one group of people. [But] to be more than just a genre work, a play has to be written with a larger dimension. The Irish plays are larger than just the specific environment. Shakespeare's plays also deal with relatives, but on a poetic level. As much as I admired *Awake and Sing*, as much as I thought it a remarkable work, I did not feel that I could or would design it as an abstract concept of a middle-class house where all sorts of people could live. Although heartbreak occurs in it, it's not *Heartbreak House*. When Thornton Wilder writes *Our Town*, he conceives this kind of environment; it's a part of his concept; it has a certain intended design as a part of it." To Aronson, Odets hadn't written that kind of stylized play: "If you enlarge something which has so much to do with relatives to something bigger than it is, I thought you would make it pretentious.

"The play called for a number of rooms which had to be simultaneously revealed on stage. It was in no way a designer's great masterpiece, but it was of service to a play which, like all plays in the tradition of Chekhov, are really based on sensitively observed and executed details. That is what distinguished this play from the ordinary play about a Jewish family. In an ordinary Jewish play, the dialogue is recorded dialogue—the way people actually speak. What was poetic about *Awake* was Cliff's personal handwriting. He was talking [through] these people. This finally became so clear to me that I started to appreciate the play on a different level, although I still thought it wasn't as daring as *Lefty*."

PARADISE LOST (1935)

In *Paradise Lost*, Odets made more of an attempt to stylize a Depression family. The characters were not specifically Jewish, for the most part, and their language was more poetic. Harold Clurman, who directed it, thought the play captured the "dreamlike unclarity" of the Depression: "The little people of the small middle-class world were fumbling about in an environment they didn't control or understand,

3 A conflict between realism and poetic symbolism: Odets' *Paradise Lost* (1935), with Robert Lewis, Morris Carnovsky, and Luther Adler.

their hearts full of fond dreams, their eyes beclouded with illusions inherited from the past, while their hands groped in a void that was full of terror. When facts finally confronted them with unmistakable concreteness, they were the facts of bankruptcy and destitution, a house empty of all its foolish and kindly furniture, forever shaken and damaged in its ancient comfort. Nothing was left these people except their basic sweetness." Stella Adler, who appeared in *Paradise Lost*, found that she and the other actors had trouble finding the play's style—and so, in her opinion, did Aronson. "It was semi-realistic, poetic, symbolic—but *we* were all realistic."

From the outset, Odets and Clurman were conscious of the play's look. According to Aronson, "They said that it's not about Jews necessarily; it's about the middle class." The designer found *Paradise Lost* difficult to design, because he didn't share the playwright and direc-

tor's view that "it was written in an epic style like a Brecht or Toller play." Aronson "didn't know who [the characters] were." To him, they still seemed the same people who were in *Awake and Sing*, but "in some kind of a disguise." And he found Odets' writing pretentious as a result. He thought that the dialogue was not organic to the characters, but represented a conscious decision on the author's part to be "modern." "[Odets] wasn't completely himself—he was under the influence of something."

Aronson saw the failings of *Paradise Lost* as paradigmatic of Odets' subsequent career: "The tragedy of Cliff, from my point of view, is that—as bright and as intelligent and as informed as he was—he never knew his limitations. . . . His abilities were enormous, [but] without knowing his limitations, he attempted everything in every possible way—and it just can't be done."

BROADWAY IN THE THIRTIES

The approach to research varies with each play. A designer becomes a detective, looking for fingerprints. The architecture of a room is constant, but its character changes according to who inhabits the room and what they do within its walls. These "fingerprints" are selected and enlarged to convey an atmosphere—to make a point. In researching, I find almost anything can serve as a source of inspiration: a toy, a Japanese woodcut, a tool. But you don't lean on research. Steep yourself in a given period or environment and then forget about it when you start designing.

THREE MEN ON A HORSE   (1935)

While Aronson worked on Clifford Odets' *Awake and Sing*, he also did his first George Abbott farce, *Three Men on a Horse.* He loved the play for its vitality and naïve, unsophisticated humor: "After all that heavy breathing with the Group, I was suddenly enchanted with superficiality."

Written by Abbott and John Cecil Holm, the play is about Erwin Trowbridge, a greeting-card writer from Ozone Heights, Long Island, who has an uncanny knack for picking winners at the races when sitting on a certain seat on the bus. Erwin bets only for the fun of it, until one night when he meets three racetrack touts who decide to capitalize on his genius.

Aronson had no knowledge of Ozone Heights. "To me, it was like deepest Africa. And gamblers, too, were people that were foreign to me. At first, I didn't know how to approach the thing." For inspiration, the designer went to his usual source, the five-and-ten—an institution that, to him, epitomized the America of that moment. "I was overwhelmed by the kind of exquisite banalities which you could buy for five or ten cents. I used to buy workingmen's gloves because, from the point of view of design, they presented something to me that was

so American—so unique, so fresh, without precedent. The American environment—the five-and-ten, Sears, Roebuck—had not yet been canonized. America still had no patina; it did not have the mark of sainthood on it. And the contemporary reality of America interested me more than America's heritage. I wanted to make a style of its young and exuberant lack of style—to capture the essence of a hotel room in Los Angeles, a bar on Third Avenue, a living room in the Bronx, the banality of Staten Island."

At the five-and-ten, Aronson trailed customers similar to the characters in *Three Men.* "I followed a woman who I thought could be the lady in the negligee in the play. Everything she purchased, I purchased. I wound up with a cuckoo clock, two cast-iron sconces, a footed urn, a do-it-yourself centerpiece, and a musical cake plate that played 'Happy Birthday' as it turned. I used these articles as research for the settings. In fact, I reversed the standard procedure. Starting from the bric-a-brac, I created the home environment, and then I proceeded to define the walls and doors around them. I wanted to make the settings sleazy; the Trowbridge home was consistently cluttered. The tendency, of course, was to do beautiful sets, but there's nothing

1   *Three Men on a Horse* (1935): a Manhattan bar.

OPPOSITE

2, 3   The "ugliness" of New York suburbia.
The play's cast included Shirley Booth, Sam Levene,
and Garson Kanin.

4   The sets were changed in darkness by the fast,
efficient "jackknife" technique, whose elaborate
mechanics were explained to a curious theatregoing
public by this newspaper diagram.

2

3

4

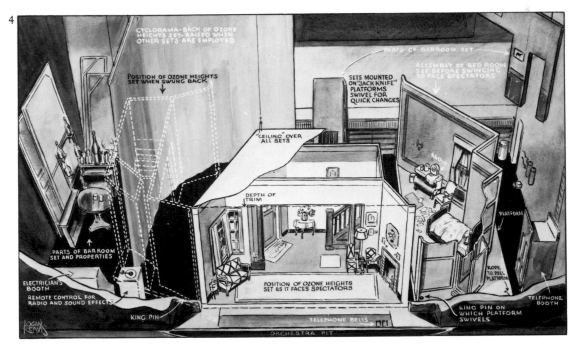

beautiful about those horse gamblers. And I thought, 'What would be the color of a home like this?' I took the ugliest colors I could think of —the brown of a cockroach, and the green of the powder used to kill a cockroach. This was my basic color scheme. Ugliness can be as exciting as beauty . . . but Warner Bros., the backers, hated the scenery. 'It should have been Colonial,' they said. 'After all, it's an American play.' "

Abbott, who'd been introduced to Aronson by the producer Courtney Burr, thought the set "quite unusual for a farce," since it departed from realism to the point of even featuring painted windows. Abbott's assistant, Garson Kanin, was impressed by Aronson's ability to "bring the real flavor of suburbia, a lowlife New York bar and hotel room on stage"—"all of which Boris had probably never seen." The three set changes were accomplished by the technical scheme called "jackknife," an efficient method for fast and noiseless set changes, then in vogue on Broadway. It was a far cry from the exposed method of scenery shifting that was Aronson's unrealized ideal. But Abbott liked fast, efficient scene changes. "Make sure the doors don't shake!" the director told the designer, expressing his major scenic concern.

THE TIME OF YOUR LIFE   (1939)

William Saroyan's barroom reverie proved an occasion for Aronson's first painful encounter with the ruthlessness of the American commercial theatre—he was fired from the production during its pre-Broadway tryout. In *Theatre Arts* magazine a year later, he recounted the ordeal and the new lessons about the Broadway system that he learned from it:

"The theatre has been built up as a gambling institution rather than a sound business. . . . The breakneck speed with which productions are whipped into shape is another concrete result of this gamblers' paradise. A scenic designer, after a long period of idleness, may suddenly get a call asking him to prepare a production which should take months of careful study, within the allotted time of a few weeks. A job of this kind will not show the designer at his best. His work, in consequence, is apt to have the quality of a series of accidents. The building and painting, done at the last feverish minute, assume the characteristics of a bombardment. There is no time to make changes

at that point or even to determine whether any material changes would be desirable. This pressure has a bad effect on managements as well.

"William Saroyan's current play, *The Time of Your Life*, for which I was engaged to design the settings, and for which Robert Lewis was the original director, is a case in point. Mr. Lewis and I planned a physical production which seemed appropriate, more stylized than the present version. The production was in rehearsal for the customary period: everything went well until the dress rehearsal. Mr. Saroyan, on his arrival, decided that both Mr. Lewis and I had the wrong conception of his play. With a few hasty changes, the play was presented in New Haven. In a few days, the management decided to scrap the entire production as given, and present a new version, using new settings and other direction.

"I don't want to argue here whether we were right or wrong. My only contention is that if we were wrong, and we may easily have been, the mistake should have been discovered weeks earlier. The management should not have waited until the last minute to make changes, with the resulting loss of time, money and talent. This state of affairs is unfortunately not limited to the above production, but is an all too frequent happening on Broadway.

"The result of such conditions leaves the earnest worker in the theatre with the double handicap of being forced to neglect the traditional path of the classics and of being kept from honest experimentation with new methods. Present-day conditions have puzzled and defeated many idealistic producing groups interested in classical repertory theatre; neither can they afford to do any experimentation with new methods under the present Broadway regime. We consequently have the woeful standardization which is apparent. This is largely due, in my opinion, to the fact that the average worker in the theatre cannot afford to experiment before he receives a commission for a production; later there is no time. . . .

"To sum up: Immediate success means too much in the present theatre. Failure teaches too little. What is needed is the organization of groups who will not work by God and by guess, but will make a sincere effort to eradicate evils past and present."

Thus did Aronson first diagnose, from a designer's perspective, Broadway ills that remained unchanged and unameliorated for the rest of his career.

5, 6   Aronson's sketch (5) for the set of Saroyan's
The Time of Your Life (1939). By the time the play
opened on Broadway, his set had been replaced by a
new one, designed by Watson Barratt (6).

7, 8 *The Merchant of Yonkers* (1938): The playwright, Thornton Wilder, and the director, Max Reinhardt, both practiced the experimental theatrical techniques that Aronson admired—but not in this Americanized adaptation of Johann Nestroy's 19th-century Viennese farce (which later would be adapted twice more for Broadway, as *The Matchmaker* and *Hello, Dolly!*). Aronson thought it "strictly a period piece of Little Old New York, directed by Reinhardt with none of the speed and pressure of America." This Yonkers hat shop was strict Victoriana, painted in café-au-lait tones (7). In a detail from *The Merchant of Yonkers*, Nydia Westman appears as Minnie Fay (8).

8

STYLIZED REALISM

In a set, a door becomes the opening through which the actor's body is framed, momentarily, as he enters or exits. It's there primarily for that transient moment and secondly for its look. You look at a painting, but you move, touch, swing, open, close, slam a door on stage.

THE GENTLE PEOPLE   (1939)

Aronson's last production for the Group Theatre became his most celebrated design for the English-speaking stage to date. Irwin Shaw's play, labeled by the author as "a Brooklyn fable," is a straightforward Depression morality tale about two innocent immigrant Coney Island fishermen (played by Roman Bohnen and Sam Jaffe) who are finally driven to murder a gangster (Franchot Tone) who has been victimizing them. The principal set was the Coney Island pier, although the play also unfolds in three other locations: a living room, a night court, and a Turkish bath, where a bankrupt businessman (Lee J. Cobb) recites his tale of woe.

There was little straightforward, however, about how Aronson approached his job. Though his sets were realistic, he arrived at them through indirect means—spurred on by the director, Harold Clurman, with whom he had his first truly satisfying collaboration. As was to become his practice, Clurman began the design process by writing lengthy letters to Aronson in which he described the mood, rather than the mechanics, of the piece.

In August 1938, Clurman wrote to the designer that Shaw's "tender fable" must have "a story quality, it is never harshly prosaic. Every characteristic of good and evil must have some fairy-tale heightening, a picture quality of charm and wonder—hence, stylization is justified.

"The *tenderness* of the play comes from a certain helplessness in these people, an unsung sweetness and humility. The play is about the lonesome, forgotten people whose little joys and sorrows are usually overlooked. The whole play, as it were, takes place in a nook. There must be some intimacy in all the scenes and the scale must be small. Here also a quality of plainness like that of an old table, or ancient fishing tackle left neglected at the water, or stones used in old bathhouses, or stones left rotting in old baskets—things that are neglected but still useful and honest. All is permeated with a feeling of love and emotion that makes all objects precious and a little sad.

"*Pier*: Must have a sense of depth, space and freedom. A feeling of open air. The audience must sense loveliness immediately in this set. They must feel a nostalgia about it, a happy sadness, a desire to go to this place and be quiet and lonely, and yet satisfied. The line in this scene becomes a dream—remote. The whole thing, in the words of one of the old men, is 'a private dream.' . . .

"*Bath*: Kind of dream world. People are protected here. Natural,

I

1   Aronson's sketch for the Coney Island pier in the Group Theatre production of Irwin Shaw's *The Gentle People* (1939).

2, 3   The dock and pier on stage (2). Elia Kazan, Sylvia Sidney, Sam Jaffe, and Roman Bohnen (3).

naked, warm, undisturbed, together. Nothing but steam and naked bodies, not much detail. The stove might be a bright homely spot glowing pleasantly and warmly. The whole place should look as though it were going to float away."

These general evocations of mood and feeling, characteristic of Clurman, gave Aronson the license and stimulation to attack a realistic set in the non-literal, imagistic manner he favored as an artist. And, as was increasingly to become the case, the designer started by experimenting with artistic stimuli that had no apparent direct bearing on the sets at hand: to design Shaw's fabulist Coney Island, he turned to the stylization of Japanese woodcuts, "a form which develops accuracy to a lyrical art."

Aronson realized that "there were tremendous possibilities of not just naturalistically reproducing the settings but of actually getting the whole spirit of the place. . . . Clurman was mainly interested in the interpretation of the play, and scenery had to become part of the whole concept. The use of Japanese woodcuts, the stylized reality, all came from conversations with Harold. Because of the nature of the play, I tried to do what the Japanese do in realistic drawings: they are highly stylized and yet recognizable; they are two-dimensional but not abstract; you can definitely recognize the locale, a specific mountain or house. But I did not make the set look Japanese or like a Japanese print; that would be wrong. These influences were not directly observable in the finished production.

"This combination of stylization (to give a certain mood) and the actual study of the environment (to re-create the special feel of Coney Island) represented something new for me." To Aronson, *The Gentle People* was a departure both from the avant-garde, Tairovesque designs he had done when first working in the Yiddish theatre and from the more realistic sets he had designed for his first plays on Broadway and with the Group Theatre. He was finding a way to blend Russian modernism and New York realism in a mix that was peculiarly his own.

To achieve this end, Aronson took another indirect design step that was to become characteristic of his method—he did a series of paintings that were not set renderings but impressions of the play's settings. "They were not concrete, and you couldn't play in them, but they had that general feeling of what I was trying eventually to do. I showed them to Clurman, and he approved in general, and that's the way we worked.

"The most important scene dramatically and scenically was the pier. The nature of the construction of a pier and the perspective of the lights—that in itself, even in reality, is so theatrical, so like the circus. It interested me so much more than the reality of a living room." In order to mask the lights, which illuminated the water and backdrop, the pier was not painted but built in perspective—and this was the exciting feature of the set, at a time when most designers would have created the pier's vanishing perspective by using a painted backdrop. Aronson also took the unusual step of draining color from the set: "The pier was seen at night, so certainly you couldn't have color there. You have to design the pier for this particular play. And so you eliminate a lot of other things which are not necessary. There are certain plays where the first thing you think of is color, but that didn't apply to this one." Aronson used stylization in the design of the surrounding water. "This was the Japanese theatre influence. [The water effect] was done with gauze, and there were fans that kept the gauze moving about. I also used a projection—so the combination of the gauze moving and the fans making the gauze go up and down and the projection of a ripple on it gave the feeling [of water]."

Just as Aronson made endless studies of Coney Island for the pier set, so he stylized the reality of Turkish baths for his bath house. "The bath scene was a comic, vaudeville scene. It lent itself to interesting designing: the very nature of the place, with the steam, with the platforms the way they are built. There's almost no way out, and it's a very hot place; it's almost like a pleasant third degree. Instead of playing it on one level, I used different levels, and I stylized the ceiling by making it much lower and heavier in order to concentrate on the few people who are there. The steam room looked much better with the actors inside the set than without them." The other two sets were handled similarly, as small units with oddly angled roofs.

Though *The Gentle People* was a classic design, cited by other designers for years afterward as a breakthrough in Aronson's development, it was not beloved by all members of the querulous Group in 1939. Clurman wrote in his memoir, *The Fervent Years*, that "the Group company was harshly critical of [the production]. Irwin Shaw himself was not altogether pleased with the results, despite the fact the play was the nearest thing to a commercial success he had ever had in the theater; and I certainly was not sure I had found the correct style for the play, which required, it seemed to me, the appearance of realism with a simplicity that was not quite that. Perhaps a more frankly fanciful treatment might have served the play better." Aronson recalled that some felt the set was "too concrete, not stylized enough," but he believed that no more fanciful stylization was called

4 Aronson's sketch for the Turkish bath house.

5 Roman Bohnen, Sam Jaffe, Lee J. Cobb, and Martin Ritt take a steam bath under Aronson's low, heavy ceiling.

for: "The play doesn't create the feeling that it is larger than just something which happens in Brooklyn at that time. And so I didn't design it as though it did. *A View from the Bridge* [the Arthur Miller play Aronson designed in 1955] also takes place in Brooklyn in a longshoreman's apartment; I did it in a very unrealistic way because it's written that way. *The Gentle People* is far closer to *Awake and Sing*, much more under the influence of Odets than it is an epic story."

Over four decades after the original production, Irwin Shaw concluded that the only failing of the set was the length of time the set changes took—and he blamed himself for writing a play that "set up [logistical] problems I couldn't solve myself." (Kazan, an actor in the production and Clurman's assistant, had to rescue the muddled staging of the murder scene at the pier.) But Shaw prized Aronson's fantastic approach to design, preferring it to the more realistic style of the Group's major designer, Mordecai Gorelik. "Gorelik was a very good designer, but very severe," Shaw said. "If you had a scene with a slum, Gorelik gave you a really ugly slum—Boris would give you a Chagall slum."

Even so, near the end of his life Aronson felt that time had diminished the nature of his achievement in *The Gentle People*. "A certain kind of naturalism is absolutely deadly in the theatre today," he said in the late 1970s, "because your eyes are tired, because you have been turning the dial on the television. You're seeing so much color, so many places, and so many environments that you don't react to them anymore. It's not exciting to see the Coney Island pier I did for the Group Theatre years ago. Then it was a great novelty." He also felt that "the whole approach to the production could be very different" in a present-day staging of *The Gentle People*: "It's not a fable now, it's a fairy tale. . . . We change and the theatre changes, and [so does] the audience."

PAINTING WITH LIGHT

Whereas most artists and designers are concerned with maintaining a personal style, or "handwriting," that characterizes all of their work, I believe that each individual project has its own specific needs, and it would be impossible to design for each in a constant style. . . . My own artistic "handwriting" is to approach each theatre piece as unique and to find the most efficient and innovative methods to convey its originality. Though I do not believe in having a style, I insist upon a consistency of style. A design has to be of a piece. If you start out with a delicate look, for instance, you have to keep that look.

THE GREAT AMERICAN GOOF (1940)

Aronson received an extraordinary commission in 1940: he was invited by Richard Pleasant, an adventurous founder of Ballet Theatre, to design a ballet for the company's opening program—and a most unusual ballet at that. Choreographed by Eugene Loring to music by Henry Brant, *The Great American Goof* was primarily conceived by William Saroyan, who wrote the ballet's scenario. Saroyan called the experiment—whose full title was *A Number of Absurd and Poetic Events in the Life of the Great American Goof*—a "ballet-play" and "a new American form." The story was, in any case, typical Saroyan: The Goof was an all-American Everyman, "the naïve white hope of the human race," who tries to save a nightmarish civilization. Constantly battered by symbolic evils—a dummy representing Conformity, a priest representing Capitalism, a dope addict representing Radicalism, et al.—the Goof forever bounces back from defeat with a winning smile.

Aronson's approach to *Goof* was to invent a new kind of theatrical scenery which he called "Painting with Light." Though he had experimented with projections in *Battleship Gertie* (1935) and some of his 1930s Radio City Music Hall projects, the projections used for *Goof* were unlike any he had designed before—and were the first ever employed in a ballet. In 1947—seven years after Ballet Theatre had dropped the production from its repertory—Aronson's innovations were still considered so novel that the Museum of Modern Art staged an exhibit of his *Goof* designs.

The scenic solution was born out of necessity. "Since *Goof* was a new ballet, there were no previous set designs. Saroyan conceived a production with ten different scenes as diverse as a church, a prison, a nightclub, and a factory. It was a necessary practical decision, as well as artistic, to find a way to design a great many sets while keeping the technical aspects rather simple. When a production runs only twenty-five minutes and in repertory, ten complete set changes are an impossibility. I eventually conceived a one-set production and incorporated a succession of slides which, when projected onto the set, created the different locales necessary to the concept of the ballet."

Almost every aspect of the design departed from the "magic lantern" effects that projections usually brought to the stage. At the time, projections were used mainly to create backdrop images—moving clouds or waterfalls or raging fires. "Slide projection was centuries old

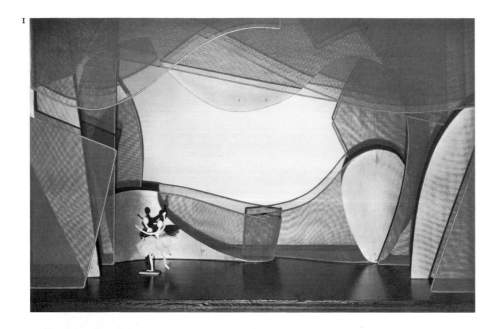

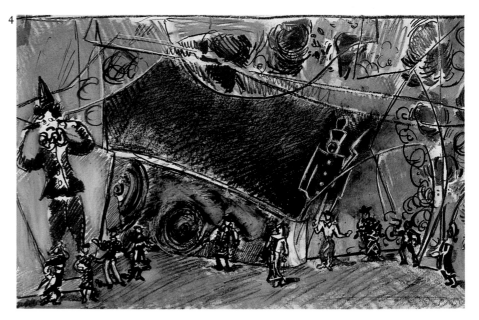

1 A model of the three-dimensional "neutral gray set" for *The Great American Goof* (1940), with transparent and opaque surfaces designed to receive front slide projections.

2 Aronson's sketch of how the set would look with projections.

3, 4 Sketches of additional designs for the ballet.

when I decided to explore the technique for *Goof*," said Aronson. "I did not regard my new use of projection in this ballet as a panacea for modern drama, but rather as a particular device to serve this particular project. The wide range of possibilities for the use of projection was hardly touched on by contemporary playwrights."

Aronson's novel use of projection in *Goof* grew out of his feeling that performers, especially dancers, did not stand out against any kind of flat, perspective-ordered scenery, whether painted or projected. Accordingly, the designer's first innovation in *Goof* was to do away with conventional flats (or flat screens) for his projections. He instead created a permanent set of interrelated abstract shapes, broken into several irregular planes. The set's surfaces were varied—transparent, translucent, and opaque materials, all in neutral grays, were used. When slides were projected onto the set, some of the imagery was refracted, reflected, absorbed, or multiplied. Because of the variations in depth and shape of the various gray screens, each slide would completely transform the basic set, sometimes seeming to alter the stationary set's structure as well as the story's mood and locale.

The slides, too, were a new invention. Aronson did not use standard slides of hand-tinted or color photographic film between glass. He treated each slide as an individually designed collage. Each collage was made up of, first, either a positive drawing, done in black line on clear unbreakable glass, or a negative drawing, done in reverse by being scratched out of black-painted glass. The drawings were sometimes combined with various fibers and textures. Through experimentation, Aronson discovered that he could use gels (the gelatin used for coloring stage lighting) instead of pigment to color the etched glass. "In this kind of projection, every little slide becomes as compact as a painting, but there is a fundamental difference between a slide and a painting. You make a diagram of a slide, but, projected on a multisurface, irregularly shaped screen, it is broken up, distorted, and multiplied. Therefore, abstract compositions serve the purpose better than representational ones." The designer sometimes consciously intensified this effect: when the plain glass of the slide was replaced by textured cut glass, yet another dimension would be added to the image when it was projected.

Aronson was able to get "depth and variety plus color." He found that "the whole technique makes possible an entire change of sets in a fraction of a second." In spite of the exclusive use of front projections, the dancers were not lost within the illuminated scenery. Strong overhead, side, and back lighting and follow spots minimized shadows,

5, 6, 7, 8 Two of Aronson's slide "collages" (5, 7), and models (6, 8) demonstrating how the slides transformed the set when projected on the models.

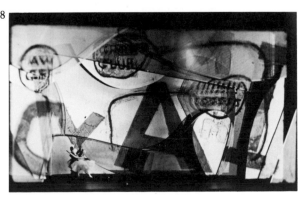

washing away the color and outlines of the projected designs from the performers when necessary. The sets had a luminous quality even as the dancers remained fully lighted.

At the time, the mixed-media theatricality and thematic ambitions of *Goof*, if not Saroyan's story, were enthusiastically received. Walter Terry, who had joined other major dance critics in praising the production initially, looked back from the perspective of 1980 to write that while the ballet "didn't last long . . . it represented the principle of total collaboration in the theater arts; it spoke for a specific period in our history; it was wholly American in word, movement, social concept and locale, and it was unmistakably 'theatre.' "

Aronson's adventurous techniques were soon assimilated into both scenic and lighting design, for, as he predicted, they suited "the complexities of modern plays and musicals"—the need "to create new illusions of reality, to make rapid changes, and to show the actors in full light." But no such lavish and sustained an application of "Painting with Light" was attempted again. "The ballet was given only a few performances, and never repeated," Aronson reminisced years later. "Even the Center Theatre, that wonderful, costly edifice [next to Radio City Music Hall] in which it was performed, has been demolished since. Like a bolt of lightning, *The Great American Goof* came and vanished."

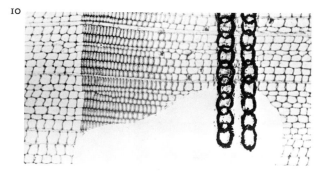

9, 10   Slide designs for a church and a prison.

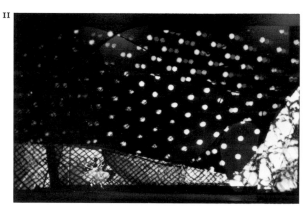

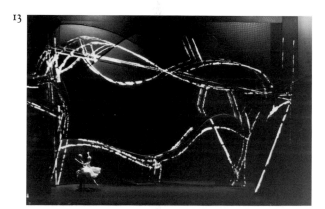

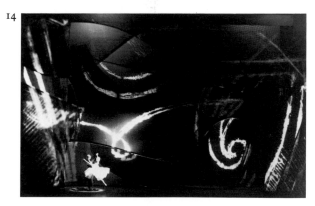

11, 12, 13, 14   From the 1947 Museum of Modern Art exhibition "Painting with Light": Models showing scenes from *The Great American Goof* as well as added projections that Aronson designed to demonstrate the possibilities of the technique. Although the innovative design survived, the ballet itself, which had appeared in the opening program of Ballet Theatre in 1940, had already been forgotten. Among its dancers had been the choreographer, Eugene Loring, Antony Tudor, and, in the corps, Lucia Chase, Donald Saddler, and Maria Karniloff (later, Karnilova). Aronson and Karnilova were reunited in two 1960s musicals, *Fiddler on the Roof* and *Zorba*.

IMPRESSIONIST MUSICAL

I am perfectly satisfied with realization of form, if a thing is designed. I don't mean a set only. I can be very much affected by a hat, by the shape of a thing. To me, it can be very moving and very meaningful.

CABIN IN THE SKY (1940)

Cabin in the Sky was the kind of bizarre collaboration that could happen only on Broadway (or in Hollywood). Three Russian émigrés—George Balanchine, Vernon Duke, and Aronson—created a musical set in a milieu that none of them had ever seen firsthand: the black American South. Such is the peculiar alchemy of show business that *Cabin* was a hit.

It didn't look that way for a while. Duke, who wrote the songs with the lyricist John Latouche, found that the "prodigiously gifted and eager" cast members—among them, Ethel Waters, Todd Duncan, Rex Ingram, Katherine Dunham, and Dooley Wilson—were "bewildered" by the three Russians: "Certain members of the cast were so alarmed by listening to our outlandish gibberish that they thought seriously about taking Russian lessons to get in on the arguments." Aronson recalled that the show's creators even had "conflicting opinions about Tolstoy." A cash shortage forced the cancellation of a pre-Broadway tryout in Boston. The producers tried and failed to fire Balanchine when the choreographer insisted on staging stylized ballets rather than tap dances for Dunham's dance troupe. The show opened "cold" on Broadway following a few public dress rehearsals and poor word of mouth. But a last-minute song addition—"Taking a Chance on Love," sung by Waters—made the show jell, and the reviews were favorable.

The story dealt with Little Joe, a poor, morally ambivalent black man whose wife's prayers bring him a six-month reprieve from hell—and who finally gets to heaven after God's and Lucifer's henchmen battle for his everlasting soul. Balanchine, according to the designer, "hired a Negro cook to immerse himself in the proper milieu"; Duke "wrote the music and got closer to Tchaikovsky than ever before." Aronson went off to Richmond, Virginia, to study the matter firsthand.

Once in the South, the designer learned a new lesson about the reality of the American scene—that the "eternal quest for beauty remains even among the inarticulate." Aronson visited the homes of poor blacks. He found that they were " 'aged' as painted scenery is when it is given a 'bath.' The homes looked dried out, like a discarded apple—wrinkled and spotted. The people, too, looked as though they stemmed from some ageless time and place. I came into poverty-ridden shacks where the only form of insulation was supplied by layers of old newspapers. In some cases, I found bits of odd wallpaper samples—picked up wherever they could be found and hung with dazzling irregularity in a sort of mosaic pattern. Without knowing it, the [occupants] had created exquisite collages." In one home, Aronson found a color lithographic print from a Sunday newspaper—a Louis XIV interior—slapped arrestingly atop a background of yellowed old newspaper remnants. In a shabby hotel room, he found that two girls had taken a colorful Cab Calloway promotional poster and rearranged

its letters into a new, abstract pattern on the wall. Aronson said: "Poor people often make themselves poorer than they really are by saving anything and everything. They would keep every bottle or can in the belief that someday it might prove useful. But, without being conscious of it, they were artists, because they had free taste and courage. It was this flavor of poverty mixed with sun, misery, and imagination that I sought to capture."

1 Aronson's costume designs for *Cabin in the Sky* (1940), built around the contrast between tropical vegetation and dark skins. "Nature was imitating Utrillo," he said of the American South.

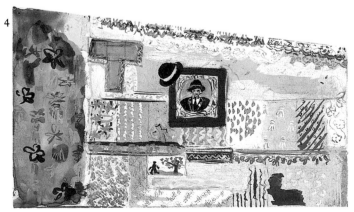

2, 3, 4 As research for *Cabin in the Sky*, Aronson took photographs of the naïve collages he found in the homes of poor blacks in Richmond, Virginia (3): "Homes leave indelible impressions of the people who have lived in them." Out of this came his sketch for the set of Little Joe's room (2). A detail from the wall of the set model (4) shows the final transformation of the Richmond documentary material.

5

5   Sketch of Joe's backyard for *Cabin in the Sky*.

OPPOSITE   6   A *Life* photo of the set in use.

7, 8   Sketches of the costumes for the devil and angel who battle for Joe's soul.

9, 10   Models for Lucifer's headquarters (9) and for a
dance scene in hell (10). Both sets preserved the same
upper architectural structure; both used the poles
which, in Joe's backyard, reached toward clotheslines.
Lucifer's office in Hades was visualized as the inside
of a refrigerator, to reflect the occupant's privileged
position in a fiery hell. In the dance scene, which
featured Katherine Dunham, the poles are lighted
from inside. It was the first time that Aronson used
plastic in a set.

THE FORTIES

The designer is seldom a part of the theatrical triumvirate: author, director, producer. Although he can make or break a play, he is mostly consulted in the men's room or when the show is facing disaster— a change of script in which it turns out that the play now takes place in a Turkish bath instead of a sunlit porch.

If the 1940s were a lean period for Aronson's career, it was nonetheless a time when he worked on more projects, traveled more widely, and pursued more varied endeavors than he did in times of plenty. He wrote outlines for two musicals, one of which (titled *44 Simple Mistakes, or What's Wrong with This Picture?*) was intended to star Ed Wynn and got far enough along to be announced in the papers. Another unproduced project was written by others—*Miss Underground*, a circus musical for the fabled Christiani family, set in Paris during the Occupation. Aronson also wrote poems, among them a parody of Hollywood that was published, and tried to enlist in the Army as a specialist in camouflage.

The most challenging theatrical assignments for Aronson in the 1940s were in the musical and ballet theatre. In between the elaborate productions that opened the decade (*The Great American Goof, Cabin in the Sky*) and closed it (*Love Life*) came a number of problematic realistic plays, as well as a quintet of more exotic tasks: *The Snow Maiden, What's Up, Pictures at an Exhibition, Sadie Thompson, Sweet Bye and Bye.*

1 "Hopscotch" (1947): In this painting of the period, as in his sets, Aronson begins to make the transition from realism to abstraction.

2

3

2, 3, 4 For Bronislava Nijinska's Ballet Russe de Monte Carlo production of the fairy-tale ballet *The Snow Maiden* (1942), Aronson designed both sets, as seen in this sketch (2), and costumes fancifully representing a birch tree (3) and a raven (4).

4

5, 6, 7, 8 *What's Up* (1943), a wartime musical about the farcical entanglements of an Army plane crew and a Virginia girls' school, marked the first collaboration of the songwriting team of Alan Jay Lerner and Frederick Loewe, who would later know more success than they did here. The choreographer was George Balanchine. Among several sets representing different locales within Miss Langley's School for Girls were a trio of picture-book bedrooms (5, 6, 7) one of which (5) was occupied by the comic Jimmy Savo (8). Savo played the entire show in pantomime. He was a tiny man, and his bedroom was scaled accordingly. To the audience, the set at first looked like just a scaled-down painted backdrop, but as a scene depicting Savo's morning ritual progressed, the drop proved to be not as flat as it seemed. Savo took the slippers from under the bed and put them on, retrieved the hat and cane, rolled up the rug and put it in the satchel, removed a pearl necklace and a box from the chair, and so on. He used every prop in the drop, whether real or painted. To punctuate the effect, just before exiting he picked a flower from the ceiling wallpaper and put it in his buttonhole.

9

10

11

9, 10, 11, 12   Aronson was able to dip into his Russian past for Nijinska's Ballet International production of *Pictures at an Exhibition* (1944). In a program note, Nijinska wrote, "I have tried to imagine how I would have staged Moussorgsky in one of the Russian theatres today. A luxurious production, complete with rich scenery and costumes, would not only be impossible to obtain, but would also be strange and unacceptable to the Russian audience. This audience, with its unusual creative inspiration, refined, further-more, by the experience of recent events, is able to accept the essential spirit of a work of art without the addition of lavish production details." Her choreography recalled Meyerhold's "biomechanics" of the 1920s; the critic Edwin Denby described it as "a sort of mechanized Russian farm-celebration." Aronson designed a simple set—seen here as a sketch (9) and on stage (12)—using a few props (Meyerholdian ladders, ropes, and benches) set against two large, crossed golden sheaves of wheat. The set could be used by dancers in different formations to create such "pictures" as gates or an oxcart or a ringing of the bells, as sketched by Aronson at rehearsal (10, 11). The homespun materials were pine wood, monk's cloth, and straw.

12

13, 14　In *Sadie Thompson* (1944), to no particular
avail, Somerset Maugham's tale of a missionary and a
tramp in Pago Pago received a musical treatment at
the hands of the songwriters Vernon Duke and
Howard Dietz and the director Rouben Mamoulian.
The show's commercial fate was sealed when Ethel
Merman dropped out of the title role in preproduction, to be succeeded by June Havoc. But
Aronson's scenic inventions included a jungle scene, a
curtain of actual rain, and Trader Joe's general store,
seen here as sketched (14) and on stage (13). "I regarded
the play as a clash between the Reverend and the
natives," said Aronson. "That meant if I gave the
show a native setting, I had to show the freedom and
lack of inhibition which the Reverend tries to destroy.
At the same time, I had to make sets that could be
seen and understood and felt. So I couldn't have the
simplified realism of genuine leaves. I made some of
them 15 feet high. They needed to be photogenic." For
the color and the lushness of the leaves, the designer
turned in part to Gauguin for inspiration.

13

14

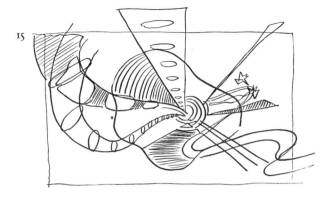

15

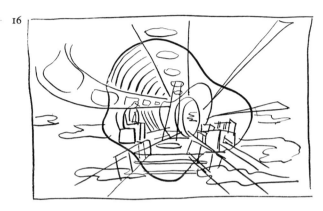

16

17

15, 16, 17 *Sweet Bye and Bye* (1946), with a book by S. J. Perelman and Aronson's close friend Al Hirschfeld, music by Vernon Duke, and lyrics by Ogden Nash, was an unlikely candidate for oblivion. Nonetheless, this lavish musical closed in the midst of its tryout in Philadelphia. The show was a comic fantasy about a meek hero who in 2076 finds corporate stock in a 1939 World's Fair capsule and briefly inherits the Futurosy Candy Corporation. For Aronson, it was bewildering even to imagine what a doorknob might look like 130 years hence. "This was a show in which I couldn't use research and there were no standards to go by. . . . My own feeling of bewilderment gave me the idea of using as a theme a jigsaw puzzle. There is a certain excitement when all the pieces of a puzzle are put into their proper places one by one. . . . I introduced the theme by two curtains, one in front of the other, which are solid in the beginning but when moved apart form different patterns, dissolve, break up, and move back again into solid form. Then, within basic permanent structures designed to create the illusion of space, I inserted various backgrounds usually based on the shapes of a jigsaw puzzle. Transparencies are used to give the illusion of endless space." These sketches show how Aronson achieved the finished design for a scene set in a spaceship: first (15), the basic pattern; second (16), the spaceship in relation to the pattern; finally (17), the completed setting, with actors.

18 For the office of a candy mogul in *Sweet Bye and Bye*, a futuristic material, plastic, was used in abundance—even for the furniture, which in 1946 could not be purchased ready-made and had to be specially built. People (in the form of dummies) would come down the plastic chute (center left) like merchandise (or money). Said Aronson: "The approach was to imagine the future in theatrical terms, not to determine the shapes of things to come or to calculate the waves of the future. Who knows? The future may be old-fashioned."

18

THE FIRST
"CONCEPT MUSICAL"

LOVE LIFE (1948)

By the late 1960s, the vogue term "concept musical" had become common Broadway parlance. A "concept musical"—the term was coined by critics, not the shows' creators—was one that eschewed a traditional story line for a theme and illustrated that theme with songs, dances, and scenes that were as much ironic commentary as dramatic action. Aronson was born to design such Americanized Brechtian musicals, and, beginning with Harold Prince's *Cabaret* in 1966, he did many of the most celebrated examples. But long before "concept musicals" came into fashion, Aronson designed an early, largely unremarked precursor of the genre, *Love Life.* Fittingly enough, the composer was Kurt Weill, who had essentially invented the form with Brecht in Berlin in the 1920s. Weill was brought into the project by the producer, Cheryl Crawford, who had just had a Broadway success with the more conventional Alan Jay Lerner–Frederick Loewe musical *Brigadoon.* Lerner, then feuding with Loewe, signed on to do the book and lyrics for *Love Life.* In keeping with the production's adventurous ambitions, the surprising choice for director was Elia Kazan, who had staged one previous musical, *One Touch of Venus,* but was not primarily associated with the musical theatre. Kazan postponed rehearsals of *Death of a Salesman* to undertake the project.

The show was a mild critical and commercial success, running for the better part of a season. *Love Life* fell short of its high ambitions for several reasons. Although it contained several Weill standards (including "Here I'll Stay"), it was a cold and sour piece, out of sync with an audience that expected its musicals to be infused with postwar optimism of the Rodgers and Hammerstein school. Yet the show didn't fail simply because it was ahead of its time; even on its own terms, *Love Life* had artistic shortcomings. Its theme—the "decline of American homelife in the past century or so and the resultant unhappiness and confusions of the average family," according to Lerner—was illustrated with vaudeville turns, but such "acts" (or at least good ones) can take years to develop; the musical's creators deluded themselves in believing they could mass-produce a full evening of them. What's more, Kazan soon discovered that Weill on Broadway was not always as daring as Weill in Germany. "Weill was the strong one of the bunch," the director recalled. "Though we kept saying that this shouldn't be like other musicals, Weill wanted the performers down center, down front, facing the audience for his songs. He was the most traditional of the authors—he wanted success very badly. Boris held his own, but he didn't have to deal with Weill."

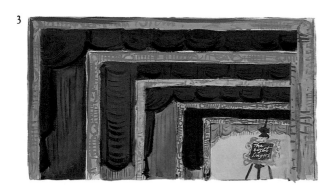

1, 2, 3, 4, 5   *Love Life* (1948): A series of vaudeville-style curtains and an olio drop (5).

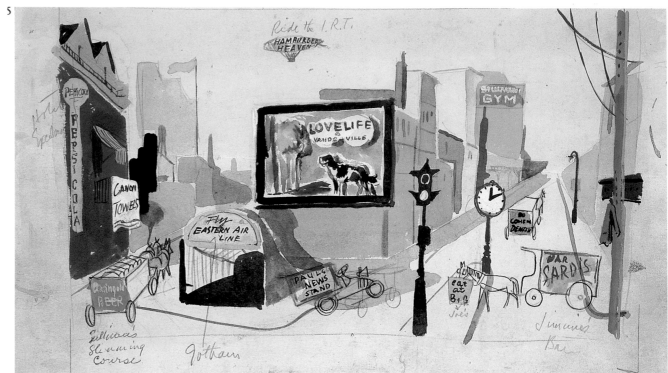

6   A sketch for the prologue's vaudeville act. A magician prefigures the Coopers' 150-year-long marital disintegration by levitating Sam and sawing Susan in half.

7   In the vaudeville epilogue, performed on a set echoing the magic-act prologue, Susan and Sam are tightrope walkers tentatively moving toward each other to repair their broken marriage.

8, 9, 10 Outside the Cooper home in Connecticut, 1791, an idyllic Yankee scene (8) is transformed by the first signs of industrialization (9). A period song-and-dance number, "Green Up Time," utilizes the industrialized Mayville of 1821, in which the pastoral landscape is now blighted by smokestack factories (10).

OPPOSITE

11, 12   The bedroom of the prosperous Cooper house in *Love Life*, 1857—as sketched (11) and as occupied by Nanette Fabray and Ray Middleton on stage (12).

13, 14   Susan envisions the perils of child-rearing in a trapeze act, "Mother's Gettin' Nervous"—as sketched (13) and as performed (14).

15, 16   Sketches of the porch (15) and living room (16) of the Coopers' early 1890s Victorian home.

17, 18   A sketch (17) and production photo (18) of the Act I finale in *Love Life*, in which Susan and Sam flirt with other partners on a luxury cruise in the 1920s. The scene was done in the style of a musical of the period, and Aronson's set somewhat recalls Cole Porter's 1934 musical *Anything Goes*.

19   As *Love Life* prefigured a later "concept musical" about modern marriage, the Prince-Sondheim *Company* of 1970, so Aronson's design for the Coopers' present-day (1948) New York apartment anticipated his modular, cube-motif design of modern Manhattan apartments in the later show.

20   A sketch of the locker room of Sam's present-day Turkish bath in New York.

21, 22   For the scene in which Sam and Susan go to court to dissolve their marriage, Aronson created a courtroom (21) that was designed to serve for a mock puppet-style ballet titled "Punch and Judy Get a Divorce" (22).

OPPOSITE

23   In the musical's largest and climactic production number, a minstrel show, the characters each sing about the meaning of love. One musical-theatre historian, Charles Willard, has noted that the sequence anticipates the surreal Follies-show climax, "Loveland," of *Follies*, which was designed by Aronson more than three decades after *Love Life*.

23

The married couple in *Love Life*, Susan and Sam Cooper (Nanette Fabray and Ray Middleton) of Mayville, Connecticut, never age during the musical's 150-year time frame. As their story progresses through every stage of American social history, Weill and Lerner use a variety of musical forms to fit the various periods—ballads, madrigals, minstrel numbers—intermingled with trapeze, magic, soft-shoe, and tightrope acts. "There were enough ideas in this show for twenty musicals," said Aronson. "*Love Life* attempted to chronicle the cavalcade of America, from the beginning to modern times, and to show the effect of the Industrial Revolution on marriage. The show started out as a vaudeville, with a lady being sawed in half, and ended with a husband and wife meeting each other halfway across a high wire."

Throughout, the vaudeville numbers served as comments on the preceding scenes. . . . *Love Life* required a light touch, charm, humor, and pure theatricality. Kazan attempted to unify the show, to give it logic and continuity, but the musical was basically written in the form of a revue. I followed the vaudeville approach by designing a variety of sketchy scenes and vaudeville drops, each making a comment of its own."

By the time "concept musicals" became the rage, in the 1960s, Lerner had made his name with more straightforward musicals, such as *My Fair Lady* and *Camelot*. But in the program of *Love Life* he wrote, "We do not rest on our oars. Today's invention is tomorrow's cliché. We must continue to invent and improvise. That is the only way that theatre—and we of the theatre—can remain healthy."

24

25

24, 25   In a ballet sequence that was designed but never staged, newspapers become the revolving doors of modern urban life.

26

26   Act curtain for *Love Life*.

DOCUMENTARY REALISM

Acting areas are the most important thing. I have my own characteristics. I like obstacles. Very seldom have I designed a symmetrical set, with one half of the set precisely balancing the other.

DETECTIVE STORY (1949)

As much as Aronson tried to escape realistic plays and realistic sets, the demands of the New York theatre dictated that he take them on. Perhaps his most distinguished and literal-minded realistic set was for the detectives' squad room of Sidney Kingsley's documentary melodrama *Detective Story*.

Kingsley had spent nearly two years sitting in police stations to collect material and atmosphere for his play, which was set in a fictional precinct. In addition to writing down details, the playwright had had photographs taken of the stations, to ensure that even window screens would be accurately represented on stage. He gave twenty-three photos to Aronson, but the designer took a hundred more of his own. To make certain that everything in the set would be standard police issue rather than an exception found in only one station, the photos were taken at stations all over town. As one newspaper account noted, "When builders suggested better and cheaper methods of constructing the setting, the pictures were the referee. It would have been easier to have the cord of the clock, which is a functional prop and runs throughout the play, come from behind the set, thus saving a baseboard connection and eliminating the danger of accidentally pulling out the plug. Every picture of a station clock, however, showed a cord running to a baseboard plug, and so the clock on the Hudson [Theatre] stage has a cord, a plug and a baseboard connec-

tion. . . . The painters visited local police stations to obtain the exact effect and values of the faded and often begrimed colors. The effect of age on the walls, cabinets, files and furniture is exact. All the items were colored to match color sketches made in the police stations. The calendar on the wall is an official police department calendar; the 'Courtesy' sign on the door is a copy of the sign issued by the Police Commissioner and found on the wall of every station. The desks, the billies, the measuring rod were all obtained from the shops which supply the Police Department."

After the play opened, the *Times* critic, Brooks Atkinson, wrote that "some of us were discussing the aesthetics of [Aronson's setting]. On literal terms the squad room is ugly, cheerless, shabbily utilitarian and musty. Although the setting faithfully records these unbeautiful factors, it is a beautiful piece of work. How is this possible? Someone suggested that the set gives life and vitality to the ugly squad room, which is an airless area scooped out of life, and this is the element that creates the beauty. In a way the explanation begs the question, because it does not explain how an artist gives life to an object that is apparently dead. But it at least analyzes the difference between life, which in this case is diffuse and boring, and a reproduction of life, which is exhilarating. Something of the same sort applies to *Detective Story*."

1, 2   *Detective Story* (1949): Aronson's detective squad rooms as sketched (1) and as occupied by the Manhattan denizens of Sidney Kingsley's police melodrama (2).

THE FIFTIES

In the theatre, it is permissible to say the same thing again and again. Nowhere is the technique of paraphrasing more accepted. In the greatest of plays, the plot is often simple and obvious: mistaken identity, love conquers all, all's well that ends well. Audiences relax with the familiar—they become aware of the same old facts—but it is the originality in the method of presenting these facts that allows the repetition of the same thing over and over again.

The theatre always functions on two levels: one is the familiar and obvious, where people identify; they know the message and have heard it before. The other level is intellectual—the philosophical, which makes the observer think—the qualities of arousal or surprise which lead to a reaction of anger or approval. Even on the most familiar level, there is magic about the theatre, and the magic is doing old clichés in fresh and original ways. In the old stock Yiddish theatre, at the moment when the heroine was reunited with her lover after forty years apart, the audience would cry and applaud so loudly that the lovers would repeat the scene, like an encore. No one questions this kind of theatrical convention, nor does anyone question the reworking of old formulas in startling and remarkably original ways. But when this becomes a purely mechanical thing, with no doubts and no feeling of questioning or expectation, then the magic goes out of the theatre.

During most of the 1950s, a period of solid if not always daring American theatre, Aronson designed a cross-section of plays by the writers who defined the decade on Broadway—from the reigning heavyweight trinity of Tennessee Williams, Arthur Miller, and William Inge to the veteran playwrights S. N. Behrman, John van Druten, Clifford Odets, Maxwell Anderson, and Robert E. Sherwood, to such popular boulevard entertainers as N. Richard Nash, Arnold Schulman, and Sam and Bella Spewack. Not all of the plays were interesting, and neither were all of the sets, but amidst the rush of activity were some outstanding examples of Aronson's art.

SEASON IN THE SUN (1950)

Wolcott Gibbs, the drama critic of *The New Yorker*, adapted his own short stories into a comedy about a *New Yorker* journalist who decides to become a serious novelist. The setting is a weather-beaten summer bungalow on the Fire Island beach. Aronson visited Fire Island and designed a realistic set, but with an important principle in mind: "On a place like Fire Island, even a cat or dog should count. The actors should look large." He made the house smaller than full scale to emphasize the ample sky and sand.

The play's director, Burgess Meredith, found that "the main problem Boris had to solve was doing an outdoor set on a beach. That included having real sand. At first, the sand he brought in was actually sea sand from Coney Island or some such place. But that sand was so drab-looking that I was dissatisfied. Boris then asked me if I had any suggestions, because sand was sand. I told him that in the spittoons at the 21 Club in New York, where people put out their cigarettes, they always had pure white sand. I explained this was more the color I wanted. I suggested that Boris call the 21 Club and ask them where they got such lovely sand for their spittoons. He called them and asked them the question, and this became a great joke. But, at any rate, they gave us the source from which this angel-white sand came. And Boris ordered quite a bit of it, which he sprinkled over the other sand like whipped cream over a cake. Courtney Burr, the producer, wouldn't let him order too much of it because it turned out to be very expensive. It seems they have to bleach it to get that pristine color."

I, 2   The set for Wolcott Gibbs' *Season in the Sun* (1950), as sketched (2) and on stage (1) with the actors, who loomed large against the bleached sand.

3 Harold Clurman, who directed Arthur Laurents' early play *The Bird Cage* (1950), described it as "a provocative but unfulfilled piece [attempting] to make routine material (melodramatic action in [the backrooms of] a metropolitan night club) serve the purposes of an allegory about the all-pervasive fear and concomitant power-hunger that are characteristic of our society." Clurman thought Aronson's set "the most original and striking of the season—an illustration of how the discoveries of modern art can be made to serve both the functional and atmospheric problems of a many-scened play without striking an audience as too obviously stylized or 'unrealistic.' " Aronson's design, as seen in this sketch, uses exposed poles, mirrored walls, and an abstract New York cityscape; the piano platform revolved to reveal a dressing room. A partial curtain made up of black vertical lines at times covered the upstairs office— in birdcage fashion—and anticipated the linear urban feeling of Aronson's *Company* twenty years later.

4

4, 5 A sketch (4) for the empty stage in Clifford Odets' *The Country Girl* (1950), which Aronson intended to contrast with the actor's cluttered home (5).

5

THE COUNTRY GIRL (1950)

"There is nothing more glamorous and more sad than backstage in the theatre," said Aronson about the milieu of Clifford Odets' play. In productions from Robert Rossen's *The Body Beautiful* (1935) to the musical *Follies* (1971), Aronson created designs for backstage plays that were meant to capture both the glamour and disillusionments of working in the theatre.

The Country Girl is about an aging, has-been Broadway star who has thrown away his youthful promise on booze and is suddenly given an unexpected chance for a comeback. Though Odets saw Georgie, the actor's wife, as the principal character, Aronson envisioned the play in terms of the actor, Frank Elgin. "The reason I lean toward Frank is because Georgie didn't have a chance to create a permanent home. So I couldn't dramatize it." In a story defined by Frank's ups and downs in the theatre, the wife "doesn't have the chance to do anything about where they are."

The designer saw the play as "mostly about two people on stage" and as "a study of contrasts between the places where the characters find themselves." The first scenes take place on an empty Broadway stage where a new play is being rehearsed and in the shabby furnished room where Frank and Georgie live. "No setting can be more effective than an empty stage. There is something about the very *nakedness* of a rehearsal which is dramatic because it is stripped of all the superficiality that's added later. I felt the feeling of bareness during the rehearsal scene should be contrasted with the very limited, condensed, and tiny place where the couple lives. Their furnished room is just a corner, crowded, cluttered, with hardly room to move. There is no closet. A trunk is used to store clothes. As with so many actors, if they walked out, you'd feel that they had never lived there at all."

The rest of *The Country Girl* unfolds in dressing rooms—first in Boston, where Frank's comeback play has its tryout, and then on Broadway, on opening night. "The Boston dressing room is very depressing: the beams overhead, the steam pipes showing, and the walls broken down. That's because the play at that time is at its lowest point. Frank is drunk, he is failing." But when Frank triumphs in New York, the dressing room is orderly, clean, and painted a "soothing" greenish-blue. "This is where there's hope, where they succeed and can look forward to life confidently."

To Aronson, the play had "a very human quality" that would not be served by "beautifying" its theatrical setting. "I tried to get the backstage of backstage."

6, 7 As a washed-up actor at first fails and then succeeds in his comeback attempt, he moves from a dilapidated dressing room in Boston (6) to a well-maintained one in New York. Uta Hagen, a co-star in the play, recalled that when Aronson doubled as lighting designer, as he did in this case, he was more concerned about lighting the scenery than the actors: "He told me one day that he thought I was the greatest actress because I always had a way of finding my way into the light."

8, 9 For *The Rose Tattoo* (1951), Tennessee Williams'
warm comic hymn to the sexually reborn widow
Serafina delle Rose, Aronson had to summon up
"a village populated mostly by Sicilians somewhere
along the Gulf Coast between New Orleans and
Mobile." He did so with an earthy landscape, the
colorful Latin interior of Serafina's frame cottage,
and a backdrop suggesting the industrialized South
beyond (8). Here Aronson started painting sets in a
more unrealistic manner by painting the deepest part
of the set the lightest in color, to give it an inner
glow, "like the heart of the candle." Aronson was
guided by Williams' precise scenic directions in the
script. Among other things, the playwright called for
a sky of a "delicate blue with an opalescent shimmer
more like water than air," "an interior that is as
colorful as a booth at a carnival"—with "everything
. . . exclamatory in its brightness like the projection
of a woman's heart passionately in love." "I wouldn't
stylize *The Rose Tattoo*," said Aronson. "To me,
it's a romantic folk play in the terms of Tennessee
Williams." The playwright loved the two aprons
that extended over the orchestra pit, allowing the
cottage to extend almost to the proscenium. In a
preproduction note, he asked the designer to "please
keep in mind that the goat must be led across the
forestage, from the rear of house on one side to the
other." Aronson complied (9).

Aronson designed both stage adaptations of the Sally Bowles tale from Christopher Isherwood's *Berlin Stories*—this John van Druten play, *I Am a Camera* (1951), and, 15 years later, the much different musical version, *Cabaret.* The setting of *Camera* is a properly bourgeois rented room in Berlin, c. 1930. Drawing on his own memories of living in Berlin in the 1920s, Aronson designed a shabby-genteel but meticulously neat Germanic interior. "When I lived there, I was always impressed by the mingling of order and Gemütlichkeit, of shining cleanliness and heaviness, of cozy cheer and regimentation. I recalled the striking of the clocks in the house where I roomed— a clamor of unsynchronized chiming which seemed to jar the orderly calm of the surroundings. I tried to assemble some of these elements in the play's middle-class bedroom with its partly concealed bed, washstand, tiled stove, and antler hatrack by the door." He was struck by the fact that the play's sole intimation of the forthcoming holocaust was disposed of casually, with a beaten-up Jew being given a bandage—and yet that van Druten "spent four days" rehearsing a piece of business involving a hangover remedy made with raw eggs. "And I learned a lesson about the beauty of being superficial," Aronson said. "Because after you work with Clurman and Strasberg, it's a joy to do a thing which is pure champagne. I did a number of shows with van Druten, and I enjoyed his genuine finesse."

THE CRUCIBLE (1953)

The Crucible was the first of Aronson's five collaborations with Arthur Miller over a two-decade span. Miller and Elia Kazan had severed their creative partnership early in the McCarthy era, and, as a consequence, this play about the Salem witch trials of 1692 was directed by Jed Harris.

Aronson went to Salem to do research. There he found that houses built by the earliest settlers, shipbuilders, were made of heavy, hand-hewn beams, with tiny windows and oddly angled roofs, like prows of ships. The dark interiors, stark and sparsely furnished, had huge fireplaces with high-backed benches flanking them; thick doors were mounted on heavy iron hinges. To Aronson, the interiors felt mysterious—"One sensed the forbidding severity of daily living"— and he tried to incorporate that feeling in his initial designs for the sets. Never the most beloved man on Broadway, Harris angered Aronson by rejecting the designs entirely and asking for nightmarish, *Caligari*-like Expressionist sets—only to reject the new designs, too, once they'd been sketched. The director then demanded conventional sets in the form of beautiful Dutch interiors, and Aronson once again tried to incorporate his extensive research.

Neither Aronson nor Miller was happy with the final results. According to the playwright, "Harris wanted Dutch painting out of his idea that he had to make *The Crucible* look like a classic play, as if it had been an old play. [It was staged] like Racine. The actors couldn't move their feet. It was operatic—they moved between positions for speeches; there were extremely long entrances.

"Harris had it completely opposite from the way it was. I envisioned *The Crucible* not as a classic, but as a very contentious play. In Salem in those days, they couldn't even agree on what time it was; the parish had six priests who argued all the time. Boris' [original] set was unstable, with an ambiance of mystery and unexpectedness; you didn't know what the hell was going to come next. What we used was predictable.

"The stability of a classic is defeating. *The Crucible* was thought to be a cold play. [After the opening] we weren't doing enough business to stay alive unless costs were lowered. We had to reduce the number of stagehands. Harris was gone, so I had to remove scenery and just use black velours in back." Along with the set alterations, Miller revised, restaged, and recast *The Crucible*—and returning critics gave the play better reviews than they had on opening night.

11, 12 *The Crucible* (1953): The meetinghouse, as sketched (11) and on stage (12), with Beatrice Straight and E. G. Marshall.

13

13, 14   Aronson's sketches for Arthur Miller's bill of one-acts, *A Memory of Two Mondays* . . .

A VIEW FROM THE BRIDGE   (1955)

Aronson's next Miller project—a bill of two one-act plays, *A View from the Bridge* and *A Memory of Two Mondays*—was also somewhat problematic. The designer had to create a basic unit set to fit both plays, even though the plays were written in completely different styles. *Memory*, the curtain-raiser, was an intimate, poetic work set indoors, while *Bridge* had exterior scenes and was more distant and overtly dramatic. Aronson treated the sets in terms of that contrast, but unified them with a basic platform.

Memory was a reminiscence about men and women working in the shipping room of a large, dingy auto-parts warehouse in Depression-era Manhattan. The play's time frame advanced from a hot summer morning to a chill winter morning—allowing Aronson to make atmospheric use of the light that entered through the dirty windows. The designer had done research at a Brooklyn garage suggested by Miller, but he also drew on Paul Klee's paintings for inspiration. In an abstract, painterly way, Aronson treated the solid surfaces to create

14

. . . and *A View from the Bridge* (1955).

the effect that light was coming through the windows from the fourth wall (the audience's side of the set). However, the play was jettisoned from the bill early in the run, after the critics uniformly dismissed it.

To Miller, *Memory* was about looking "from the inside out," about "trying to get through the muddy panes of a window." *A View from the Bridge* was about "looking in from the sea." The play was set in and around the apartment of Eddie Carbone, who lives in Red Hook, on the bay, seaward from the Brooklyn Bridge. Carbone is a

longshoreman whose incestuous passion for a niece leads him to inform the police about the niece's illegal-immigrant suitor.

Miller wrote the play as a tragedy—complete with a Greek chorus in the form of a neighborhood lawyer who narrated the action. Aronson designed it accordingly, with a sweeping ocean vista and a strong hint of Greek columns at the entrance to the Carbone apartment. The producer, Robert Whitehead, thought from the beginning that a simpler approach was called for. Indeed, the play's genesis had been

15, 16, 17   Aronson's sets for Jean Anouilh's *Mademoiselle Colombe* (1954), in which the dressing rooms and backstage corridors of a 1900 Parisian theatre are seen at odd angles (15, 16). In the final scene (17), the audience sees a play performed from the perspective of the wings.

OPPOSITE

18   Edna Best and Julie Harris in the climax of *Mademoiselle Colombe*. The critic Eric Bentley wrote that Anouilh's "particular blend of French reality with theatrical unreality" has been "translated into color and shape."

far humbler than the set suggested. While producing Odets' *The Flowering Peach*, Whitehead had noticed that when the set (by Mordecai Gorelik) was struck each night, "it looked like a circus ring. All that was left on stage was the ring and a cyclorama; with only a work light on it, it looked beautiful and evocative." The producer thought that the struck *Peach* set might be used on Sunday nights for informal stagings of one-act plays. He called Miller, who first came up with *From Under the Sea* (the original title of *View*) and then *Memory*—two plays about New York. But agents said no to Whitehead's idea of a Sunday-night presentation.

Instead, the producer mounted the Broadway production, arguing all the way with Miller about the "suggestively classic element" of *View*. "Why reinforce the classic element with the set?" Whitehead asked. "Why not make it as simple as possible? Aronson's set was beautiful to look at, but it worried me. The Greek classicism separated *View* from *Memory*, which was just as poetic. Everyone got carried away into Greek tragedy, including Arthur. Maybe it should have been done as originally planned, without the tragic aura, with just a cyclorama. The point of the play was that people come to America to work, but the romantic poetic quality of the ocean suggested we were on the coast of Calabria or something."

After *View* failed on Broadway, Miller rewrote it—expanding the play to full length and removing some of its portentous excesses, including the use of verse. Subsequent productions, all more successful than the original, used more realistic sets in keeping with the new text. *Memory* also resurfaced—a quarter-century after the first production—in a Public Broadcasting System television version. It was shot in an abandoned New York warehouse used by the city to service trucks. When Miller visited the location, he felt it uncannily resembled Aronson's original design: "Life had reproduced Boris' set!"

MADEMOISELLE COLOMBE (1954)

Aronson returned to the backstage world of the theatre in Jean Anouilh's play, but with a glamorous period panache far removed from the seedy New York theatre environments of *The Country Girl*. This time the dressing rooms, stage, and backstage areas were those of a Paris theatre circa 1900.

Harold Clurman, the director, described the intended mood in a letter to Aronson a year before the opening: "I was struck by the fact that many of the characters act like *clowns* and then I realized that in the commedia dell'arte sense they are all clowns. . . . The play is as the commedia dell'arte plays so often are, a kind of tragic farce and pure theatre. It is, in fact, a sort of serious *circus*.

"This leads me to believe that the play should be made as colorful as possible in costume and setting, in turn romantically gay and romantically sad. It must be heightened to a thoroughgoing theatrical picturesqueness. The shabby element which also exists as part of the atmosphere may be minimized in behalf of the picturesqueness. We should see the theatre with the eyes of Colombe [a young woman who falls in love with the theatrical life], who thinks of it as a fulfillment of everything she desires. . . .

"The color should not be garish, but rather *light* and tasteful in the French manner. In *Colombe*, the theatre is the world, the world which Anouilh loves and despises at the same time because it is beautiful illusion and terrible cynicism. . . . I want the set to be the most glamorous of many seasons. I intend to heighten make-ups, color of hair and characterizations in line with this feeling I have about the play. . . . One thing is sure, I am not going to have a realistic production."

Aronson executed Clurman's vision with a sumptuous series of sets that were oddly angled; they were all geared to the final set, in which the audience sees a play-within-a-play from the vantage point of a theatre's wings.

18

19

19   Aronson's set for Ibsen's *The Master Builder* (1955).

THE MASTER BUILDER (1955)

Aronson rarely had the opportunity to work on classics. This late Ibsen play, about the most successful builder in Christiania, Norway, at the self-destructive end of his career, was a perfect match for his sensibility. It deals, in part, with the limitations of the artist.

"I can't imagine a contemporary play that would say more about what happens when you reach the top, when you can't go higher," Aronson said. "Everything about my design and the detail that went into it was stylized—the essence of the powerful architecture of Norway in the 1890s. At the same time, I based my concept of the central character, Solness, on Frank Lloyd Wright. I saw *The Master Builder* as the tragedy of the visionary.

"In the theatre, great moments don't necessarily have to be 'poetic.' When Solness, the master builder, confesses his terror that 'the younger generation will come knock at my door,' youth knocks immediately—but *not* in the person of a clamoring young competitor. It is the uncompromising Hilda Wangel, the half-forgotten girl from his past and now the young woman who will determine his future. The dramatic moment of that knocking at the door is so meaningful, so true. It's saying in the simplest terms something that really hits you if you understand it. Because it's written that way, you design it that way." Aronson understood that when "youth comes knocking at the door" of a house in an Ibsen play, it isn't necessary to have a real house on stage; his design emphasized "symbolic essentials."

The sets were Nordic without being heavy and gloomy. Aronson used a light plasticity and Paul Klee–like striations. "The sketches had watercolor-like horizontal logs in shades of gray-lavender through greens," said John Keck, the scenic painter who had to interpret the designs on a large scale. "The intermixes were so subtle. When dye sank in in one color, there would be paint over it in the other color—so that there were always pinks under the green." Three revolving elements allowed the interior of Solness' office to expand into his home's drawing room and then to expand further, revealing the scaffolding and trees surrounding the builder's final creation, his tower to the sky. "Unfortunately," said Aronson, "the acting and direction lacked the size, style, and dimension that would have made it larger than life." The critic Eric Bentley agreed, writing that "in three settings, [Aronson] contrives to have the best of both worlds, the abstract and the representational, the symbolic and the actual, just like the Norwegian master himself. . . . His interpretation of Ibsen is more surefooted and more suggestive than anything else that happens."

20, 21 As *The Master Builder* grew from act to act toward the symbolic, so did the set.

22

23

24

OPPOSITE

22, 23   In William Inge's *Bus Stop* (1955), a bus is waylaid by a blizzard and deposits its few weary passengers overnight at a diner. "It was a romantic comedy in a very specific place, a restaurant in 'a small town 30 miles west of Kansas City,' " said Aronson. "You couldn't design it as a stylized café 'somewhere in the world.' " Aronson emphasized the contrast between the diner's warm interior and the dark storm that whirled (complete with blowing snow) beyond the plate-glass windows and above the cutaway roof (22). Aronson's lonely Americana was inspired by Edward Hopper's "Nighthawks" (23).

24   Inge's fast overnight friends in Aronson's diner: Albert Salmi, Kim Stanley. "When that design went up, it *worked*," said Robert Whitehead, the play's producer.

25

25   Though Aronson had never been to Florida, this did not stop him from designing *A Hole in the Head* (1957), Arnold Schulman's comedy about a widower (Paul Douglas) coping with his 12-year-old son and a tacky, bankrupt Miami hotel (as seen in the sketch). "We needed a lobby, living quarters, back porch, and a staircase for guests to come in and go out," said Garson Kanin, the director. "I asked Boris if we could fix it in such a way that in each scene we see the hotel areas from a different point of view. We talked about it at length and I didn't hear from him for about ten days. Then he called me up and I went up to his apartment/studio. We began to look at the model. It was simply one great big platform that shifted so that you looked at it one way and then, the next time, the whole thing had shifted again. It wasn't a circle. It was a *swivel*. The aspect kept changing. It looked like a different set every time." The producer, Robert Whitehead, felt the set properly "stressed the cheapness of the milieu" but was initially against the bulky shifting of it from scene to scene. In the end, he decided that the tilting "brought another kind of reality to the play—movie technique."

OPPOSITE

26, 27   In production photographs, the set is seen in two different positions.

26

27

28

29

30

OPPOSITE

28, 29, 30   The dry-goods store of *Orpheus Descending* (1957) as Tennessee Williams requested it—seen in the sketch (28) and on stage, in both its transparent (29) and opaque (30) modes.

31   Harold Clurman's production of *Orpheus Descending* starred Maureen Stapleton and Cliff Robertson.

ORPHEUS DESCENDING   (1957)

"Of all the authors I worked with," said Aronson, "the one whose scene descriptions were the most helpful was Tennessee Williams."

Williams' manuscript for this revision of his first produced play, originally seen as *Battle of Angels* in 1940, began: "The set represents in non-realistic fashion a general dry-goods store and part of a connecting 'confectionery' in a small Southern town. The ceiling is high and the upper walls are dark, as if streaked with moisture and cobwebbed. A great dusty window upstage offers a view of disturbing emptiness, then fades into late dusk. The action of the play occurs during a rainy season, late winter and early spring, and sometimes the window turns opaque but glistening silver with sheets of rain. 'TORRANCE MERCANTILE STORE' is lettered on the window in gilt of old-fashioned design. Merchandise is represented very sparsely and it is not realistic. Bolts of pepperel and percale stand upright on large spools, the black skeleton of a dressmaker's dummy stands meaningless against a thin white column, and there is a motionless ceiling fan with strips of flypaper hanging from it. There are stairs that lead to a landing and disappear above it, and on the landing there is a sinister-looking artificial palm-tree in a greenish-brown jardiniere. But the confectionary which is seen partly through a wide arched door is shadowy and poetic as some inner dimension of the play. Another, much smaller, playing area is a tiny bedroom alcove which is usually masked by an oriental drapery which is worn dim but bears the formal design of gold tree with scarlet fruit and fantastic birds."

Aronson's final set matches that description, but his first one did not. Robert Whitehead, the producer, rejected the original design as "too French"—"Boris was designing ballets and doing watercolors at the time." As a result, Aronson got research material depicting a real-life dry-goods store from the small Mississippi town, near Greenville, where Williams' *Baby Doll* had been filmed. Even so, the original design's French arches persisted.

THE ROPE DANCERS   (1957)

A first play by Morton Wishengrad, a radio and television writer, *The Rope Dancers* also marked the Broadway debut of the English director Peter Hall, then twenty-six years old. Aronson was "a hero" to Hall, who had first seen his designs in *A View from the Bridge* and *The*

32

32, 33, 34   Aronson's design for Morton Wishengrad's
The Rope Dancers, as sketched (32) and as seen on
stage (33). Its abstract use of color was inspired by
Matisse's "Red Studio" (34).

Diary of Anne Frank a few years earlier. The play was about a shift-less husband, his wife, and their deformed daughter in a turn-of-the-century New York tenement. Neither Hall nor Aronson was happy with the script. "It had a streak of sentimentality about it," the director said. "It was a twentieth-century retelling of a nineteenth-century melodrama. But it had wonderful acting parts and a sense of place and time. Though the cast was very fine—Siobhan McKenna, Art Carney, Joan Blondell, Theodore Bikel—the joy to me was making a complete statement on stage with Boris. He was the first designer who absolutely sucked me dry. He took absolutely everything out of me. He wanted to know exactly what I thought and why, and if I didn't think, he wanted to know why I didn't think. He wanted to know my opinion about every facet of the play and production."

Another theatre artist who first collaborated with Aronson on *The Rope Dancers* was the costume designer Patricia Zipprodt, who later worked with him on the musicals *Fiddler on the Roof, Cabaret,* and *Zorba.* "Boris had me come out to his painting studio. He was or-chestrating the whole design, and he taught me the difference between warm and cool colors, the relativity of values. In one area, we were both working in white. I designed a white-blue nightie for the daughter, and he made her bed sheets white-beige so she'd show up against them. We went to the balcony to check, and it worked. During the New Haven tryout, we spent a lot of time in the basement fixing things up—the kinds of details that used to be handled by costume and wardrobe people. The girl-next-door in the play had a plaid dress in my sketch; I found a light plaid dress, took it home, and painted it gray-green between the stripes to work with the set."

Aronson's principal inspiration for his color treatment of the set was one of his favorite paintings, Matisse's "Red Studio" of 1911. From it, he took the notion of using a uniform tone throughout the set—greenish-gray in the case of *The Rope Dancers*—and of dotting it with carefully placed color accents, such as those used for the bed-spread, a colored glass panel over a door, and the view through the window. The painting minimized the realism of the architecture, treating it as two-dimensional—a device that had also been used in *A Memory of Two Mondays.* The result was a set more abstract than naturalistic, designed to help lift the play out of its kitchen-sink origins.

35   Peter Hall and Aronson at work on *The Rope Dancers.*

ATMOSPHERIC REALISM

Stages are too cluttered. Why so much luggage for so short a trip! A property man supplies four vodka bottles, flaming swords, empty tables, full-length mirrors (rented), and bouquets of roses—all this in order for an actor to say, "Looking for your hat, Mister!" But in Waiting for Godot *a single half-carrot can symbolize an entire meal; in* A Streetcar Named Desire *one naked lightbulb stands for an entire mood.*

THE DIARY OF ANNE FRANK   (1955)

The Diary of Anne Frank was the longest-running Broadway hit that Aronson worked on during the 1950s. As a design project, it illustrates the subtle and profound differences a set can make to what might seem a straightforward realistic play. The script by Frances Goodrich and Albert Hackett was a dramatization of a famous document—the diary of a young Jewish girl who, with family and friends, hid successfully for two years in an Amsterdam garret before being discovered and sent to a Nazi death camp. The diary was a sacred text that could not be fictionalized for the stage; the garret was not an imaginary place, but a real one that had survived the war with its occupants' furnishings intact. Yet within these tight coordinates dictated by actual history there were many aesthetic decisions to be made. As it happened, Aronson's set—which grew out of his close collaboration with the director, Garson Kanin—had an impact on the Hacketts' adaptation as well as on the finished production.

The process began when the producer, Kermit Bloomgarden, sent the Hacketts' script to Kanin. Bloomgarden told the director that the production had already been designed, by Howard Bay—at the request of the authors, who needed a graphic visualization of the diary in order to write their play. Kanin took the job on the condition that the Bay set not be used. "I did not want to be handed a physical production," Kanin later said, "since one of the principal things that a director must do is to convey to the designer, or work out with the designer, some concept of how the whole play is going to be produced.

"When *Diary* was first sent to me, it was a multiple-scene, multiple-set play. It required some fourteen or fifteen separate settings, and the problem was how could you go from one set to the other swiftly enough to keep the flow of the story going. I could visualize this as being an evening of stage waits—the lights going down, the noisy shifting of scenery; whatever you did—revolves, platforms—it was going to be a mess. I wanted to make it a single set, but they were troubled by the fact that I didn't intend to do the old stage convention of putting all the lights out on the areas that were not in use, but was going to keep the whole thing alive all the time. They said, 'When Peter [van Dam] is playing the tender little love scene with Anne, wouldn't that be so distracting?' I said, 'Not at all, because that's life. The mother and father will be playing cards, somebody will be knitting, somebody will be sleeping. It will be all right.'

1   Aronson's sketch for *The Diary of Anne Frank* (1955).

2   The occupants of the garret, each in his or her separate room, fulfilling Kanin's idea that the entire stage be kept "alive" at all times.

"I told Bloomgarden that I did not want to even look at the other set design because I wanted to start from scratch, and he agreed. I told him there was only one man in the world to do it if he could be interested, and that was Boris. Bloomgarden sent Boris the play. I was living in Europe at the time, and I wrote Boris and said that I was very, very anxious somehow not to have it be a multiple-scene play. I asked him if he saw any possible way of turning it into a single unit set that would live the whole time, not with some areas being live while others go dead."

Aronson agreed with Kanin. Instead of using different successive sets for the several living areas of the garret—each one filling the stage —the whole garret would be on stage, its various "rooms" reduced accordingly in scale.

This decision served not only to improve the play's flow but also to enhance its mood and substance; Aronson's design came not merely out of Kanin's desire for streamlined theatrical logistics but out of the designer's emotional relationship to the material. As Aronson explained, "I don't start from a plan. I start by asking what is the nature of this material, what is it trying to say, what does it stand for? If you get a play written by a girl who is not an artist and not a playwright, the quality of the whole thing is documentary. It's as if you were lucky enough to take a picture of a plane which is on fire because you happened to have a camera at that time. *The Diary* is also the story of a young girl in love with life who manages to squeeze bitterness and sweetness out of every moment. It is the story of boredom, search for comfort, dreams, fears, anger, and joy. It so happened that I also was familiar with danger and with death from pogroms in Kiev. And what is the worst thing about being cooped up in a place where the Nazis could come in any minute? The most unbearable thing is lack of privacy—to be constantly exposed to other people, with no exit, twenty-four hours a day. It is so horrible that Anne walks around from place to place and can never for one second in any human fashion be alone; that's what I have to design. But there is a great discrepancy in doing this on the stage. On the stage, it would seem ridiculous, because, visually, you have the opposite. You have so much space, and yet still you have to create the feeling that [Anne] is caught, her claustrophobia." At the same time, a densely packed set could not solve this problem: "A crowded dwelling on the stage doesn't look crowded; it looks cluttered."

In the end, Aronson decided to "create a sense of organized clutter. The single setting—essential to accentuate the confinement—actually consisted of many small compartments. These tiny rooms for the family and the strangers present—each had a character all its own. The longer the occupants lived there, the more home-like the garret became. But to accentuate the sense of the lack of privacy, all rooms were exposed at all times to the 'naked' eye of the audience. The final look of the setting was that of a very authentic cross-section of an attic converted into a temporary dwelling." The acting areas were conceived of in terms of staging the play; the details were documentary.

Aronson also had to deal with other physical and atmospheric matters that Kanin specified in a preproduction letter, written after script revisions and a tour of the actual Frank garret in Amsterdam: "The pattern of the play itself does not follow the actual layout [of the garret], since this would not have been possible. In actual fact, the people in hiding made use of various parts of the building when it was empty, in the evenings, and also on Saturday afternoons and Sundays, but the Hacketts feel, and I agree, that the play will be better if a greater sense of confinement and isolation is suggested.

"Further, the actual hiding place was the back portion of the building. The title of the original diary in Dutch is *Het Achterhuis*, which, translated literally, means *The Back House*, but for the purposes of the play the Hacketts feel it important that from one of the windows the street be visible. Thus, the playing area now consists of three rooms: Peter's room, Anne's room, and the principal room. Mr. and Mrs. Frank sleep in the principal room, later joined by Margot [Frank]. This is also the room which was used for cooking and eating, and general assemblies. . . .

"I feel that the rooms should be as small as possible, again to emphasize the sense of cramped, confined quarters. The center room is, of course, the largest, and contains the sink, the stove, the food cupboard, the principal table, a daybed . . . and Margot's bed. . . . Anne's room is smaller, and should grow to become the prettiest room of the three. It contains the two cots, a work table, and a dresser, or dressing-table of some sort. . . . Peter's room is not properly a room at all, it is a passageway to the attic, and has, as you have seen, a ladder-step arrangement which leads up into the attic. The skylight in Peter's room is important . . . it is the only place through which the outer world can be freely seen. I think, too, that it will be valuable as a way to mirror the changing seasons. . . .

"Please disregard any indications in the script which you have about lights dimming on and off in various portions of the stage. I do

3, 4, 5 The kitchen area in the actual Frank hiding place (3) and the same area as seen on stage (4). On the reverse of Kanin's Amsterdam photograph is a detailed caption provided by him and the Hacketts for Aronson (5).

5

The kitchen part of
the main room.
A stove (gas 2-burner)
stood where I have
marked it —
There were pots and pans
where the bottles now
stand.
Note the _single_ faucet.

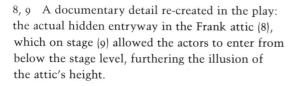

6, 7   The wall in Anne Frank's room (6), with its homely decorations of postcards and magazine pictures, and Anne's room on stage (7).

8, 9   A documentary detail re-created in the play: the actual hidden entryway in the Frank attic (8), which on stage (9) allowed the actors to enter from below the stage level, furthering the illusion of the attic's height.

not consider this plan stageworthy, and the Hacketts and I are now agreed that the full playing area, all three rooms, be visible and alive at all times."

Nonetheless, Kanin also requested set changes of a sort that would occur throughout the play during dim-outs: a redressing of the rooms that would indicate the passing of time. "Actually, I see this play as a ten-set play," the director explained, "since each time we see the rooms, some change has taken place. Furniture shifted, furniture added, furniture painted or repainted, a chair covered. Perhaps, later on, instead of the blackout curtains being drawn, one section of a window has been painted out. I should think it valuable for the room to have a more and more homelike appearance as time goes by, the place itself becoming increasingly attractive and livable as the inhabitants become shabbier and thinner. . . ." In this way, the set became a character in the play, with Aronson designing every detail that gradually transformed a bare attic into a civilized, decorated home.

Kanin then added "one final comment: I do not regard this a sad play, nor an unhappy one, but rather as an exalting comment on the human spirit. Therefore, I hope that the graphic side of the play will not unnecessarily emphasize the tragic tone."

Though the play would take liberties with some of the real garret's architecture, its furnishings were scrupulously based on dozens of photographs that Kanin hired a photographer to take of the interior and exterior of the Frank house at 263 Prinsengracht, down to individual doorknobs and moldings. Kanin also spent a whole night in the house: "I wanted to know something about the sounds, which I knew would be different in wartime than in peacetime. And what you heard in the streets as far as traffic was concerned. I wanted to know, could you really hear a truck go by? If someone was talking in the street, or soldiers singing, could you really have heard them up there? Then I sent all the photographs to Boris and that was my contribution to the setting. The rest of it is all Boris, except for one thing. I insisted that the main entrance had to be a trapdoor. The only way the audience will have the illusion that these people are actually in an attic is if they come up through the floor. As it turned out, the theatre they gave us was the Cort, which had a steel girder running right where we needed that entrance, and we were absolutely mad, beside ourselves." In the end, a complex solution was found: the entire set was built on a platform above the stage level, adding further to the illusion of the attic's height.

According to Kanin, the set's color scheme was Aronson's idea:

10   The set of *Diary* as seen by actors arriving from the stairs below stage.

11, 12   A panoramic view of Amsterdam (11) remade by Aronson into a drop (detail, 12) suggesting the "vivid city life" outside the Frank hiding place.

"Boris said that Amsterdam means only one thing to him—Rembrandt. And the entire palette for *Diary* was Rembrandt: browns, maroons, deep blues, beiges, yellows. There was nothing arty about this. It was simply that Boris said, 'The reason that the Impressionists painted as they did in and around Avignon or the reason that Matisse paints the Côte d'Azur as he does is because that's the colors that his eyes see.'" Thus was Aronson able to use ideas about national characteristics in art that he had first advanced in 1923, when he wrote his treatise on Jewish graphic art in Berlin.

But perhaps the designer's most imaginative addition to the set was the cyclorama surrounding it. Among the many photographs Kanin had sent were views from the top of Amsterdam's principal ca-

thedral, and Aronson used them to create a painted bird's-eye view of Amsterdam that wrapped around the attic. The panoramic perspective on the city was not that of the characters, but that of the audience—as if the audience were looking over the roof to the Amsterdam beyond. "This wasn't just a question of putting up a drop," said Aronson. "It was not a decorative effect, but a concept. Kanin said that the environment should not unduly emphasize the tragic tone. My solution was to emphasize the isolation of the occupants from the outside world. I felt it necessary to contrast their confinement with the vivid city life going on below and around them. The idea was to have Amsterdam, which is a beautiful city, in full glory—as a contrast to all the horror taking place inside."

EPIC THEATRE

No matter what space I am trying to create on stage, I will wind up with actors. The challenge is that the architectural, spatial aspect of a stage set, no matter how fascinating, can achieve its fullest aesthetic value only if the actor enhances it. The passing of time brings changes—enormous changes in architecture, decorative changes in costumes— but the size of the human figure does not change. Designing begins with the size of the human body— a constant—the size of the actor establishes the scale. The environment surrounding the actor serves to emphasize—to put the actor into focus. Space is created around the performer.

At the end of the 1950s, Aronson finally got the chance he had yearned for throughout his career—to design sets for plays that were entirely removed from living rooms, bars, dressing rooms, and kitchens. The plays were, in his view, "epic"—not necessarily because they were superior in quality to other plays he had designed, but because they dealt with large themes in exotic, even fantastic, environments. Aronson's imagination was given free rein. One of the sets of this period, for Archibald MacLeish's *J.B.*, was, to many, the most significant achievement in American theatre design since the Mielziner sets for *Death of a Salesman* and *A Streetcar Named Desire* a decade earlier. In retrospect, it can also be seen that Aronson's epic designs in the late 1950s were a limbering up for the new style of sets he would design for the new style of musicals of the 1960s and 1970s.

THE FIRSTBORN (1958)

Anthony Quayle and Katharine Cornell starred in this production of Christopher Fry's 1945 meditation on the Book of Exodus, with Quayle doubling as director. Set in 1200 B.C., *The Firstborn* is about the battle between Moses, leader of the Jews, and the Pharaoh over the bondage of the Israelites.

"A pyramid by its nature is monumental, timeless, sundrenched," said Aronson. His set aimed to distill the essential characteristics of Egypt. The blazing sun seeped through a straw-colored, highly textured papyrus cyclorama, drenching the stage with the illusion of sweltering heat. Before it was a sculptural, abstract design of complete plasticity: a huge, hieroglyph-engraved Egyptian wall that stood in stark, symbolic contrast to the modest, unpretentious tent of the Jews seen in a later scene. Even the floor was elaborately designed. Ming Cho Lee, who became an assistant to Aronson a year later, "was always envious" that *The Firstborn* was not one of his assignments: "It was design that is not just illustration. That wall is the essence of Egyptian—surfaces and textures." Aronson started to work in a medium that he had been favoring in his painting, encaustics. These hard, wax-based paints, which had to be heated to be used, produced a sketchy, spontaneous look while retaining a high color intensity.

The design process was not untroubled. Anthony Quayle traveled from London to New York to begin work on the production and found that "Boris had already made a start on the play and had some prelimi-

1, 2 The abstract, "timeless" Egypt of the design, as sketched (1) and on stage (2), for Christopher Fry's *The Firstborn* (1958).

nary models. They were too realistic, too literal, for this play of ideas about Moses and ancient Egypt. But I was a bit nervous of saying so. I held Boris in considerable awe. But Boris seized on everything I had to say with a wonderful openness of mind. 'Come back in a couple of days,' he said, 'and I will have something different to show you.'

"I came back, and still I didn't think he was quite on the right lines. And then I remember noticing some small, exquisite pieces of work he had done in quite another medium. (Were they enamel? I think so.) They were vivid in color, detailed but irregular, organic but seemingly haphazard. And they glowed like the wings of an exotic beetle. And I said, 'Look, Boris. There! That's the clue you are looking for.

"And Boris picked up that tiny suggestion, and developed it, and made it both concrete and abstract at the same time, until he had evolved this wonderful setting that seemed to embody the very essence of ancient Egypt. It was positive without being over-dominant, and it held the suggestion of pyramids, of hieroglyphs, of long-dead pharaohs, and of scarab beetles. And without humility he could never have achieved it; he could never have gone through the long, laborious search.

"I remember a dreadful day when we were both very concerned about a certain costume in the show. [Katharine Cornell had privately had her costumes redone to her own specifications, without regard to the production's color scheme.] We were playing in Boston, just prior to opening in New York. Boris flew to Boston for the last Saturday matinee and was appalled. He stood in my dressing room, white in the face, and said, 'Tony, if that costume appears on the stage in New York, I give you solemn warning that I will set fire to the scenery with my own hands.' And I had not the slightest doubt that he meant it. He could have found some way to destroy his own work. And that takes great certainty, great (and true) pride."

CORIOLANUS (1959)

After his happy partnership with the designer on *The Rope Dancers* on Broadway, Peter Hall, then director-designate at Stratford-on-Avon and about to form the Royal Shakespeare Company, invited Aronson to do his one and only Shakespeare project. *Coriolanus* was Hall's second production since arriving at Stratford, and it was part of the theatre's hundredth-anniversary season. The cast included Laurence

3 The Aronson encaustic that Quayle saw: "That's the clue you are looking for!"

4 Aronson's epic theatre designs reflected the new, more plastic phase of his own art, as in "Night Image," a metal relief of the period.

5

6

5, 6   An aerial view of the model for Peter Hall's 1959
production of *Coriolanus* at Stratford-on-Avon (5),
and the "barbaric," Etruscan-colored sketch that led
to it (6).

7, 8 On stage in *Coriolanus*, the walls open to reveal an interior scene with more of a Renaissance feeling (7); Edith Evans and Laurence Olivier inhabit it (8).

Olivier, Edith Evans, Vanessa Redgrave, Albert Finney, Harry Andrews, and Mary Ure.

"The whole basis of the production," Hall explained, "was to try to relate the play to tribal society. I did not want what we think of as a classical set—pale and rain-washed and proportionate." What Hall did want was indicated in a series of letters he wrote to Aronson—from London, Stratford, and Hollywood—during a period of months that encompassed the initial planning of the set, Aronson's preliminary sketches, and the delivery of the final model.

Hall initiated the process by sending the designer "a few rough jottings" laying out his view of the play: "One of the main themes—if not *the* main theme—is the individual against the State. Therefore one must feel a dignity and a community about Rome. The difficulty is that the Roman plays of Shakespeare usually end up very arid and white and architectural, and this somehow makes him seem very classical in the wrong sense, and inhuman. The fable of *Coriolanus*, if it is true at all, happened some four centuries before Christ, at a time when Italy and Rome had not yet attained the grandeur that we think of as 'Roman.' I would like the design to be very strong in colour in a way more Etruscan than Roman; or anyway, with the colours that one finds on many of the wall friezes of Pompeii—deep reds and terra cottas, and a marvellous dark blue-black. . . .

"I don't think we can have a lot of scenery in this play, nor very much in the way of scene changes. The action has to flow more or less continuously so that the set will have to be more or less permanent. Any major changes will have to be confined to the intervals. The only things that I have in my mind's eye at the moment are a series of enormous pillars dividing the stage, and two, or perhaps three enormous gates. Quite apart from their use as the gates of Corioli, and the gates of Rome, when shut they could give us opportunity to prepare a sort of inner stage, or opened up they could form an inner room for the domestic scenes. I think we should limit the acting area as much as possible. The play is almost one perpetual crowd scene, and the battles hardly ever stop. We probably shan't have much more than 20 or 25 people doing the extra work, and if we keep the space down they will look far more. . . .

"The one thing essential [about the Stratford stage] is to keep the action right on the forestage. It is practically impossible to play a scene at Stratford behind the setting line. This means that the set must be only a background. . . .

"Some people say that *Coriolanus* is a cold play. I don't feel it is this way. I think that passions run high, the battles are continuous, there are strong emotions between Volumnia and Coriolanus, and the battle between the people and the Senate is not a piece of cool politics, but a revolutionary struggle. Nor do I think that Coriolanus is a cold man. He is self-conscious and shy and immature, largely I suppose because of that strange relationship with his mother. He would rather 'do' than speak or be spoken to. All these passions, and all the blood, should, I think, be mirrored in the way the production is designed.

"Obviously the play has enormous contemporary significance. For that reason I had thought for some time of doing it in a kind of modern dress. I still haven't quite given up the idea, except that I usually find modern-dress Shakespeare to be disturbing in that some aspects of the play may come out clearer, but an awful lot gets lost and confused. I imagine that the parallels one would draw in the play are strong enough to take care of themselves."

Aronson requested, as always, a more specific sense of the production's playing areas; he also questioned the strict specificity of Hall's period design scheme. The director reassured him: "Of course I don't want to make the production archeologically correct, but I do want to give it some overall *period* flavour—a sort of barbaric reality. Because I really can't bear abstract theatre, particularly for Shakespeare, who is so warm, human and even dirty and smelly. I think your idea, however, that what we must work on is playing areas rather than sets is absolutely right. The quality of the reality must come from the costumes, properties and the actors themselves."

After more discussion, Hall refined his notions further: "I hope I haven't gone too far in insisting the play is barbaric. It is certainly barbaric rather than civilized, but it is *heroic* rather than specifically barbaric. The tone and texture of the play is always heroical and hyperbolical, and it is vital to have a heroical, stark, *hard romantic* set. All this could be Etruscan, but it's the dark greens and umbers of this period, rather than the light blues. But this you feel already. . . . I've been looking at the Skira volume of Roman painting, and there are things there which seem enormously apt for *Coriolanus*. . . . This is B.C. Rome, not CinemaScope and *Julius Caesar*. . . . The play is not *all* barbaric. Things like the Valeria scene and the character of Menenius have Renaissance elements and belong to the world of Veronese and Mantegna. In fact, as we said on Saturday, the ideal design cannot be too period-tied. . . . This play requires many levels. There is scarcely a scene where steps would not help the staging." Hall provided other general observations as well: "These men are dressed in metals, hides and furs rather than in cloth. It is a play written for *animals* rather than men. . . . Be sparing with colour. Browns, ochres and black, the dark Etruscan green. . . . Would it help to establish the city-state ethos if the set was somehow wall-backed—like the walled towns in medieval paintings? . . . The gates are very important—they are required in the action and also suggest war-based societies. Could we have two gates thus [shown in sketch]? . . . Archeological accuracy could *not* be less important. We need to take from all periods, as Shakespeare did himself."

A subsequent Aronson sketch of the design, incorporating nearly all of Hall's instructions, left the director with a few "worries": "It seemed to me that the new sketch was beginning to lose something of the mosaic effect on the steps. I thought this was a pity, but perhaps I won't when I see the completed colour sketch. . . . Do watch the cool greys. They will light very white and if we're not careful will land us back in abstract, ancient Rome. I think the dirty ochres and chrome browns that you were experimenting with were much safer."

A month later, the design was completed. "The model arrived safely," Hall wrote to Aronson. "I shall look forward to seeing the colour sketch on my return. Don't lose that marvellous crude strength that was in the early sketch. . . . I was a *little* disturbed by the copy that you sent to John Goodwin [Hall's assistant], in that I felt it was becoming light and rather pale, and losing its masculine vigour; but I understand you have since wired him and told him not to use it. . . . It is the dark rich colours that you had in the early sketch with their thick patina that I found so stirring. . . . I really think it is a quite beautiful set, and the simplicity and strength of it is now undoubted."

Even by the low American standard for designers' pay, the standard Stratford fee for a set design was minimal—£250, plus £50 for the model, and one-way fare from New York to England. But for various reasons, not all of them intrinsic to *Coriolanus* itself, Aronson found the production an unusually invigorating experience.

Part of the thrill came from watching Hall and his actors use the set. Because Aronson had fulfilled the director's wish that twenty-five extras look like fifty, Hall could stage an opening sequence in which the vast main gates disgorged what looked like a mass of barbaric humanity; the Roman mob erupted out of the earth, frightening the audience. Another theatrical virtue of the set—unplanned—was discovered by Olivier: when stabbed in Coriolanus' death scene, he plunged headlong over the edge of the upper platform (backstage, it was jokingly called "the diving board") and was caught by his heels to

end up dangling by his feet, Mussolini-style, from the eight-foot rostrum. The plunge was a sensation, eliciting gasps from the audience. The star didn't complain about the acrobatics involved: "I just have to learn to use a whole new set of muscles," he explained.

Aronson was equally impressed by his first exposure to a state-supported repertory theatre, which in no way resembled the Broadway theatre. "I was so flabbergasted and bewildered that there is such a thing as working without the pressures, without all the difficulties, without the deadlines. They had so much space for rehearsal that they were able to make a skeleton of the set to rehearse on from the first day. And Larry would come there all by himself between rehearsals, which impressed me so much, trying out and walking on the thing. The whole method of working was so pleasant. . . . They have a shop where the costumes and props are made, [and the artisans pass on their skills] from generation to generation. The master carpenter embraced problems and took pride in solving them. The artisans (painters and carpenters) took pride in their work and attended the opening night; they were an integral part of the production. It made it possible to do the type of work which is almost impossible to achieve in New York."

JUDITH (1962)

With *Judith*, Aronson tackled another Christopher Fry script based on biblical legend, this time with Harold Clurman as director. *Judith* is Fry's adaptation of Jean Giraudoux's most difficult play; it was staged at Her Majesty's Theatre in London's West End. As with *The Firstborn, Coriolanus*, and *J.B.*, Aronson pursued an "epic" design that relied on surface textures, plasticity, and a hand-crafted look.

In the play, Giraudoux offers a revisionist view of a story from the Apocrypha. The title character is a beautiful, rich young woman who decides to save her people, the Jews of ancient Palestine, by visiting the Assyrian conqueror, Holofernes, in his tent, luring him into bed, and then murdering him. Clurman, like his designer, regarded the work as far removed from "the modern psychological or naturalistic play," in part because "its speech is stylized, often close to verse." In his preparatory notes on the script, the director said he wanted the audience to enjoy "a heroic (and philosophic) tale—told with modern wit and sophistication, in a blaze of beautiful color—sumptuous and noble."

9

10

9 Act I of Jean Giraudoux's *Judith* (1962): a millionaire's home where all is "luxe, calme et volupté."

10 Act II: An "ultracivilized" French vision of Assyrian barbarism.

11 One-inch-scale color details of the wall in *Judith* showing Aronson's use of a textured, simulated fresco technique. John Keck, who worked on painting the half-inch-scale model from Aronson's sketch, brought the wall to Aronson on a separate piece of paper before gluing it into place. "Boris took it to the back room and put Scotch tape on it and tore it off, and dropped solder on it, and burned it around the edges, and tore little pieces off and taped them somewhere else. And I did a new one, with all that damage built into it. He thought that was just peachy, and he took that one away, and it came back all crumpled and wrinkled and scorched. After about three tries, I eventually did one with all those changes, with the scorching and everything all in the paint job— and we glued that one into the model."

11

As preproduction began, Clurman wrote Aronson a letter about what the "visual aspect" of *Judith* should be:

"The first act [an anteroom in Judith's house] is a banker's or millionaire's home. ('There is no lack of mirrors in the house.') There may be a fountain of running water (referred to as a 'glass of water' in the text), etc. In other words: the first act is a *salon*—the dwelling place of wealth and sophistication as the French might imagine it—except that the names and locale are semi-Biblical. 'You mirror luxury and gold,' someone says to Judith. Here all is, to quote Baudelaire, *luxe, calme et volupté.*

"The second act is rougher, more barbaric, with an alcove masked by a curtain in which Holofernes presumably sleeps and works and from which, when the curtain is drawn or lifted, he makes his first splendid appearance. Holofernes is the Man of This World—a synthesis of physical and mental keenness. . . .

"The play is fundamentally French classic—like Racine—stripped, noble, elegant, and, so to speak, motionless. But such a style is unacceptable (boring) to the Anglo-American audience. On its clas-

sic purity, savage, violent colors must be splashed in discreet proportion to lend the setting its Near-Eastern orientalism and vibrancy. In brief, it is necessary to create a classicism out of decorative and dramatic elements which being somewhat primitive and Near Eastern are not classic at all! We must avoid a totally flat stage. Perhaps an arrangement of levels or platforms can serve. The play, being all rhetoric, requires *a stage to move the actors.* Otherwise the play will strike our audiences as intolerably static. (There should be an opulent couch in Act One for Judith to lie down on. And some places to sit!) . . .

"Above all, the production must be sumptuously lovely—most attractive—without giving the impression of complication or overproduction. We want it to be a joy to the eye in which every figure on the stage may stand out with picturesque impressiveness. The play is both virile and *trés raffiné;* it is addressed to the mind and to the senses—a combination of French *esprit* (or intellectual agility) and aristocratic physicality. There is absolutely nothing Jewish in the modern sense or Hebrew in the Biblical sense in the play. Can you be a French (ultra-civilized) Assyrian—scenically, at least?"

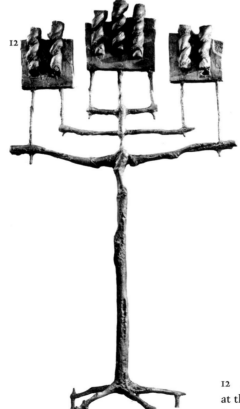

12

12 Aronson's mania for sculptured, textured surfaces at this time also resulted in this design of a menorah for Temple Sinai, a synagogue in Washington, D. C.

A CIRCUS OF ESSENTIALS

Against the ocean, even a bird counts. Against a street in Paris, the human figure counts. In New York, only a parade counts. But against nature, a man counts.

J.B. (1958)

Shortly after Elia Kazan's latest Broadway hit, his production of William Inge's *The Dark at the Top of the Stairs*, opened in 1957, Aronson ran into the director on the street. The designer told Kazan, "Look—for the rest of your life you can do that type of show. And it's very well done, well written, well acted, well designed, well lit, well directed. But you have to do something which is much less safe but much more daring, much more satisfying. Something which also has a very good chance of failing. But I think you can afford it. You're at a point in your career where you need something else." Aronson was so emphatic about his directive that, later on, he liked to think Kazan had taken his advice. It was soon after that chance encounter in New York that the director wired Aronson in Tel Aviv, where he was touring with *The Firstborn*, and invited him to read the script of a new play, Archibald MacLeish's *J.B.*, with an eye to working on it. Kazan, who was in Athens, asked Aronson to stop there for a meeting on the way home.

"When I read the play while flying to Greece," Aronson said, "it hit me immediately. I was fascinated by the idea of placing Job in a modern setting, and I was doubly fascinated by the fact that the locale was to be a circus. I had traveled with the circus as a painter—it was an atmosphere that I knew and loved."

MacLeish's script described the setting as "a traveling circus which has been on the roads of the world for a long time." Two out-of-work actors, the old Mr. Zuss and the young Nickles, have been reduced to selling balloons and popcorn in the circus, which has been playing a sideshow version of the Old Testament story of the sufferings of Job. Late one night, when the tent is empty, Zuss and Nickles pick up the masks of God and Satan to try improvising their own version of the tale. They quickly get caught up in the story of J.B., a wealthy and esteemed contemporary American industrialist who loses his fortune, family, house, and health in a series of ever more horrifying disasters. As J.B. wrestles with his soul, Zuss and Nickles provide their own commentary, built around Satan's wager that Job will be driven to curse God.

Aronson considered the Book of Job, which he had first read at *cheder* as a child in Russia, to be (along with *Don Quixote*) one of the two most influential literary works of his life. "The story of Job is one that has happened before and will happen again. It is timeless." He immediately envisioned Job "in terms of today" as "crude and raw," with "everything reduced to big and small, the giant and the midget, God's will and Job."

Aronson also felt that the circus, "where fear is mixed with pleasure, horror with excitement," was "an ideal locale for an allegorical play"—and, in general, an ideal setting. "When you get a play which takes place in the circus, half of it is already designed, from my point of view, because it takes place in an environment which is almost impossible to ruin. The nature of the environment you are called upon to create has a concrete form already, a 'basic design': the rings, the trapeze, ladders, tightrope wires, tent. . . . There are two locales which come alive only when they are used—the gymnasium and the circus. But in my first meeting with Kazan I questioned why the Book of Job takes place in a circus. I was told that, as Shakespeare says that the world is a stage, MacLeish says it is bread and circuses."

Once Aronson realized that MacLeish's circus stood for "the whole world," he knew how to design it. "The interpretation could be very personal—not a place where you sell peanuts and popcorn. This was a monumental work, and it should be sculpted. There's nothing circusy or gay about it—no balloons. Very early on, I decided not to use the stage curtain. People walk into this play as they walk into the circus."

A previous production of J.B. had been done at Yale, and the play's Broadway producers wanted to use that production's designer, Donald Oenslager, for New York. Kazan insisted on Aronson, some of whose circus paintings he owned. When the director and designer met in Greece in June 1958, they challenged each other with ideas about the play. Kazan needed a "vision" of the script to go with MacLeish's words, and after Aronson returned to New York the director sent him a detailed memo summarizing their discussions in Athens.

In his memo, Kazan defined both the epic design and the staging concepts, which were now inextricably linked:

"1. It is not a circus. It *looks* like a circus. It is not an illustration of anything. It is the plastic rendition of essences. . . . [The set contains a] family 'circle.' . . . There is another circle, a bigger one, which includes the restricted area of the family and which is the World (where Satan walks back and forth). This 'world,' a circle, too, includes the audience and in fact tips down towards them. . . . The small circle of the family is within the large circle of the world.

"2. This is a show. It is a circus or vaudeville show. It does not take place in a make-believe place bound by a picture frame. It is frankly a show. We may never use a curtain to begin with. The actors do not act as if the audience does not exist—except at the beginning. . . . The style of the direction and the acting is vaudeville-like, big, presentational, out front. People represent essences, they are not individuals. . . . They are what the Russians call 'masks'—broad types, significantly rendered.

"3. The course of action of the play is the spiritual history of the America of our time and of our memory. From 1912 to 1958 and on into the immediate future as we anxiously await the next war or cataclysmic possibility. The symbols of the story and the events are all from our recent memory—achieved by recognizable signs and images of our time. The play is, in a way, the dream or nightmare of an America starting from Anxiety about what our fate is to be and ending in an affirmation of life.

"4. The tent is the whole apparatus which man put up to stand over his head, protect him and shelter him, and which, in fact, stood between him and God. . . . The ecclesiastical claptrap, the churches, the pagan and oriental and eastern and western religions, from the caveman till today—the whole apparatus which man put up to shut out the black mysterious and frightening void, but which also in fact blocked man's view from the hard, stern, frightening questions of Where am I? How small am I really? Is anyone aware of me? Is there anyone else? Is there any meaning to it all? Within this tent, from time before memory the whole drama of Man's drama vis-à-vis God has been played. . . .

"5. Visually the progression of the play is that Nickles [Satan], piece by piece and one by one, tears down these symbols of security and solidity and safety. And as each piece is torn down he reveals the entrance and locale of the next disaster coming.

"It is the circus of the world—a phrase which suggests the ESSENTIALS which [are] torn down. Nickles leaves man naked and alone, helpless, defenseless. That is man's actual condition today. His Gods are gone. There is no more tent. There is no more protection. There [are] no more illusions. Man is up against his own cosmic isolation and insignificance. Above is black void. The final disaster that Nickles perpetrates on J.B. is to leave him this way, isolated and alone. . . .

"This is a circus where magic is combined with meaning. Visually. The setting should be spare and suggestive, 'simple,' abstracted. The bits of props, the working props, the costumes, the types of actors, the makeups, the sounds, the business, the dances, the songs, the movement, the clothes all must be terrifically saturated in the

1

1 As the audience entered the theatre for Elia Kazan's production of Archibald MacLeish's *J.B.* (1958), the set stood revealed, but the tent was not visible, except for its slack ropes. (This photograph was taken before the proscenium had been painted black and the house curtain removed.) As the play started, two roustabouts slowly raised the tent while Zuss and Nickles walked down the aisles with their trays and balloons, arriving on stage and starting the play. The tent collapsed late in Act I, and at the end of the play the set looked as it had at the start. Like a circus performance, the story of Job can happen again and again. Kenneth Tynan wrote: "Boris Aronson's setting, a desolate, cavernous circus tent, is one of the most majestic I can remember; it prepares the heart for events of towering grandeur and cosmic repercussion. In every department the presentation is flawless. The same, unfortunately, cannot be said of the thing presented."

OPPOSITE

2, 3, 4   The preliminary, unsimplified Aronson sketch for the epic circus of *J.B.* (2), the final sketch, after revisions requested by Kazan (3), and the set as it appeared on stage (4).

5   The circus after the apocalyptic tent collapse. When J.B. confronts the void, the sideshow banners marking the entry of his house (at right) are also gone, leaving only bare platforms for a universe.

6

7

6   The precisely defined playing areas in use:
God (Raymond Massey) looks down on Nickles
(Christopher Plummer).

7   An Aronson sketch of *J.B.*, Act II.

color and meaning of what they are designed to represent. . . . The set is the universe, step by step revealed. The props and personalities are the American in the universe.

"The POLE. It is the finger of [the] question [with which] man reaches into the black, unfriendly, impersonal void. It is not dramatically prominent at the beginning. It may not even be noticed. But it is made prominent and dramatic and meaningful by the stripping down of the tent of standards—it then stands alone; as *the* question. . . .

"VISUAL PROGRESSION. By the end of Act One the TENT HAS COLLAPSED. The protection of dogma etc. is no longer there etc. Act two is played under open sky on a couple of circular platforms. . . ."

Aronson was soon "bursting with ideas." He knew "the design required a solution with a certain grandeur," yet he was also aware of Kazan's necessary "restrictions," which would be needed to stage the play. These were the three playing areas: the "family circle," the pulpit-like acrobats' platform where God appears, and the large circle of the "world" inhabited by Satan and, implicitly, the audience. Still, Aronson saw the possibility for "a kind of total theatre" that would involve the audience "the minute they walked into the auditorium." Because of Kazan's clout, the designer was able to execute two ideas then unheard of on Broadway: he eliminated the house curtain and he painted the proscenium arch black to blend the set into the auditorium. "I wanted to change the looks of the theatre," said Aronson, and "only a person with great influence" like Kazan could have fought and won the battles needed to achieve that.

Once Aronson had completed his initial design, he invited Kazan to see it. The director revealed his response in a letter that led to further refinement of the set—and that also revealed the close collaborative process on this "epic" show. "As Archie says, [the set] makes his play possible," Kazan wrote in September 1958. "Now I am urging you in the direction of simplification. I'll put it constructively: Let the main design speak. Anything that stands in the way of your main design statement should be simplified out, or blended into the whole.

"The simplification . . . is not in the direction of 'simple' props. For example, ladders instead of stairs. It is deeper than that. It is the elimination of all unessentials. Excuse the reference to another designer, but it was the one great gift [Robert Edmond] Jones had. . . . Your basic statement is so right and so strong that anything that is added decoratively, or not absolutely necessary, should be eliminated.

"Above all, the tipped-up pattern of the ring, and paths leading to the ring and Heaven and Home . . . should all be blended into one unified design with a cohesion of its own. What you have now, especially on stage right, is a collection of elements. . . .

"Now we come to the problem of color. Archie said in his letter that we all agreed that the tent should be made up of patches and pieces inherited from all the religions of history, from the witch doctors down to the Roman Catholic Church. But he stressed that these pieces have been woven into the fabric of the tent for so long that the colors have all faded. And I would add, FADED INTO ONE. Of all your sketches that I have seen, I still like the black and white best. I have never felt this about a design of yours before because you are brilliant at color. . . . But essentially the simplicity of this play demands a simplicity in its design. Furthermore, simply technically, I don't want J.B. to be backed up by a mottled background. I want him to stand out from it. I don't want him part of it. I want him dominant in front of it. I don't want him minimized, I want him maximized. . . .

"Let us think of making this show no bigger than necessary. But I'm not nearly so much concerned about the scale as I am about the 'busyness' of the colors. As we both commented yesterday, Archie has simplified the canvas of the world. There is a purity in his nature that only a man who sees life simply can have. . . .

"[When the atom bomb hits,] it's as though the place where J.B. lives is suddenly twisted by an enormous force. If you will look at some of the pictures of Hiroshima or any city that has been hit by modern high explosives, you will see that the structural elements have been taken and twisted into designs that tell-tale the force of the explosion. . . .

"This show, more than any other I've done, requires the designer and director to work hand in hand. It's almost as though the line of demarcation between your work and mine was not clearly marked at certain points."

Aronson was not without reservations about the play. He wasn't sure that the script entirely realized the "tremendous" idea of combining the American present with the story of Job. He was also dissatisfied with the sentimental ending: "I said to MacLeish, 'You can't wind up a situation like this with the wife coming back to J.B. and bringing him a branch and a candle—and it's all straightened out.'" Aronson told MacLeish that he believed in doubts, not happy endings. But, such objections notwithstanding, Aronson found that "working on *J.B.* came nearest to what I would like to do in the theatre [after] thirty-five years of designing in New York. It offered scope for freedom and imagination. It takes you out of your own little environment and gives you a chance to do things bigger than life. Not every play can offer that opportunity, of course, but when one does, it is a most satisfying experience."

Among other ideas, Aronson used the set's hanging lights to suggest a constellation of stars and planets; the peepshow suggested a Catholic confessional. He used sideshow banners to create an entrance to J.B.'s house, but the banners depicted signs of the Zodiac instead of circus acts. "Sometimes the decision to put a plain barrel on an empty stage does more for the actor than a lot of Pompeiian ornaments, pressed molding, and marquee enrichments. The table and chairs had the basic shape of a cube or a bench. The props were skeletonized to the same extent as the structural elements of the set."

Aronson wanted to stress visually that tension is what keeps the tent in a firmly upright position—with the tension being "suppressed excitement . . . produced by forces pulling against each other." Within the tent, man's relationship to God is played out. When the tent crashes down, "man is left naked and alone." But there were problems with collapsing the tent. "Calamities like this have to be organized,"

Aronson said. A movie studio was rented in which to experiment with the effect before trying it in the theatre. An even greater challenge was to arrive at the final ground plan—to find the "living geometry" of the play. "It was arrived at after I had the most intimate knowledge about the action. It had to be refined so as to blend the pattern of movement, as well as the various vignettes of J.B.'s life and disasters, into an organic whole."

After the opening, MacLeish wrote to Aronson: "You made *visible* the peculiar tone of the play—half tragic, half ironic—so that no audience could miss it. You established its scope which, but for you, might have seemed pretentious. Most miraculous of all you gave it a place in space and time without destroying its ability to exist outside of space and in no time at all."

But, for Aronson, the particular excitement of working on *J.B.* had a lot to do with working hand-in-hand with Kazan. He felt that "in a sense, Kazan choreographed the play." Kazan, conversely, felt that his "ideas for movement all came out of the set," that his choreography was all built around Aronson's design—because it was possible "to talk in poetic terms about what Boris did."

8 "Rhythm in the Ring," a 1938 Aronson circus painting owned by Kazan at the time he started working on *J.B.*

COLLAGE MUSICAL

Spatial ideas on paper or in model form are not the same as space on stage. It takes experience to look at a scale model. A quarter-inch chair looks like something out of Tiffany's window. It looks like a work of art to start with—a beautiful toy which you enjoy so much because of its smallness. But how will it look within a thirty-eight- or forty-foot opening? That takes almost a lifetime to know.

DO RE MI (1960)

Do Re Mi, a musical (with songs by Jule Styne, Betty Comden, and Adolph Green) about small-time hustlers in the booming jukebox industry, was written by Garson Kanin in a Runyonesque comic style reminiscent of *Guys and Dolls.* As produced by David Merrick and directed by Kanin, it was most of all a vehicle for its stars, Phil Silvers and Nancy Walker. But for Aronson, *Do Re Mi* was a rare opportunity to create sets for a multiple-locale, non-realistic musical—an assignment that rarely came his way at this point in his career.

Aronson was also taken with the aesthetic implications of the jukebox. "A jukebox visually and symbolically is a most characteristic American idea," he said. "Not only the noise but the lights, the impossible textures—put together, they have a grotesque vulgarity that just sends me." He took the show as an invitation to try out some wild imaginative flights, most of which involved the use of collage. More than fifteen years later, collage figured in another, vastly different, Aronson musical design, *Pacific Overtures* (1976), and by then Broadway musicals were ready for his sophisticated level of abstract scenic invention. In *Do Re Mi*, Aronson's designs were at once advanced art works and impractical, at times even unworkable, sets that took a

path at odds with a conventional show. "As often happens," the designer later said, "while I was working on the sets, demonstrating them to the director and producer, they were highly pleased with the concept. But when they saw it on stage, they weren't. On stage, they didn't fit a show that turned out to be more like the usual musical of the day. It was a terrible disappointment for me, to be used that way. Not only is the novelty of the sets lost, but so is the point I wanted to make with them." After the musical's disappointing season-long run, many theatre hands, Aronson included, thought that a few of the show's many problems might have been solved had it been assigned to one of the more traditional designers who specialized in Broadway musicals of the time.

Aronson's scenic plan derived from his belief that a jukebox was itself "a collage," and that, symbolically, it represented "the cathedral of youth of our time." To execute this notion on the grandest possible scale, he drew on Kanin's conception for an overture sequence in his original script. The author envisioned that a series of seven jukeboxes, each defined by a bright, abstract color pattern and "suspended in space" on stage, would consecutively play seven different "records"

1

1, 2, 3, 4, 5, 6, 7 *Do Re Mi* (1960): The model of the show curtain (1), and the individual collages (2, 3, 4, 5, 6) that contributed to the overall design of a cathedral-size jukebox made up of smaller, abstract jukeboxes. On stage, Phil Silvers and company appear in front of it (7). Aronson described the show as "a razzle-dazzle musical based on the decorative patterns of a jukebox," with a tone of "fabulous vulgarity."

2

3

4
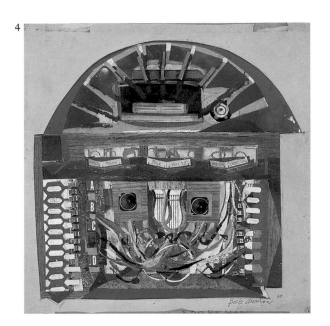

5

7

6
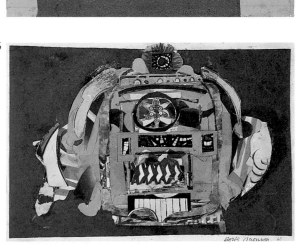

8

9

8, 9   Aronson's design for the "Casablanca" nightclub in *Do Re Mi* (8) used the large fake palm trees he had photographed in the actual Copacabana club (9). It also used three-dimensional and large cut-out mannequins to represent the club's patrons. Garson Kanin, the director, recalled that "Boris insisted on dressing the mannequins, putting the right makeup on them. They were always interspersed with live performers— so that if a man was sitting with a female mannequin, he flirted with her and grabbed her. Boris continued the idea of the mannequins onto the drop; the way it was lighted, you would swear you were looking at a thousand people. You couldn't really tell where the drop began and the mannequins and the people left off."

10

10   On stage, Phil Silvers, Nancy Walker, and the mannequins survey a chorus line.

11

12

11, 12 A collage sketch (11) for a hotel's "Imperial Room" (based on the Waldorf-Astoria grand ballroom) and its realization with dancers in the London production of *Do Re Mi* (12).

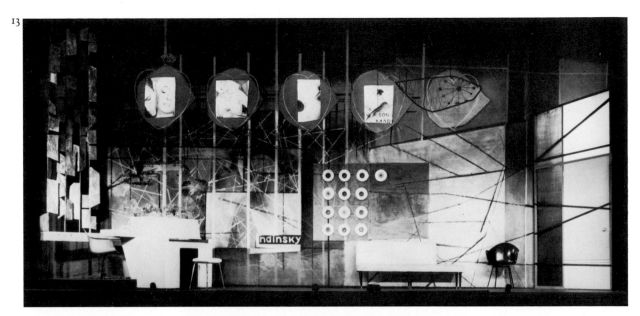

13, 14   The office of a music-industry "gangster of today": Aronson's original sketch (14) and on stage prior to tryout-tour revisions (13). The set was a Pop Art collage (pre–Pop Art) containing a Marilyn Monroe image (changed to gold records by the time the show reached New York) and a specific calligraphic homage to (Ka)ndinsky. Aronson saw the modern-day gangster as a smooth, well-educated, "legitimate" businessman with a record company, a Fifth Avenue office, and a modern-art collection.

15

16

17

18

18, 19   A recording studio—seen as a model (18) and on stage (19)—used newspaper clippings (from *Billboard*) and Paul Klee's arrow iconography, as well as microphones arranged in an overall pattern suggesting an Alexander Calder mobile.

19

OPPOSITE

15, 16, 17   A design for a Broadway bar in *Do Re Mi* began with a collage sketch (15) that was then divided into planes that included an abstract, Stuart Davis–like drop, again anticipating Pop Art (16). It was no easy task to transform the basic design into a three-dimensional set (17) usable on stage.

of songs from the *Do Re Mi* score. After the song and lights of the last jukebox had faded, all seven would light up and blare out at once, forming "a single, colorful, pulsating, avaricious, and loquacious monster."

The show curtain Aronson devised in response consisted of eight collages. Seven individual jukeboxes, each a large and fanciful plastic collage of intricate design done in sculptured relief, were assembled into an enormous eighth collage—a cathedral-size "fabulous monster" jukebox that towered to the top of the proscenium arch. "Lighted separately and sometimes together," Aronson explained, "the jukeboxes created the effect of a cathedral stained-glass window in a jazzy vein." The other creators of the show loved this and the other collage-motif sets to come, but they were also frightened of their novelty. When *Do Re Mi* opened its tryout tour in Boston, the fears proved justified. As chorus people representing teenagers inserted dimes into each of the collage jukeboxes, gradually lighting them all up in a cacophony of color matching the steady rise in the music's volume, the effect was so overpowering that it stopped the show—and no one could get the show started again. Soon the lighting was toned down, and the entire sequence was moved to the opening of Act II.

In his other sets for *Do Re Mi*, Aronson maintained the jukebox idea of collage. He worked in patterns reminiscent of Klee and Calder —gaudy signs would be both inside and outside the sets—and again he fought normal architectural perspective in a painterly way. Ming Cho Lee, who assisted Aronson on the designs, felt that both the method and the final results were way ahead of their time. "The abstraction took off from the idea of the jukebox, the idea of big crooks and little crooks. To Boris, the jukebox was *American*. Boris said the whole American look is really collage. Americans can never leave anything alone, it's all patchwork. Even if we patch a jacket, it's never with the same material.

"We kept going along, not caring about how the hell the show would actually work technically. We'd do an abstraction, then break it into planes to make it into a set for a scene in the show. We'd cover newspapers with turpentine, then rub a spoon on top for texture. We were always painting, rubbing, pasting, painting again. . . . But none of us could make the sets work. Finally, Bob Randolph [another set designer] came in to figure out a scheme which would work for the show. He was in one part of the apartment, me in another. He planned the show from the mechanical point of view for the St. James stage, which was only twenty-eight feet deep, but his allowances for room

had nothing to do with the design. In the end, *Do Re Mi* didn't work too badly technically; it used drops and wagons. But the final product did not look as well as Boris visualized because we didn't really know how to do it and the precision wasn't there. Though each sketch was turned into a model, in the show the sets looked exaggerated and rough. The newspaper collage [for a scene set at a Washington, D. C., hearing] was done at the shop as a painted copy rather than a photo blow-up, because it was cheaper that way. . . .

"Boris saw a show about grotesque behavior—a Weill-Brecht show with the edge of *Happy End, Threepenny Opera, Mahagonny*. The physical production of *Do Re Mi* was out on a limb—the theme in the set was not in the show itself." The sets were, indeed, so misunderstood that Aronson did not get another musical until four years later—*Fiddler on the Roof*—and even then he was hired by the director, Jerome Robbins, over the objections of the producer, Harold Prince, whose opposition was based on his dislike of the designs for *Do Re Mi*.

20

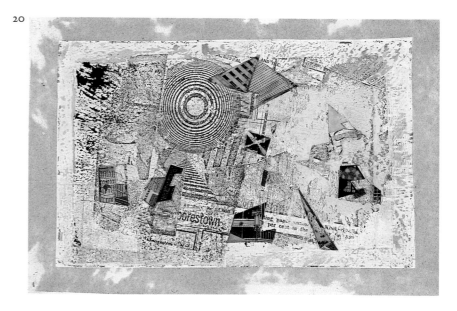

20 "City," an Aronson collage typical of his artwork of the period of *Do Re Mi*.

PLAYS OF THE SIXTIES AND EARLY SEVENTIES

Shortly after the war, first in the European theatre and later here, the use of new materials started to be prevalent in the theatre: plastics, metal, the mechanization of scenery, mirrors, polyester, and, later on, fiberglass, Lexan, and now photographic enlargements. It hasn't stopped yet (TV, lighting innovations, projections, etc.). Modern times ask for more inventiveness, expertise, perfection. A designer is always curious about new materials and new possibilities. He has to work constantly because the theatre changes quickly. Unless a designer continues to function, he will lose touch with new possibilities through which he can interpret plays. But he must use these things guardedly. You should not praise a revolving stage or treadmill for being what they are— but for being the best and most suitable scenic device for that particular show.

During the final two decades of his career, Aronson turned down more plays than he accepted—especially once *Fiddler on the Roof* brought about a sudden increase in the demand for his skills as a designer for musical theatre, whether on Broadway or at the Metropolitan Opera. Those plays Aronson did take on were the new projects of such longtime colleagues as Garson Kanin, Arthur Miller, and Harold Clurman.

A GIFT OF TIME (1962)

This documentary play was adapted and directed by Garson Kanin from the memoir *Death of a Man* by Lael Tucker Wertenbaker, who wrote about the final months in the life of her cancer-stricken husband, Charles Christian Wertenbaker (played by Henry Fonda).

Like *The Diary of Anne Frank, A Gift of Time* deals with suffering in the midst of a sunny environment. To help draw the necessary contrasts, Kanin decided that, as with *Diary*, he wanted to have multiple settings on stage, with a minimum of stage waits. "When we began to put the play together, I spent two months in Biarritz, driving every day to Ciboure, where most of the story happened," he recalled. "I went to all the locales, and each one seemed to relate so importantly to the show and the story. The couple *had* to be seen sitting in the little sidewalk café, he *had* to be in his bed in the hospital, she *had* to talk to the doctor, he *had* to be in his workroom. But I hate the idea of a play where the lights keep going on and off—that was the movie influence in my career.

"I sat in the town, to be really sure of the atmosphere. And I knew I had to have that number of sets. And then I began to see how it could work out—if we could put three sets on stage, then three more, then three more, we could manage it. Often Boris was inclined to be a little impatient when too much was asked of him: he would experience a sudden terror of something that seemed impossible to realize. But somehow, when I mentioned this notion to him, he liked it.

"I think I admired Boris' work on *A Gift of Time* more than anything because of the breadth of it. On the same stage, the same evening, you saw a hospital room, a shipboard. The shipboard had a stateroom, the purser's lounge, and the deck, so that the life of the

1

1   In a triptych set for *A Gift of Time* (1962), the different living areas of a home in the French town of Ciboure, near Biarritz, are all revealed.

2

2   Three simultaneously displayed locations in the neighboring village of Saint-Jean-de-Luz.

3

3   The angular, darker precincts of a New York hospital.

4

4   A cruise ship with stateroom, purser's office, and deck area.

5   The complex sets for *A Gift of Time* are installed
at the Barrymore Theatre on Broadway.

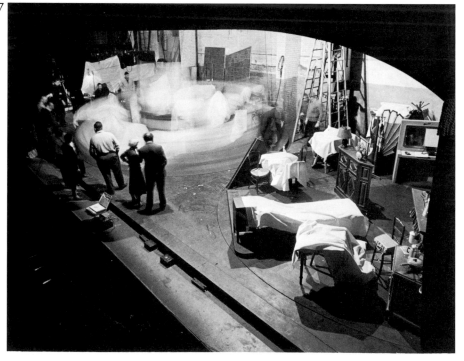

6, 7   Aerial views—from the mezzanine and a box—
of the incompletely installed sets as the production
staff tests out the turntable rotations that facilitated
the fast changes the director Garson Kanin required.

ship was reproduced. And then in Ciboure, the couple's home, there were servants' quarters, his workroom. . . . Each one was a vignette. And when the play had a scene set in New York, Boris and Jean Rosenthal [the lighting designer] probed into the differences between Mediterranean and New York light."

INCIDENT AT VICHY (1964)

In Arthur Miller's play, ten men are held in a detention room in the occupied Vichy France of 1942, waiting to be called into an inner office where an inquisition will determine whether they live or die. Though the play unfolds against the same historical background as *The Diary of Anne Frank*, the design demands were totally dissimilar —not in the least because *Vichy* was performed on the thrust stage of the ANTA Washington Square Theatre, the temporary, first home of the fledgling Repertory Company of Lincoln Center.

In his notes for the production, the director, Harold Clurman, describes an early conversation with Aronson about the design: "It must seem constructed of metal and stone. Its locale not too specific. (Originally it was called 'a police station.' Changed by Miller to 'a place of detention.') The fact that the play presumably takes place in Vichy is not important."

"This is the third play of Miller's I've done," Aronson told an interviewer as the production opened. "He is a very precise and definite writer. His script calls for a place where the prisoners are interrogated, a place where they wait and a corridor where the police stand guard. There was nothing to be fancy about. It had to have these elements." Still, the designer discovered that "it's not easy to take an open stage 65 feet across and make it into an enclosed space with no exit." Aronson started by laying down a floor covering, a mosaic of bleak blues, greens, and black—the irregular remnants of a once-spiffy tile floor. The interrogation office, small and to the rear, allowed for the projection of shadowy, menacing silhouettes on a large, translucent window within. The only entrance was a skeletonized corridor leading into the detention basement. Over the set's center was an arch of metal beams, suggesting the bared structure of a nineteenth-century French institutional building. "When you walk into the theatre," Aronson said, "you have to feel right away that you are in an enclosed area."

While Clurman approved Aronson's initial set design, two of the Repertory Company's directors, Robert Whitehead and Elia Kazan,

8, 9 The sketch (8) and model (9) for the detention room of Harold Clurman's production of Arthur Miller's *Incident at Vichy* (1964).

10   The *Incident at Vichy* set in the ANTA
Washington Square Theatre, transforming an open
stage into "an enclosed space with no exit."

11   A menacing silhouette in the interrogation
room threatens the waiting detainees.

objected to it. When the finished set was installed at the theatre, Whitehead thought the colors on the floor had been painted too bright and didn't match the subdued colors of the final model he'd seen in Aronson's studio. "At the ANTA, you had to design the floor," Whitehead said, "and Boris couldn't resist *over*-designing it. We had to spray it down." (Aronson may have been carried away by his own paintings of the time; he was working with brilliantly colored encaustics.) Kazan believed that the overall plan of the set was right, but that the look was too decorative. The playwright agreed: to him, the set "looked like an Art Nouveau subway entrance." The revised final set had more of what Clurman called "a macabre . . . hard, mysterious, 'Kafka-like' . . . 'no man's land' " look.

THE PRICE (1968)

In Arthur Miller's Ibsenesque drama, two brothers who haven't seen each other in sixteen years reunite in an old brownstone's dusty attic to dispose of their late father's furniture and to battle over the past that the furniture represents. The unofficial referee in their dispute is an aged Jewish antique dealer, Solomon, whose funny, philosophical maxims were modeled somewhat on Aronson's own idiosyncratic verbal style.

For the designer, however, the most important character in *The Price* was neither Solomon nor the warring brothers but the furniture in the attic. "Usually, furniture is an element in a set," he said, "but in this play the furniture is the fifth character. It tells its own story of another time, of another people. It has to create the mood of a period that no longer exists; it has to tell what kind of people owned it."

Though Aronson went to Bucks County and the Salvation Army to look for the appropriate secondhand furniture, what he found was not used "as is" on stage. "The real thing is not necessarily theatrical-looking," he explained. "On the stage, it has to be larger than life." Inspired by Miller's script, which viewed the furniture as a metaphor for the tension within a family, and by an Edward Kienholz sculpture, "The Waiting," Aronson took the furniture apart in the studio, broke it into abstract forms and shapes, and began redesigning it. Some pieces ended up larger than they were originally; others were smaller; still others were constructs combining odd fragments of several old pieces. The new furniture was then arranged in a carefully conceived, cluttered arrangement designed to give the room an atmosphere of physical discomfort parallel to the characters' psychological distress.

Although Miller at first was in favor of using real furniture unchanged, he came around to Aronson's way of thinking. "The play is a fixation on time," its author said years later. "The house was a metaphor to start with; it struck me that we shouldn't be buying or renting furniture—that you can't take it out of a showroom and use it. The furniture should not be real—but more than real." It was his idea, upheld by Aronson, that the actors should seem almost lost in the furniture as the play begins. The set was designed so that the director—and, with him, the audience—would gradually pick out the actors within the jumbled room, as a film director might use a close-up to focus on characters within a busy panorama.

According to most of the play's collaborators, however, the director, Ulu Grosbard, wanted to take a more conventionally naturalistic approach. Grosbard used the set as a background and focused his staging on a central playing area downstage center that contained the standard, symmetrical living-room arrangement of a couch, a table, and two chairs. The final run-through at the New Amsterdam Theatre was a disaster—so much so that Aronson was moved to write Miller a memo expressing his feelings about what had gone wrong:

"Key words (for what it needs): physical discomfort, burdensome, tension, restlessness, impatience, lack of involvement—till the point when, towards the end, Victor and Walter [the brothers] clash head on. The avoidance of real conflict up to that point.

"The only one or two moments of genuine sentiment are when the brothers do get together on some point remembered—such as the radio—but only momentarily.

"No patting sentimentally the furniture—after all, Victor wants to get rid of it. It must be a burden throughout the play and the action.

"Fill the front area—now completely empty—with furniture—obstacles. Let the actors be uncomfortable to the point of exhaustion. On their feet 80% of the time; lose them behind furniture, circle around the screen, etc. Let them pull up furniture, or push it out of their way. Let them lean on furniture (such as phonograph closed), sit on edge of a table. Possibly a trunk downstage—use stacked chairs and take [them] down as needed.

"NO COUCH! If settee or small couch is used, cover it with a throw and pull part of it aside—just enough to be able to sit in a corner of it. Only after lap robe is thrown on couch does it seem more comfortable to sit on. The key sentence, ' . . . not a conducive atmosphere,' which comes late in the play, must have been felt at this point by the audience and can only be expressed by physical discomfort—not the words alone.

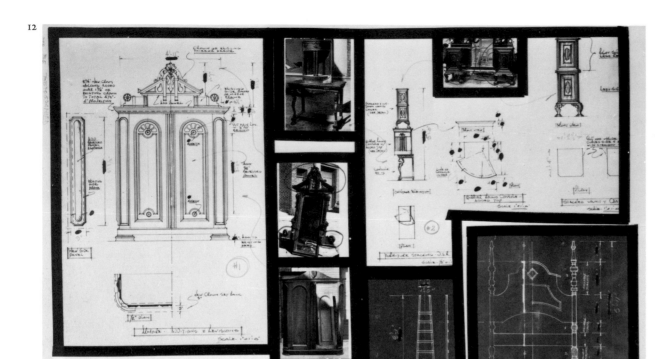

12   Working drawings for Arthur Miller's *The Price* (1968) demonstrate how Aronson took apart and redesigned the secondhand furniture that appears in the accompanying photographs.

13, 14   The model for the set, with the reconstructed furniture unpainted (14). The center-stage furnishings reflect Aronson's fascination with Kienholz's sculpture "The Waiting" (13).

15, 16   *The Price* on stage (15), and as acted by
Kate Reid and Pat Hingle (16).

"Victor, Walter, Esther [Victor's wife], these are people of today—restless, nervous, dissatisfied—vs. the placidity, the seeming stability of the era presented in the furniture on stage (that is more important than how elaborately one piece of furniture is carved or how 'rich' it looks)—and, of course, vs. Solomon—the eternal Jew—who is timeless. . . .

"The play is timed in two hours time—

"Victor and Walter and Esther, they have no time—

"The play is a race against time—

"Only the Jew has time (he is timeless)."

Much of what Aronson wrote echoed the playwright's own views about *The Price.* When the play opened weeks later, Miller had unofficially taken over the director's duties himself and had restored much of the disorder that had originally been intended.

THE CREATION OF THE WORLD AND
OTHER BUSINESS (1972)

"A very interesting assignment—the creation of the world," said Aronson. "You don't get to create a Garden of Eden every other day."

Arthur Miller's play is a straightforward retelling of Genesis that begins with the creation of Adam and Eve (Act I), moves on to the couple's expulsion from Paradise (Act II), and concludes with Cain's murder of Abel (Act III). In a letter to Aronson setting out his views of this "philosophic comedy," the director, Harold Clurman, provided a vague recipe for the physical production. "Whatever else we accomplish," he wrote, "the *Words* and *Sense* of the play are more important than the Spectacle. . . . Therefore we must consider how to make the speakers stand out above everything else. The setting and background must be beautifully *Simple.* (When the world was created, it was bare. There wasn't very much there!) . . . We must forget the *Setting,* once we have admired and felt its tone." What Clurman envisioned was a circle to represent the "World itself," with boulders for seats and a heavenly circular area above the "clear space" below. "The Total Effect and Style is *Magical,*" he summarized. "Let's not worry too much about *realism.*"

To create such a modern view of the origins of Earth, Aronson turned for inspiration to the engravings of William Blake, the later work of Joan Miró, and, given the God-as-scientist dialogue in the play, photographs of molecular formations from the magazine *Scientific American.* These photographs were blown up to suggest an abstract pattern for the stage floor, which was then sculpted out of a relatively new material for scenic construction, fiberglass. To complete the illusion of an elliptical "world" that was floating in space, the sky was a frieze with a gauzy texture, unified with the floor. The lighting scheme—accomplished with projections as well as lights placed beneath the fiberglass stage—changed the unit set from the verdant Paradise of Act I (conveyed in the colors of Blake's palette) to the heavenly void of Act II (with flashes of lightning beneath the now cloud-like floor) to the bleak, primitive hues of the man-made barbarism of Cain.

The logic by which Aronson created this set is less apparent in Miller's text than in the notes the designer made after digesting Clurman's directives:

"If I think of the STAGE representing 'THE WORLD,' then, in terms of unity, ACT II is key to play, basic unity and space—it is *the* 'empty stage.' The universe dominates—man is lost, fall from Paradise. Man is small, the Universe looms large.

"ACT I: Eden is a 'children's playground' built on the empty stage. Playful and protected. Man is close to God (sky). 'Paradise' is a state of mind (joy, bliss, balance, Blake, color). The Universe is close to man (equal)—Man is large—'Paradise' is unreal, a visual experience rather than a concrete place (except the apple tree).

"ACT III: Empty stage is 'torn' into. A built-up man-made surround. Sense of primitive force but also domesticity. Man creates his world. Universe becomes removed, becomes science, weather. Man now large and real—Universe abstract. . . .

"To emphasize word and gesture—horizontal frieze shapes (intimacy) rather than height (vastness). Frieze idea rather than sky above, earth below. Adam and Eve relate to ground: sit—lie down—squat—lounge—roll—run—skip (especially Act I). . . . I don't sense the cosmos, in the play, in terms of a huge space. The cosmos is more a background (secondary) to the play than a spatial necessity."

As both a play and a production, *Paradise* was bedeviled by problems at nearly every step. After Aronson's quarter-inch scale model of the set was approved, his half-inch scale model was challenged—largely, in the designer's view, because of management's latent realization of the sizable budget required. Aronson didn't want to alter the set radically; Miller wanted to simplify it and add some gauze columns. Years after the play's Broadway failure, the author put much of

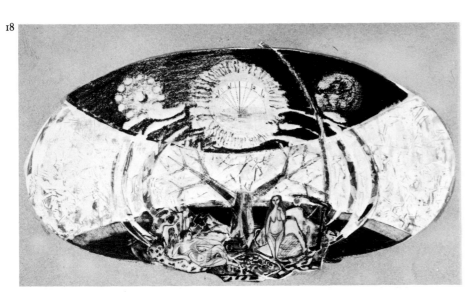

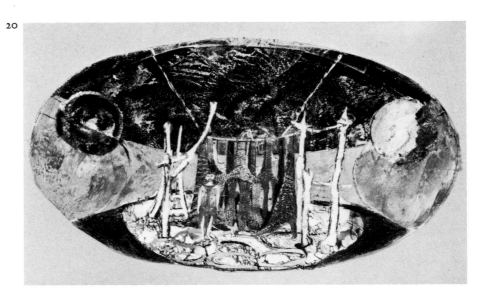

17, 18, 19, 20   Arthur Miller's *The Creation of the World* (1972): Sketches of Eden as a "children's paradise" in Act I (17, 18); the "pure weather" of Act II, after Adam and Eve have been expelled from Paradise (19); and the primitive, domestic man-made world of Cain and Abel (20).

21

21, 22   Early models of the molecular-based universe of *The Creation of the World*.

22

OPPOSITE

23   The controversial orgy sequence on stage, with the fiberglass floor garishly illuminated by 400 lights below.

24   Zoe Caldwell (Eve) contemplates the tilted, sculptured stage floor.

25   The actor Lou Gilbert, against the microscopic imagery inspired by *Scientific American*.

the blame for the production's cross-purposes on the director's "oblique" way of backing into the physical production. "Harold loved painting," Miller said, "but never understood scenery. He had no geometrical sense; he saw a sketch as one-dimensional, as a painting. Apart from the fact that the play had problems, Boris kept saying to me, 'I don't know where heaven is—where are we?' Harold's answer was, 'You'll find out. You're talented and you'll find out.' Boris was never forced into heaven and relied on his sensibility to create his own place. I don't blame him. He kept after Harold, and Harold was relying on everyone to supply him with everything. No one could make out what he wanted them to do. This thing got out of hand, we spent thousands on objects. If we were in a simpler theatrical setting [than Broadway], we wouldn't have fallen into these traps; we should have been able to experiment with materials instead of building the whole set and spending a fortune. . . . But Harold went from scene to scene, with nothing to hold it together. The audience didn't know if they were in a farcical play or a satirical play or a quasi-tragic play. Boris was the only one who could sustain a poetic approach to the whole thing."

Ultimately, Clurman was replaced as director; there were major cast changes and rewrites as well during the pre-Broadway tryout. But, in Miller's view, one basic problem with the set could never be solved —the use of fiberglass. "It's awfully hard to make plastic look life-giving," the playwright observed. "There's something about plastic that sucks away life and emits death. It's not like wood. With plastic, your soul knows that it is dead. The funereal air killed the laughs, created the wrong mood, and didn't allow the audience to get the play's context. I tried to have them put more pink on the thing—a warmer color—but nothing would help it. I finally thought that if there were a suggestion of a maypole, the audience would know it was fun. But that was like a plastic funeral—it was horrible."

Robert Whitehead, who produced the play, found the set "effective and beautiful—with a disembodied feeling, as if the cast were walking in space." He objected only to a Dionysian orgy scene, during which the subterreanean lighting made the stage look like "a dance floor in the Warwick Room." But he also thought the strongly tilted and unevenly sculptured floor was difficult to play on. "We took the cast up to the studio in the Bronx to see how they could move on it. But every night in Washington [where *Creation* had its premiere at the Kennedy Center], Zoe [Caldwell, who played Eve] came off the stage and said, 'I want to get Boris alone and slug him.' "

26   *The Great God Brown* (1972): Directing Eugene O'Neill's early play for the non-profit New Phoenix Repertory Theatre, Harold Prince knew he had to have a unit set that cost "about two and a half dollars to build." Aronson immediately seized on O'Neill's principal theatrical conceit—the use of masks for the four major characters—to create his design. The set itself became an assemblage of masks. To Aronson, *The Great God Brown* was a play about man meeting his destiny of death, and destiny was "like a chess game where every move is determined by the first move you make." His visual equivalent of this notion was a set, seen above in model form, in which "all the elements of the play are always on stage," but "the manipulation of each move gives focus to the individual scenes." Accordingly, O'Neill's setting, a pier, was visible from beginning to end—indicated by hanging lamps and stylized water at the rear of the stage—but the playing area was reconfigured throughout the play by small, revolving set pieces. There were five of these two-sided units, turned or moved by actors and relating to one another in various combinations. Like the masks called for by O'Neill, they revealed the two-sided faces of the action and its participants. Though this visual parallel may not have registered on audiences, Prince was convinced that audiences would have observed "the *absence* of it." Aronson felt that the "rigid sameness in the arrangement" of each of his chessboard elements was essential. As death is the predestined checkmate for the characters in O'Neill's play, so the designer carefully choreographed his visual "game" to "end where it started."

FOLK-ART MUSICAL

There is a danger in arriving quickly at a design, especially when it's good-looking. One is immediately victimized by one's findings—you become your own sponsor or collector and fall in love too quickly with your own solution. I postpone for the longest time my formulation, in the mind or on paper, a scheme or pattern. Scenery has to evolve—the design kept incomplete, changeable, until almost the very end. Scenery best fulfills its function when it captures the spontaneous, natural excitement of rehearsal.

FIDDLER ON THE ROOF (1964)

When Aronson heard that a musical was to be adapted from Sholom Aleichem's stories about Tevye the dairyman and his daughters, the designer did something he had hardly ever done before in his Broadway career: he actively sought the assignment. The reason for Aronson's eagerness had nothing to do with any prescient perception that the musical would be a huge commercial and critical success; in fact, no one much believed that this seemingly parochial project would have mass appeal until it was well into its pre-Broadway tryout tour. Rather, Aronson simply knew that he was right for *Fiddler*. The musical was set in the *shtetl* of Anatevka in 1905—roughly five years after Aronson had been born into the family of the Chief Rabbi of Kiev. Aronson had designed an Aleichem play for Maurice Schwartz's Yiddish Art Theatre not long after arriving in New York and felt a kinship with the writer. What's more, the title of the musical was inspired by a Chagall painting; Aronson had first encountered Chagall in Moscow, where the painter designed sets for Aleichem plays at the Jewish Kamerny Theatre, and it was in part Aronson's early monograph about Chagall, published in Berlin in 1923, that gave him the wherewithal to emigrate to America.

However, *Fiddler*'s producer, Harold Prince, did not want Aronson for the show. Prince regarded the designer's work as heavy; he joked that if he ever hired Aronson, it would be to do *The Lower Depths*. He leaned instead toward William and Jean Eckart, who had designed past musicals produced or directed by Prince, including *Fiorello!* and *She Loves Me*.

The logjam was resolved by the production's most dominant force, the director-choreographer Jerome Robbins. Robbins had suggested Aronson to start with, and his choice was confirmed when he and the show's authors (playwright Joseph Stein, composer Jerry Bock, and lyricist Sheldon Harnick) visited an exhibition of Aronson's artwork and theatre designs at the Storm King Art Center in upstate New York. Robbins was particularly impressed by the design for *J.B.* "This is a perfect set," Robbins told Harnick, "because it is a perfect work of art and yet it won't be complete until there are actors in it."

Once Aronson was hired, little about *Fiddler* came easily. As had always been his reputation, Robbins proved to be a perfectionist and a severe taskmaster. He also preferred that Aronson and Patricia Zip-

1, 2   Early sketches—of the village (1) and the tailor shop (2)—for *Fiddler on the Roof* (1964). They were among many that the director, Jerome Robbins, rejected.

prodt, the costume designer, work separately, answering only to him. As a result, they had to have secret meetings to coordinate their designs. Robbins also rejected many designs before making his final choice. "He wears you down," said one of the director's theatrical collaborators. "He wants to try every possibility. He's like the man who asks to see a shirt in seventy-five colors before making his decision. He doesn't fully understand the time it can take a designer—or writer or songwriter—to do so many different versions." It was typical of the process that Aronson designed dozens of show curtains for *Fiddler*—none of which, in the end, was used in the production.

However exasperating it may have been, Robbins' behavior was rooted in a desire to grapple with the meaning of the piece. He kept reminding the authors that if *Fiddler* struck the audience as simply a story about a dairyman and his daughters, it would end up being an ethnic domestic comedy about "the previous adventures of the Goldberg family—and it's not enough." The real theme, in Robbins' view, was the dissolution of a whole way of life. It was this thinking that led to the creation of one of the last songs Bock and Harnick wrote for the score—the opening number, "Tradition," which establishes the *shtetl* traditions that are gradually dissolved and which becomes, in Harnick's phrase, "the tapestry against which the whole show plays." Robbins was also struck by the visual image of a circle, which suggests both the notion of a tight community and the patterns of folk dancing. Robbins used a circular formation for his choreography of "Tradition," and, two acts later, he ended the musical with the breaking up of that communal circle, to symbolize the dispersal of the Jews who were forced out of Russia by pogroms.

Aronson and Zipprodt spent hours at Robbins' apartment looking at films about *shtetl* life. At Aronson's suggestion, a photographer was hired to take stills of the main research film, *Through Laughter and Tears*, so that the smallest details could be captured—a broken-down fence, or the layout of a room. At the same time, there was a great deal of discussion about how Chagall should be used in the design. "Throughout his life, Chagall has been the one Jewish artist to paint the *shtetl*," said Aronson. "Chagall's colorful fantasy—a man flying through the air, head in hand, a fiddler on the roof—his love for the homey little things in life (a shoe, a cat, a rooster)—is closest to the folk art of Aleichem. . . . It was the emotion of Chagall's paintings I tried to incorporate into *Fiddler*, but the show needed to be solved in terms of its own problems."

Robbins eventually decided that Chagall-like fantasy should be incorporated only into the background of the designs, and that the homely realism of poverty should be in the foreground and in the costumes. Aronson decided to interpret and synthesize Chagall rather than to copy or imitate him. He took from the painter textures, colors, and a few props, but never the characteristic figures (the green fiddler included) that are central to Chagall's pictorial scheme. Aronson composed his sets very carefully—even to the exact placement of Tevye's milk can—so that they would be complete only when performers like Zero Mostel inhabited them.

From an early production meeting with Robbins—in October 1963, nearly a year before the Broadway opening—Aronson took away notes that were largely upheld in the finished design: "Color—Chagall, simple-naïve-buoyant-primitive-childlike-charming-delightful to look at . . . Set not fill out stage at all times . . . Musician [the Fiddler, ultimately a minor character] starts show, establishes the tone of play, is guide to show (fantastic)—he is 'magician' throughout show, knows what happens . . . A sense of village people owning village, possess it . . . Richness of communal life—all is shared. Evocation (memory) without sentimentality (not sugary) . . . Combine elements of fantasy and reality . . . Backgrounds not reality, but fantasy . . . Overall scheme: establish entity of town, bringing it on—making it come to life. The opening and the closing of the circle of the story . . . End of show, when people are cast off the land, the village goes too, leaving Tevye on cart . . . Essence of show: (may be) tradition of an existence impregnated and altered by time and events . . . Tevye is traditionalist. Daughters are affected by the changes . . . Jewishness is a way of life . . . The *shtetl* was a life connected, it gets broken up."

A principal design feature of the production was the use of two concentric turntables—a small one placed asymmetrically within a larger one. They were designed to move the people of Anatevka and the ramshackle dwellings against the backdrops of delicately colored skies and trees. The idea for this device came from a sentence Aronson found in Aleichem: "Tevye's family is like a small circle within the larger community of the town of Anatevka." The designer had always believed that the only justification for a mechanical technique on stage was "to reflect the show it builds on," and the turntables proved to be a crucial factor in the show's staging, right through the choreographed curtain call that Robbins added in final New York previews. But Robbins, who had decided not to use the traditional turntable in Brecht's *Mother Courage,* his last Broadway production, at first objected to the idea. He felt that Tevye's house and village were steady and stable, and

3

3 The unpainted model of the basic set for *Fiddler.* "At first I was disappointed," said Sheldon Harnick, the lyricist. "The sets were modest—not splashy, grandiose. Only by living with the show was I able to see how right they were—that they provided the right atmosphere for what happened on that stage."

4, 5, 6, 7   Tevye's house. The design is a variation on "a little house in the woods" that opened up in Aronson's design for Maurice Schwartz's *The Tenth Commandment*, the opening production of the Yiddish Art Theatre on Second Avenue in 1926. When first seen, the house is closed (4); when the turntable moved the house downstage, the house opened up to reveal its interior—as seen in the sketch (5) and on stage in London (6), during the performance of the song "Matchmaker, Matchmaker." A different backdrop was used for the Sabbath scene, as sketched (7).

5

6

7

8

9

10

shouldn't dance around the stage (an effect created by the asymmetric position of the inner turntable).

Eventually, the director was won over. To suggest the "stable" circumference of the little town of Anatevka, Aronson designed a proscenium border of upside-down houses, in a Chagall-like manner, which framed the show. A few small houses "danced" along almost every backdrop to complete or echo the circle. At the end, when the inhabitants are forced to leave and the traditions of the *shtetl* collapse, the company formed a circle (on the turntable) for the last time, bowed to each other, and retreated. As their communal circle disintegrated, so the little houses in the background and the arch of houses on the proscenium border slowly lifted out of sight, leaving Tevye with his family and milk cart on an empty stage against a rosy-gray sky. At that point, Tevye and the symbolic fiddler described the community's circle one last time by ritualistically walking around it, in silhouette, just before taking the final, deliberate exit upstage. Thus did Robbins, Aronson, Zero Mostel (Tevye), and the lighting designer, Jean Rosenthal, work together to produce one of the most moving final curtains of the American musical theatre.

Robbins was also concerned about the size of the sets. He constantly argued for more empty space, which he needed for dance numbers. Aronson scaled down Tevye's house by reducing the size and sweep of its roof; the inn set had to be redesigned in three sections so it could open up and pull away to allow for the major Act I production number, "To Life." A greater problem, in Aronson's view, was to duplicate in shop-painted scenery the Chagall-like qualities of glowing, translucent colors and free brushstrokes. Aronson himself liked working in mixed media, which was often difficult to reproduce on a large scale. In sketches for the sets, he emulated Chagall's loose painting style in his own favorite medium at that time, encaustics—the heated, wax-based paints which are deployed quickly to produce a spontaneous, loosely sketched look. Most of the sketches for *Fiddler* combined encaustics, pastel, and a bit of gouache—all done on blotter paper, which further added to the hazy, atmospheric quality of the designs. In order to translate these techniques into the large-scale painting of backdrops (almost all of which had to be translucent), many samples were made. The desired surface textures were achieved by such devices as strewing pebbles on a drop and artfully spraying over them with various dyes. Often there existed several versions of the same drop, and Aronson would ask scenic artists to combine the background from one sketch with some detail from another. He was very

II

OPPOSITE

8, 9, 10 Drops for *Fiddler* demonstrate Aronson's distillation of Chagall colors, textures, and fantasy images, as well as the seasonal flow of the story: the setting advances from spring (a barn scene backdrop, seen as sketched [8]), to summer (the wedding) to autumn (a railroad station where Tevye says goodbye to his daughter Hodel, as sketched [9]), to winter (again the barn, as the villagers prepare to leave Anatevka, drop as sketched [10]). The spring and winter drops show the same trees, with and without leaves. In Act II, the leaves on the three-dimensional tree beside Tevye's house also vanish.

11 The spring barn scene on stage in London.

12 Zero Mostel as Tevye completes the picture
carefully composed by Aronson.

13 Detail of the night drop sketch for the wedding
scene, with a translucent moon and a loosely painted,
swirling Chagall sky, all developed through Aronson's
use of a mixture of paint media. "Chagall will forever
paint *Fiddler on the Roof*," Aronson said. "He takes
Anatevka with him wherever he goes. I only got to
do it once."

14

14, 15   A gauze traveler curtain of a street in Anatevka (14), used for the least memorable song in *Fiddler*— "I Just Heard," performed in Act II (15). The point of the number, which has never been included on *Fiddler* cast recordings, was to allow scenery to be changed behind the curtain. It was the last time this traditional Broadway-musical device would be used in an Aronson set; in the Harold Prince–directed shows to follow, Aronson provided a "limbo" setting that fulfilled his long-held belief that all of the movement of stage scenery should be revealed to the audience.

15

16, 17, 18, 19, 20 This sequence of sketches shows the first of many versions Aronson designed for a proposed Act II "Chava" ballet. Here it was conceived as a demonic nightmare, prompted by Tevye's discovery that his eldest daughter is to marry a gentile. A scenario by Robbins describes its "general premise and atmosphere": "[Tevye's] world begins to tilt, careen and come apart. Realistic time and place changes: events are condensed, only strong meaningful confrontations and exchanges get through to him: his world becomes flooded with associative fantasies. As he rushes about, the real, the feared and the wanted mix, confuse and fly by. . . . He is always haunted by the illusive presence of Chava, imagining her as she is, was, and will be. Through the village he charges in pain, and the *shtetl* comes apart, fragmentizes and flies around him: people and places . . . sail past, linger mockingly or float commiseratingly. . . . The traditions he has lived by crack apart. . . . The total effect is of seeing a man trying, within his own limitations, to deal with an event too catastrophic for his capabilities to handle. . . . In between in fluid state is the town—its people—the wood—the roads. . . . What pieces of scenery appear are treated normally at first, but as the sequence progresses, the bits and wisps of props etc. representing village etc. become transparent, unrealistic— swimming—detached and loose—a Chagall swirling past in pieces."

21 The discarded "Chava" ballet was replaced by a brief song for Tevye, "Chavaleh," and an accompanying small-scale dance that took place behind this gauze drop, as seen in the London West End production. Around the drop, one sees the upside-down houses that framed the proscenium; the motif was continued with a few tiny houses in the drop itself.

22

22, 23 Aronson worked hard to translate the sketchy, loosely painted quality of Chagall's canvases into large-scale scenery. But those qualities were not always upheld in the many productions of *Fiddler* around the world. The designer, who had long theorized about the national characteristics of art, was pleased and amused to find that his beliefs were borne out as his sets for this hit musical were replicated in different countries. Though the theatre artisans who built the scenery for each *Fiddler* all worked from the same blueprints and samples that guided the original Broadway production, they managed to imbue the sets with distinctively local characteristics. Compared with the successful London duplication of the Broadway production (22), the Paris *Fiddler* (23) has much busier brushstrokes—as if the Impressionists, rather than Chagall, had been the inspiration for the design.

23

24

25

26

27

24, 25, 26, 27 The models for the Tokyo production —as represented here by the interior of Tevye's house (24), its exterior (25), the inn (26), and the railroad station (27)—are so calmly and two-dimensionally painted that the house, though technically the same as Aronson's original, has the feeling of a Japanese shrine and all the sets have the aesthetics of Japanese prints. Because the Tokyo production used a 54-foot turntable, roughly twice the diameter of the one on Broadway, the show also had the horizontal feeling of Kabuki theatre.

28, 29, 30, 31   In the late Act I sequence that the producer Harold Prince considered the most abstract and successful scenic solution of the show, a scene in Motel the tailor's shop (28) precipitates a cinematic dissolve that leads to Motel's outdoor wedding to Tevye's daughter (the song "Sunrise, Sunset" [29]), which is then followed by a spirited wedding dance (30). The set for the wedding is shown on stage, without performers (31).

32   The wedding as sketched by Aronson.

much dependent on the individual artistry of the scenic painters; he needed person-to-person contact with them. While some found his method of working exasperating, the best of them felt that the final results were rewarding.

In the end, Aronson and Robbins achieved a kind of peace in their often difficult creative relationship. The designer told friends that however much he suffered during the genesis of *Fiddler*, "Jerry suffered more." Richard Altman, who was Robbins' assistant on the show, was standing between Aronson and Robbins at the back of the theatre the night Robbins' last piece of choreography went into the musical during previews—a wedding-scene dance in which male dancers balance wine bottles on their hats. When the number was over, Altman saw that tears were running down Aronson's cheeks.

"Any man who can do that," said the designer, "I forgive everything."

Harold Prince, by contrast, did not think the Aronson-Robbins collaboration was a "good" one. He felt the design was at its best when it approached the abstract: the most successfully solved scenic problem occurred late in Act I, transforming a tailor's shop into the outdoor wedding scene before the audience's eyes. Otherwise, in his view, Robbins' constant rejecting of designs inhibited Aronson's creativity. But *Fiddler* made Prince into an Aronson enthusiast; he used the designer on nearly every musical he directed over the next dozen years. A decade after *Fiddler*, Prince had decided that Aronson was second only to George Abbott as a theatrical colleague who had influenced his own work: "I thank Jerry Robbins for Boris Aronson every day of my life."

33   In the final image, Mostel's Tevye, in silhouette, joins the exodus that has dispersed the village of Anatevka, taking leave of a now empty stage.

THE FIRST PRINCE MUSICALS

*Scenery is still hand-crafted. Therefore the involve-
ment of everyone working on it is essential, from the
scenic artist and prop builder down to the stagehand
who handles the scenery and the propman.*

In three shows over a brief period—*West Side Story* (1957), *Gypsy*
(1959), and *Fiddler on the Roof* (1964)—Jerome Robbins and his collaborators had begun a radical transformation in the style of the Broadway musical. The Robbins shows still had conventional musical plots,
but they also had serious themes that coexisted with the various love
stories of their librettos. The staging techniques, meanwhile, became
more and more cinematic. Robbins musicals didn't necessarily have
more dancing, but, increasingly, they were choreographed to achieve a
seamless flow in which scenes, dances, and songs were inextricably
interwoven.

Robbins left the Broadway musical theatre after *Fiddler*, and his
ideas were taken to their next stage of development by Harold Prince.
After producing *Fiddler*, Prince had decided to turn his principal career focus to directing. Like Robbins, he chose to do musicals built
around themes and metaphors; he also hoped to do away altogether
with the vestiges of the old-fashioned musical book—the paired ro-
mances, happy endings, and symmetrical narratives. He did not fully
achieve this goal until the musicals he did with Stephen Sondheim, beginning with *Company* in 1970. But both *Cabaret* (1966) and *Zorba*
(1968), each with songs by John Kander and Fred Ebb, took transitional

steps that departed from the conventional musical format more than
Fiddler had.

The theatrical ideas that Robbins and then Prince championed required accompanying changes in design. If a musical was to be an organic piece rather than an alternation of scenes and songs—and if a
well-made story was to be dispensed with—the sets would have to be
less naturalistic and more fluid in movement; they, too, would have to
be choreographed into the whole. "What I liked about Hal's shows,"
explained J. J. Moore, an Aronson assistant at the time, "was that the
method of getting from scene A to scene B was as important as the
scenes themselves." The concepts involved were not new—except to
the commercial theatre of Broadway; they were the ideas of total
theatre that had first captivated Aronson in the revolutionary Moscow
theatres of Meyerhold and Tairov almost half a century earlier and
that he had later seen in their Brechtian incarnation in Germany. At
last, the Broadway theatre was ready to accept those techniques, as
adapted by Prince to the indigenously American form of the musical.
It was surely serendipitous that Prince chose Aronson to design these
shows; this was the kind of theatre that the designer had been waiting
for a lifetime to do in America. "I have been fortunate enough late in

my career to begin an association with a director who knows my strong points and limitations and who uses me for what I am best suited," said Aronson at the time. "Hal knows how to challenge me. He also challenges himself with each production."

CABARET (1966)

Appropriately enough, Prince's liberated staging notions for his first adventurous musical—an adaptation of Christopher Isherwood's *Berlin Stories* and John van Druten's previous theatrical adaptation *I Am a Camera*—were directly inspired by both Meyerhold and Brecht. The material itself was set in Brecht's Weimar Germany; accordingly, Kander and Ebb wrote a score somewhat flavored by Brecht-Weill, and one of the lead roles was tailored to the talents of Weill's widow, Lotte Lenya. If anything, *Cabaret* had the general, if somewhat softened, form of a Brecht-Weill musical: the musical numbers didn't always advance the show's story, as was the common practice on Broadway, but instead served as acidic, ironic commentary on the story and its themes.

Meyerhold's influence on *Cabaret* was a direct result of a trip Prince took to the Soviet Union while the musical was in its planning stages. In Moscow, the director visited the Taganka Theatre—the descendant of Meyerhold's experimental company of the 1920s—and was startled by the techniques he saw in a revue suggested by John Reed's *Ten Days That Shook the World.* Among other things, Prince saw "an apron built out over the orchestra pit . . . a curtain of light behind which the scenery was changed . . . black velour drapes instead of painted canvas [which] made possible [the use of surprising] source[s] and colors of light." Some of these ideas were executed in *Cabaret* by Aronson and the lighting designer, Jean Rosenthal; others turned up in later Prince musicals, including those designed by Aronson and those not (*Candide, Evita, Sweeney Todd*).

With *Cabaret,* Prince realized for the first time that a designer shouldn't just design "sets" but should design an abstract space—a "limbo" area—that could contain the entire action of a show. Instead of illustrating a story, Aronson was designing a space that contained the ambiance of that story. For the director, whose formative years had been spent producing shows directed by the veteran George Abbott, it was a whole new way of working. "With Abbott," Prince explained, "I did the scenery. He didn't care about it—he didn't even have lighting—he just wanted to know where the doors were going to

be. He'd arrive the first day of rehearsal and be shown the scenery. Boris made it clear to me just how advisable it could be to start the design of the show at the moment it was being written—when there was nothing on paper except an idea. Some designers are authors—Boris was an author."

The idea of *Cabaret* was to use a seedy, decadent Berlin nightclub, the Kit Kat Klub, and its grotesquely clownish emcee (played by Joel Grey), as metaphorical representatives of a chaotic German society rapidly skidding into a Nazi apocalypse. The musical was adapted from the same stories that had served as the basis for John van Druten's *I Am a Camera,* which Aronson had designed on Broadway fifteen years earlier, but the two stage versions had little in common. "My experience illustrates how the same basic material when differently used can be—indeed, must be—approached from a fundamentally different point of view," said Aronson. "Van Druten's adaptation combined his characteristic light touch with the darker side of the situation represented by the threatening menace of Hitler and Nazism. . . . In *Cabaret,* on the other hand, I was seeking to project quite a different aspect of Germany before World War II. Coexisting with the predominant sense of order was the bizarre defiance of the Berlin cabarets. Neither theatre nor vaudeville, political cabaret was improvisational satire, and the German performers were masters of it. I visited many of these cabarets [while living in Berlin in 1923] and my recollections helped me greatly in designing the show." He and the costume designer, Patricia Zipprodt, also looked at Pabst and Dietrich films at the Museum of Modern Art's film archive to get ideas for atmospheric touches.

As *Cabaret* was the first Prince production to break away from the traditional musical, it was slower to develop and choppier in achievement than those to come. In an early version of the script, for instance, the cabaret numbers were all consigned to one segment at the start of the show rather than, as in the final version, dispersed throughout the evening. Even in the final version, the narrative scenes —involving the romantic fates of two couples—were conventionally written, staged, and designed. As Prince later said, "If we'd done *Cabaret* five years later, we'd never have had wagons bringing on bedrooms and living rooms. I wish we'd done the realistic scenes differently—that they had been *less* realistic." J. J. Moore remembered that "problems were solved late" on this first of the Prince experiments. "We thought we had fit in everything," he said. "We had no floor or fly space left to hide any other set, and then it turned out we had to fit in a fruit store, too! We flattened out that set so it could

1 A preliminary sketch for the "limbo" area of *Cabaret* (1966). The storefronts, hanging lamps, iron staircase, and trapezoidal mirror are all in place in embryonic form—as is a hanging neon sign, itself having its own red mirror image, with an indeterminate text. Eventually the librettist, Joe Masteroff, decided that the sign should read "Cabaret."

2 A model for the limbo area, with a Joel Grey emcee doll down front. Simplified from the early sketch, it still contains gaudy red curtains that were ultimately eliminated from the design.

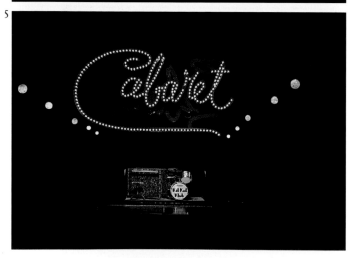

3, 4, 5   Three photographs of the limbo area on stage in London, without actors, showing its various configurations: without the mirror (3), with the illuminated mirror (4), and with the double-image "Cabaret" sign of the Kit Kat Klub (5).

be held on three or four hangers—that was my education in how Boris and I were going to function."

If the fruit store and the other rooms were too realistic for Prince, they nonetheless floated in the stylized limbo space. And the production's other advances were considerable. Whereas Robbins in *Fiddler* had had to clear the stage of scenery to have a dance number, the stage of *Cabaret* was empty for much of the evening. Through experience, Prince began to learn to do without doors and props; by the time he and Aronson got to *Company* and *Follies* five years later, there would be no doors, few props, and almost no chairs. In *Cabaret*, there were no longer the usual painted curtains—as there had been in *Fiddler*—to mask set changes. Rosenthal created a curtain of light, augmented by a curtain of silver streamers, that duplicated a curtain for a stage-within-the-stage in Aronson's design for the Kit Kat Klub; in addition to signifying to the audience that a number was taking place in the cabaret itself, the light "curtain" camouflaged some set movements. The lights embedded downstage to form this "curtain" were on 180-degree swivels. When tilted up, the lights formed the "curtain." Another bank of lights faced into the auditorium and temporarily "blinded" the audience at the end of scenes. The set changes were in the open. Prince was learning that just as "you shouldn't be able to pull a song out of the second act and put it in the first act and say that it still works, so the same is true of a set. The scenery should feed itself, so something that happens at the end of the evening would be a payoff of what happened throughout the evening."

The space Aronson designed had black walls with roughly seven-foot-high black-rope curtains along the bottom of each to allow actors' entrances; the panels would lift up suddenly to allow the wagons to bring on parts of rooms which assembled into complete sets on stage. A huge iron spiral staircase at stage left—suggestive of one backstage at a cabaret—ran up and offstage as part of the permanent set-up. Prince had a couple of onlookers stationed on it, serving as a "surrogate German population" who would sullenly and silently observe scenes happening below, further heightening the undisguised theatricality of the show. (The device dovetailed with Aronson's long-stated desire to expose the artifice of theatre to the audience; it was Prince's equivalent to Brecht's "alienation" effect.) The abstract limbo area was further defined by hanging streetlamps and expressionistically lighted storefronts that, following strict perspective, converged toward a central vanishing point. As in *J.B.*, no house curtain was used. The setting existed indoors and outdoors simultaneously.

6

6, 7, 8 "Wilkommen," the opening number of *Cabaret*, with Joel Grey and chorus performers under the mirror ceiling. Earlier, the audience had entered to find no show curtain—just the mirror in its vertical position, reflecting the arriving theatregoers. The musical began with a blackout and a drumroll, during which each letter on the "Cabaret" sign in front of the mirror lighted up individually, culminating in the flashing of the entire sign. The emcee entered to sing "Wilkommen" as the mirror rose to become the "ceiling" of the cabaret (6). The mirror tilted to distort the garish Brechtian cabaret turns (7, 8).

7

8

9

9 One of the relatively realistic sets, a fruit peddler's
shop, as seen in its sketch. In his review of *Cabaret*,
Walter Kerr wrote, "Aronson's scenery is so
imaginative that even a gray-green fruit store comes
up like a warm summer dawn."

10

10, 11 The fruit shop on stage (10), where it floats
against the still-visible abstract limbo area, with
its storefronts suggesting the urbanscape of a sickly
Weimar-era Berlin. In London (11), Judi Dench starred
as Sally Bowles, and, at left, Lila Kedrova played
Fräulein Schneider—roles originated in New York
by Jill Haworth and Lotte Lenya.

11

12

12, 13, 14 The other principal interior of *Cabaret*, the room of the landlady, Fräulein Schneider—as sketched (12), seen on stage in London (13), and occupied by Lotte Lenya and Jack Gilford on Broadway (14).

15

15 The Kit Kat Klub in *Cabaret*.

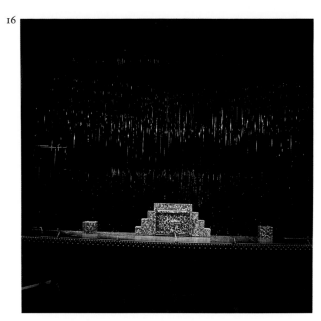

16, 17   To indicate that production numbers were
taking place on the stage of the Kit Kat Klub, a curtain
of shiny plastic streamers filled the entire proscenium
(16). Those streamers simulated the silvery curtain
within the Kit Kat Klub set, as seen onstage in
London with Judi Dench as Sally Bowles in a cabaret
number (17).

18

19

18, 19, 20   An elaborate projection of a nightmarish
official Berlin—as sketched (18) and seen on stage
in the Boston tryout (19)—during the song "Why
Should I Wake Up?" (It was reminiscent of Aronson's
"Painting with Light" experiments of a quarter-
century earlier.) Prince provided an accompanying
shadow-play sequence, seen in Boston (20), but he
could never stage it to his satisfaction; it was cut
from the show prior to the Broadway opening.
"[The sequence] was set at the lowest point of the
German depression," Prince said. "Germany was
humbled, but fighting back in the wrong way.
Joel Grey was put on wheels, playing a legless man
on a cart; we dropped a curtain and did a shadow
play showing the whole panoply of poverty.
But I couldn't get it right, and, visually, it didn't
work. I finally figured out the right technique in
the bedlam sequence of *Sweeney Todd* [in 1979]."

20

But the key element of Aronson's set—and the designer's own contribution—was a large trapezoidal mirror that hung center stage and in which the audience saw their own reflections as they took their seats. "When Hal Prince and I first discussed the project," Aronson said, "I asked him why he wanted to use the Isherwood material again and to revive its period. He answered that he saw political similarities between what had happened in Germany and what was happening in the United States [during the civil rights confrontations of Selma and Little Rock]. So I decided to use a mirror that would almost fill the stage. Tilted one way, it would reflect the audience, saying, 'Look at yourselves.' It was a mirror of life—of a society." Tilted at another angle, it reflected the cabaret performers from a distorting perspective and emphasized "the intentionally grotesque quality of the cabaret numbers."

For Prince and *Cabaret*, the mirror proved to be the crucial element in the design—it at once reinforced the cabaret's value as a political metaphor, augmented the abstraction of the limbo area, and gave a literal ceiling to the Kit Kat Klub. Like the turntables in *Fiddler*, the mobile mirror underscored the staging, but it also upheld Aronson's conviction that any such mechanical apparatus must spring from the meaning of the play. When it was set up for the first time in Boston, as the show was being installed at the Shubert Theatre, the only three faces the mirror reflected were those of Aronson, Prince, and the choreographer, Ron Field. Aronson liked to recall: "We were sitting in the otherwise empty theatre. Since the house lights were on, our three small figures were conspicuously reflected in the enormous mirror at the front of the stage. Hal wondered out loud about the justification for such a costly effect. 'I'm sorry,' I said. 'This mirror calls for a full house. It won't register otherwise. You have to have a full house.' Fortunately, large audiences continued discovering their images in the *Cabaret* mirror for years." In addition to its long Broadway run, *Cabaret* thrived on the road and in London. It brought mirrors on stage into fashion—so much so that they subsequently turned up in works as varied as the National Theater production of Tom Stoppard's *Jumpers* in London and the musical *A Chorus Line*.

ZORBA (1968)

To define a limbo area for *Zorba*, his musical version of the Nikos Kazantzakis novel *Zorba the Greek*, Prince put his show within the framework of a bouzouki circle in an imaginary Greek café. The mu-

sical opened with the entire cast seated in a semicircle facing the audience; the company posed as a contemporary Greek chorus that then proceeded to act out the legend of Zorba, with the chorus's anonymous members portraying all the roles in the story. Gradually, the cast members forsook their street clothes for the costumes of their characters in the play-within-the-play; in a similar way, the primitive props of the initial scene gave way to a more elaborate production.

Simplicity had to be preserved, and to maintain the limbo area throughout the show, Aronson built everything around a basic amphitheatrical design. The unit set consisted of four movable sets of stairs and platforms. With the addition of a few built pieces of scenery, they could make various combinations of levels and entrances, as well as define the locale of each scene. Instead of a curtain, an elevated road or hill spanning the greater part of the stage was used, with the performers acting or singing on and around it to bridge the open scene changes. A translucent, gauzy sky drop surrounded the rear upper half of the stage.

Even so, the design process was sophisticated. For a path into the theme of the musical, Aronson turned to the lyric of the Greek chorus's opening song: "Life is what you do . . . while you're waiting to die." To the designer, "the basic theme of the play was about Life and Death in equally strong force," and this dictated a color scheme dominated by blacks and whites. "I used the brilliance of the white-washed mountain villages with their deep shadows rather than the pictorial blues and greens of the Mediterranean. I wanted the sets to look sculptural—strong in textures and contrasts." The sets were in warm and cool whites, while Patricia Zipprodt's costumes were in warm and cool blacks and browns. "Naturally, the sunlight had to be part of the locale. A miniature sculptured village hung against the sky as a sundial. It was lit so the shadows should mark the time of day." The only use of non-monochromatic colors occurred in a mine scene and during the wandering Zorba's visit to a Turkish nightclub.

Aronson felt that Kazantzakis' novel was contemporary, because "the young hero, Niko, is revolting against the mechanical—returning to something native. Hence, the sets had to be 'handmade.'" The designer went to great lengths, both in his research and his choice of scenic materials, to make sure that *Zorba* would have a hand-crafted look. The sky consisted of loosely woven layers of translucent and transparent fabrics. The mountains were made of heavy, knotted tapestries woven around wooden rods in the scenic studio. The village church and other buildings were carved out of Styrofoam; a flown-in tree was created out of individually crafted sponges and other textured

21, 22, 23, 24 *Zorba* (1968): These research photographs, brought back by Prince from Greece, gave Aronson clues to the hand-crafted look of his design for the musical.

fabrics. Even the neutral maskings, which were black on black, were appliqués of textured materials. Where *Fiddler* was designed in terms of painting, and *Cabaret* according to the glittery theatricality of a revue, *Zorba* was three-dimensional, rough-hewn, sculptured, tangible, and had small scenic elements designed like props. "'Only God can make a tree,'" said Aronson. "I couldn't imitate nature, so I made a tapestry hillside out of sticks and rope for the mine scene."

In part because *Zorba* involved creative personnel and two stars, Herschel Bernardi and Maria Karnilova, associated with *Fiddler*, the designers had to avoid making the show look like, as Patricia Zipprodt put it, "*Fiddler* in Crete." To play down any overlapping circular imagery between the two musicals, both set in impoverished ethnic communities, Zipprodt used rectangular patches on the costumes to echo the rectangular elements in the set. Another problem, which resisted solution, was the crucial scene of a mine explosion. The explosion fought the stylization of *Zorba*; it was too real an event for the musical (just as it was an ideal event for the film previously adapted from the Kazantzakis novel).

As non-realistic as Aronson's sets for *Zorba* were, they were nonetheless based on secondhand observation of the real Crete. Prince visited the setting and sent back notes that were observed in the basic design configuration: "The buildings are built on the side of hills . . . [linked by] tortuous roads . . . and piled on top of each other." (However, Aronson ignored Prince's initial preoccupation with the blues and greens of the real Crete.) According to the lighting designer, Richard Pilbrow, "Both Boris and Hal obviously took as a major element the blinding whiteness and purity of light in Greece, which is what we strove for. The marvelously sculptured setting and its links from evocative reality to almost pure sculpture took all the light one could throw on it. . . . Because of all the other moods needed in the piece, Boris evolved that remarkable backcloth that allowed one to produce an extraordinary variety of visual mood and effect. It became, however, a dense patchwork of layers of gauze—wonderful but finally something that failed to allow one quality of the Grecian sky that we needed—that is, its brightness. We had more light behind that cloth than, I would think, any backlit cloth hitherto on Broadway, but I'm not sure we ever got what I and, I suspect, Boris were looking for."

In design *Zorba* moved more in the direction of pure theatricality than *Cabaret* had: fewer individual sets had to be pulled out of the wings to augment the limbo area that defined the show. By the next Prince musical, *Company*, Aronson's entire theatrical environment would be revealed on stage from first scene to curtain call.

25

26

25, 26 The stairs-and-platform units that dominated the simple design of *Zorba*—as seen bare in model form (25) and on stage for a wedding scene (26). "White has been a stage taboo because of the glare," said Aronson, "but then Greek whites *do* glare."

27

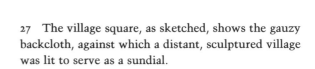

27 The village square, as sketched, shows the gauzy backcloth, against which a distant, sculptured village was lit to serve as a sundial.

28 The village square, at night, on stage.

28

29, 30, 31, 32   The hand-crafted look of *Zorba* was simulated by complex procedures at the scenery studio. Artisans wove a tapestry mountain and sculptured Cretan buildings out of Styrofoam.

33   Aronson's model for the all-purpose road in *Zorba*.

34   The house of Hortense, the aged French courtesan.

OPPOSITE

35   Hortense's house revolved to reveal its occupant's bedroom. Aronson often decorated sets with the personality of the actor in mind—in this case, Maria Karnilova. The designer was also pleased with Prince's use of the set in Hortense's death scene, which climaxes with old Greek women stripping the dead woman's room of its finery, leaving it pure white; the staging and design worked in perfect unison.

35

36 The mine scene, with the woven tapestry mountain in its background, on stage.

37 One of the few non-monochromatic settings in *Zorba*—a gaudy Turkish nightclub consisting of colorful rugs, rags, and beads that, in the show's most spectacular scenic moment, flew into the limbo area from above.

GRAND OPERA

My instructions to the craftsmen who build and paint the scenery: The patina of time is what I am trying to capture—not the dust.

MOURNING BECOMES ELECTRA   (1967)

If Aronson could never find enough epic works to design in the theatre, he could find them at the opera: even more so than most Broadway musicals, opera is, by definition, epic theatre—or can be when directors are willing to eschew musty, realistic productions. "Opera is such a stylized, unrealistic medium," Aronson explained. "It's mixed media. People die and keep singing. You have a solo and then three hundred people appear from all over the place. It's an art form that mustn't get lost in too many visual details. [But usually] in opera there are more hats, more shoes, more buttons, more swords. . . . It clutters. How about approaching the so-called great operas in a contemporary way? By contemporary, I mean the difference between Breughel and Picasso. In Picasso, you see the simplification, not the detail."

In the first of two Metropolitan Opera assignments, Aronson found a congenial director in Michael Cacoyannis. The piece itself was made to order for the designer's ambitions. *Mourning Becomes Electra*, with music by Marvin David Levy and a libretto by Henry Butler, was an adaptation of Eugene O'Neill's epic 1931 trilogy, which was itself an adaptation, transposed to New England in the Civil War era, of

Aeschylus' epic *Oresteia*. Indeed, the original Broadway production of O'Neill's marathon play had inspired one of the most famous scenic designs of the American theatre, by Robert Edmond Jones. For Aronson, who admired Jones' career without ever being particularly influenced by it, *Mourning Becomes Electra* was a chance to spin his own variations on a great theme.

As a pathway into this gargantuan work, Aronson seized on one passage from O'Neill's play for his design's guiding metaphor: "Why are the shutters still closed? I hate what's warped and twisted and eats into itself and dies for a lifetime in shadows." What followed was a design accentuating the steady disintegration of the tragic Mannon household.

As in *Zorba*, which also dealt with fundamentals of life and death, Aronson played constantly with contrasts between blackness and whiteness, negative and positive values. The Mannon mansion's exterior was black—hollow and rotting away at its center, progressively harder at its edges. White and gray were used to sketch in the closed shutters and other details. Aronson also made use of rough-hewn surfaces by heavily encrusting transparent surfaces with textured pat-

1, 2, 3 The prologue of the opera *Mourning Becomes Electra* (1967) took place on the portico of the Mannon mansion, looking down toward a valley (1); in an open change, a cinematic "reverse angle," the audience then looked *at* the portico (2), instead of from it. Aronson's design of the mansion broadly acknowledged the famous Robert Edmond Jones design for the original Broadway production of O'Neill's play in 1931 (3). Although Aronson deliberately appropriated the most famous feature of the Jones setting—a row of columns suggesting both the play's classicism and the entrance to the Mannon mansion—he stylized the columns by giving them a decayed appearance. The audience looked through the rotting pillars to the sinister house façade.

4

4 Marie Collier and Evelyn Lear as Christine and Lavinia Mannon.

terns. The interior was similarly handled; it was falling apart at its core, and even a canopied four-poster bed was distorted. With typical perception, Harold Clurman wrote that Aronson's settings for *Mourning* "tell us of the fading venerability of an old New England family, the harsh intensity of the mansion and its inhabitants, the complexity of the motives, the cross currents of impulse which create an emotional tangle sufficiently powerful to strangle those trapped within it. The total impression is that of a steel web breathing the ghostly spirit which haunts the entire drama. The contours of the set are drawn in long lines but no detail within them is smooth. The experience of life has covered every plane with jagged incrustations."

In O'Neill's stage directions for the trilogy, he had asked that the Mannons have mask-like faces. This assertion of Greek classicism was upheld by Aronson in his stark costume designs, whose minimal details served to accentuate the performers' sepulchral faces. But masks also played a major role in the set itself. A dominant feature of the design was an array of Mannon family portraits, which appeared both on a gauze front drop and in the interior of the mansion. As

Cacoyannis suggested in a letter to Aronson early on, the portraits would provide a "hallucinating effect" and be lighted "in such a way that they sometimes seem like presences rather than framed paintings." To create the portraits, Aronson once again took an elliptical path in his research—by studying photographs of English gravestones featuring sculptured, bas-relief facial images. And, again in typical fashion, he remade the images into shadow-box portraits with a favorite technique, collage.

Not the least of Aronson's concerns with *Mourning Becomes Electra* was the size of the Met—the problem of achieving intimacy on a vast stage. He and Cacoyannis worked to achieve what they called an "artificial close-up" by "cornering" the actors. For the set of Adam Brant's ship, Aronson had tall masts and rigging that reached above the proscenium: "I created a contrast with this outer air and space by the way I treated the intimacy of the ship."

Even so, Aronson found himself questioning whether operas should ever have elaborate visual productions, "because the main thing is the arias, the music—that is what makes it."

5

5, 6, 7   The initial black-and-white sketch (5) for the Mannon mansion's interior, indicating the many different gray values and textured feel, and its realization on stage at the Met (6, 7), with its various rooms and levels allowing for simultaneous action.

8   The images of English churchyard gravestones from which Aronson conceived the Mannon family portraits for *Mourning Becomes Electra.*

9, 10, 11   Aronson's remaking of the portraits into shadow-box images through abstraction and the addition of a textural surface. Lighted from the back and heavily textured, the gallery of Mannon ancestors had a creepy, mask-like apparitional quality in keeping with the opera's doom-laden atmosphere.

12 The gauze curtain, haunted by the ghostly
"masks" of the Mannon ancestors.

13 *Mourning Becomes Electra:* Adam Brant's
towering ship, with its intimate deck areas contrasting
with the open sky. Lavinia and Orin (Orestes) met on
a hooded deck immediately above the small interior
cabin in which Brant received Christine.

FIDELIO (1970)

For a bicentennial production of Beethoven's only opera, the Met's general manager, Rudolf Bing, brought together Aronson and the Austrian director Otto Schenk—apparently assuming that they would be good collaborators because, in Schenk's words, "he knew we were both mad." Even as he was preparing the Met *Fidelio* (to be conducted by Karl Böhm), Schenk was completing a *Fidelio* (conducted by Leonard Bernstein) at the Theater an der Wien in Vienna—and he had no interest in doing the same production twice. Aronson flew to meet the director in Munich, where he was working on another project. Their first meeting took place at a small pension. Severely pressed for time, Schenk, who is also an actor, performed the key scenes of *Fidelio* for Aronson—a performance which proved helpful for the designer, as it turned out.

Fidelio, with a libretto based on an incident of the French Revolution, is a tale of political oppression, set largely in a prison. Leonore, a Spanish noblewoman, has disguised herself as a male jailer's assistant (Fidelio) in order to rescue her husband, Florestan, who is being held in chained bondage on political grounds by the tyrannical governor, Don Pizarro. *Fidelio* ends with the liberation of all the prisoners; Kenneth Clark has described it as "the greatest of all hymns to liberty." To both Aronson and Schenk, the idea of freedom became the dominant factor in their conception of the production.

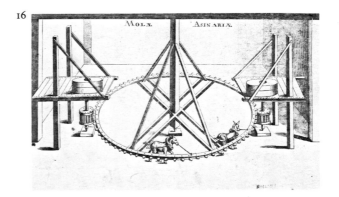

Schenk was at first startled by Aronson's choice of a visual metaphor. "In Munich," the designer recalled, "I asked Schenk—somewhat to his surprise—to take me to the science museum. There I showed him a collection of antique German locks and keys which I felt had the quality we should be looking for." The director quickly agreed. According to Schenk, "We were struck by the cruel, strange locks, all rough and handmade, at the museum. We looked at medieval locks and old architecture of salt mines; at strange, old wooden machinery—the inhuman wheels and winches." The director and designer soon agreed as well on giving the production a "handmade" look. "This was inspired by the nature of the work itself—a *Singspiel*," Aronson said. "In other words, *Fidelio* was for the people. It didn't demand an excessively clever interpretation.

"Furthermore, why set the locale in Spain for a musical expression so essentially German? I hear German in every note of this music. A Spanish locale may have been necessary in 1805 to get around the censors. But not in 1970. *Fidelio* is of a time—the last decade of the

14, 15, 16, 17 *Fidelio* (1970): The medieval locks and machines that gave Aronson his guiding visual metaphor.

18

20

19

21

18, 19, 20, 21, 22, 23 *Fidelio* as directed by Otto Schenk at the Metropolitan Opera, as seen in Aronson's sketches (above) and on stage (below). The central circular playing area (18, 19) does not change throughout the drama. The prisoners crawl out from spaces under the walls in the scene in which they are allowed a few rays of light. It is surrounded by heavily sculptured walls, which are interrupted by the structure supporting them and a gallery where guards are visible, off and on. Act II, dungeon scene (20, 21). Final scene (22, 23).

24 From the model, the textural detail of a wall.

eighteenth century. Most productions approach it in one of two ways: architecturally according to the period, or in a modern style. If you follow architecture, and particularly Piranesi, you end up with a tremendous amount of stone. But the music sings of freedom, not layers of granite. If you make *Fidelio* modern, everyone pictures Auschwitz and the like. The classical emotions—freedom, love, jealousy—are minimized when tied down too closely to any one point in time. A tree is never dated, and *Fidelio* is equally timeless.

"So what did we do? We tried to create intimacy on that huge Met stage—just as I had tried to do in *Mourning*." The idea was to devise a Shakespearean, Globe Theatre–like space—a *Fidelio* stage in which *Fidelio* and *Fidelio* only could be performed. The space itself would represent the prison and give the sense of confinement, oppression, dilapidation—a prison of a system which doesn't work, a place no longer of this world. There was to be no attempt to illustrate or interpret.

"In constructing the set," Aronson said, "we used folk-art substances: wood, metal, stone. Colors were gray-green, muted by a patina of age. The look of age can be had only by expert painting and fabric treatment. The prisoners wore ordinary clothes that looked as if they had undergone weeks and years of constant wear. The villain's silhouette is more important in creating a figure of evil than any Nazi-type outfit. In *Fidelio*, my whole concept was closer to sculpture than to painting or architecture."

With its heavily textured surfaces, the set reflected Aronson's own work in sculpture at the time of the production: wire webs, iron grilles, rotting burlap, and stone slabs were all part of the mélange. The principal sculptural medium was fiberglass—then a material much used in operatic scenery. Lightweight but capable of providing the illusion of weight and massiveness, fiberglass could also be lighted from behind to create a translucent effect. As the prisoners are freed at the end of the opera, Aronson could have blinding white light pour through the walls of the jail—thereby transforming a forbidding dungeon into an airy, abstract image of liberation. The audience was startled to see a gloomy stone-and-plaster environment so suddenly transformed by, as one critic put it, "the incandescent light of justice." The brilliance of the entering light underscored the intensity of "freedom" and the symbolism of the ending; the glaring whiteness did for the audience what the *Sonnenlicht* did for the prisoners in Act I.

The one access to the main acting area was by a small iron door within the huge gate of the prison. It was Schenk's idea that at the opera's end the huge gate, present throughout but never previously used, would lift slowly to show the mechanics—the lock, as it were—that had held the prisoners captive. It was, to the director, an "incredible" effect: "Something that had not opened for years suddenly opened. You could see the visitors outside through the gate: mothers, children. It was a very theatrical ending, showing people getting crazy about freedom. It was like my feeling after the war—when Hitler had gone—the shouting and screaming and crying and dancing in the streets, the madness and exuberance of freedom."

Schenk was satisfied with both productions of *Fidelio* he directed during that same season. He later remarked, "The interesting thing for me was that I had told both designers, Boris in New York and Günther Schneider-Siemssen in Vienna, the same things about how I saw the opera, and yet each came up with totally different and equally workable solutions."

25　*Fidelio*'s sculptured look reflected Aronson's own sculpture of the time.

RETURN TO CONSTRUCTIVISM

My main approach to theatre design is to recognize the individuality of each production in terms of theme and concept of the script. It is used to solve the unique problems that each presents. My eventual choices for creating the set for Fiddler on the Roof, *for instance, could scarcely be used satisfactorily to design* Cabaret; *no other play could be performed in my set for J.B. Each has its own special message, its own singular quality to maintain. You have to be reborn with each assignment.*

COMPANY (1970)

Almost half a century after he arrived in New York, Boris Aronson was given an assignment for which he had been preparing, in a sense, throughout his career. *Company*, a musical with a book by George Furth and songs by Stephen Sondheim, allowed Aronson to create a set in which he could synthesize and express a lifetime of thinking about the aesthetic character of New York City itself. It was also an opportunity for him to return to the Constructivist style of his formative artistic years—for the New York that emerged in *Company* was literally and figuratively a machine for playing, with its gears and tricks fully exposed to the audience. The working conditions that produced the set harked back to the theatre of Aronson's Russian youth as well: like the designers of the post-revolutionary avant-garde, Aronson could participate as a full collaborator in an innovative production, beginning with its formative stages. None of this would have been possible, of course, had it not been for the particular nature of *Company* and the other theatre artists associated with it. The musical's creative team worked in such close harmony—and thought so much alike—that it is often impossible to distinguish the authorship of individual contributions. Both behind the scenes and on stage, *Company* had an uncom-

mon artistic unity, especially by Broadway standards; the production was a watershed for the musical theatre in general and for *Company*'s creators.

For Harold Prince, the director, *Company* was the purest realization of the non-narrative "concept musical" he'd been reaching for in *Cabaret* and *Zorba*. The show was inspired by a cycle of eleven non-musical one-act plays that Furth had tried and failed to have produced on Broadway; at Prince's suggestion, the writer transformed them into a musical libretto. Yet Furth's book took an unusual form: even if no longer a set of playlets, the script remained as fractionalized as the lives and the city it describes. Offering little plot as such, *Company* is a series of thematically related vignettes about marriage as practiced by five upper-middle-class couples living in high-rise apartments in Manhattan; the couples are linked only by their friendship with Bobby, a thirty-five-year-old bachelor who visits them during the course of the show. The book's structure liberated the songs from the conventional task of furthering a story; the musical numbers instead became Brecht-Weill–like commentaries on Bobby's search to resolve his own confused feelings about love and marriage. It was an assign-

1, 2 Early quarter-inch-scale models for *Company* (1970), in which projections are used to transform the set into a Manhattan street and in which the five couples' apartments materialize in more elaborate detail than was eventually used.

ment that seemed to liberate Sondheim. In 1970, he was known mainly as a lyricist and had not written both the music and lyrics for a Broadway show since *Anyone Can Whistle*, a one-week flop of six years earlier. As it turned out, *Company* was the project that established his reputation as Broadway's premier composer—and that led to an outpouring of four more experimental Sondheim-Prince musicals (three designed by Aronson) in the 1970s. *Company* was also the turning point in the career of its choreographer, Michael Bennett, who previously had staged several unmemorable musicals, but would soon move on to *Follies* (with Prince, Sondheim, and Aronson) and then branch out on his own with *A Chorus Line*.

Aronson had worked on an experimental Broadway musical about marriage a generation before: the uneven Kurt Weill–Alan Jay Lerner *Love Life* of 1948. He was sold on this one as soon as Prince told him that the show's metaphor for the confusions of modern marriage would be Manhattan. At the time work began, the script had no resemblance to its final version; according to Prince, only fifteen to twenty percent of it was written. But the guiding conception of the show was so strong that the director easily conveyed what he wanted during three months of intense discussion—namely, a set in which the entire cast would "live on stage all night" in their individual dwellings. Specifics were left open. Instead of explicitly discussing the ages, tastes, jobs, or tax brackets of the characters, Aronson and Prince discussed mood. "We did not talk about doors or about the architecture of roofs," the director said, but about "the smell of the city, the faces of people walking in the street." What remained constant was the concept of telling the story: while the couples would be on stage throughout the show, functioning as a chorus of "observers," they would move among scenic elements that would be changing constantly. At one point, Prince thought that the apartments of all five couples would be represented by a single apartment whose rooms would be redressed in each scene: one couple's bedroom would become another's kitchen, and so on. This notion, though soon abandoned as unworkable, helped trigger the set that finally resulted.

For Aronson, another trigger was a toy he had at home—a construct of plastic cubes. "People who live in glass high-rises shouldn't throw stones—that's *Company*," he decided. "Married life in New York City isn't rocking the afternoon away on a front porch in Maine. In New York, people sit stacked on top of each other in transparent cages. We live in a Plexiglas world now." The designer's emerging concept was further sparked by the paintings of Francis Bacon. In Bacon's pictures of anguished, contorted figures sitting alone in abstracted cages, Aronson found an image that expressed the bleak mood of alienated contemporary New Yorkers who are at once trapped and exposed in their glass enclosures. When fully occupied, the set would look, in the description of Aronson's aide Robert Mitchell, like "a collage of people in metal frames, the essence of what it means to be a New Yorker." Prince later used the same idea in his staging: when the angriest character in *Company*, a much-married cynic played by Elaine Stritch, sang Sondheim's most lacerating song, "The Ladies Who Lunch," she rose from her chair during the final, acid lyric ("Rise! Everybody rise! . . .") to strike an anguished pose that almost explicitly recalled the Bacon pictures.

Aronson's overall design, though later refined, came fast: a two-level Constructivist "urban jungle gym"—a "gymnasium for acting," as Meyerhold or Tairov might have described it—whose compartments could be viewed as the character's apartments, or as a Manhattan cityscape, or, metaphorically, as glass cages. To accompany photographs of the quarter-inch-scale model, the designer wrote Prince a letter to describe it: "As we had agreed on in our preliminary meetings, the basic set is airy, transparent, silvery gray—consisting of 'floating' levels within a chrome-and-plastic framework. Against that 'neutral,' background, the stage takes on color through furniture, props, people (costumes), and various uses of projections. The set, though relatively simple in its basic structure, offers endless possibilities and variety in acting areas and in the intimacy of individual scenes. Only at the end of the show should one realize its complexity. In layout, I was working for the contrast of the intimate individual scenes and what you call the 'walk' through all the rooms simultaneously, at given moments. . . . There are two elevators, one flexible revolving door, sliding panels, moving platforms, flying 'props.'"

Into this basic plan, Aronson poured his ideas about what he considered to be the essence of New York City in 1970. During the course of his career, those ideas had changed a great deal. As he put it, "Today, I see the city differently than when I first arrived—not in its outward signs, but in terms of reflections and lack of intimacy." No longer did Aronson feel, as he had upon arriving in the 1920s, that New York was exemplified by the dazzling displays of Times Square. Nor did he any longer subscribe to the romantic-fantasy New York of *The Bronx Express* and *Walk a Little Faster* or the documentary New York of *Awake and Sing*, *Three Men on a Horse*, and *Detective Story*. "I could never have designed *Company* when I first came to New

3   A Francis Bacon painting that proved influential in establishing the caged-in look of *Company*'s Manhattan denizens.

4   A sketch, referred to by Aronson, of the theatre reference reading room at the Lincoln Center library —"a hospital for books" that influenced *Company*'s design.

5, 6, 7   Sketches of the flexible unit set for *Company*,
with figures and projections establishing scale.

8

8   The model for the set.

9

9   Projections transform the *Company* set into a
nightclub.

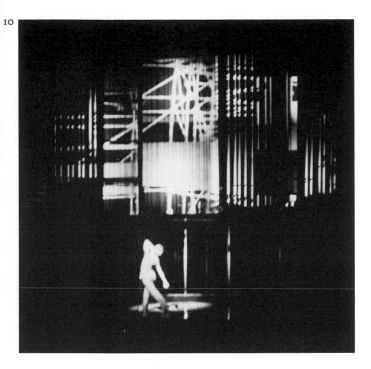

10, 11 The set in use: Donna McKechnie's solo, an angular dance number (10); one floating apartment, in the London production (11), with Elaine Stritch above in "close-up" during "The Little Things You Do Together." Although in different colors, the patterns of the fabric in a costume by D. D. Ryan and couch were intentionally chosen to match.

12   *Company:* First scene, on stage, Robert's 35th
birthday party—Aronson's "jungle gym for actors."

13   In this set for the song "Another Hundred People," Paley Park was represented by plastic trees and a waterfall, as well as chairs supplied by William Paley that matched those in the actual park. As part of the process of simplification, the set was reduced to a bench and projections during the Boston tryout.

14, 15   In production, performers combine with projections to create panoramas of a frantic Manhattan.

York," Aronson said. "It took me fifty years to know that New York is not 42nd Street, neon lights, and Coca-Cola signs. I rejected using neon signs or skyscrapers, because it is ridiculous to make a characteristic New York site seem larger or more exciting on stage than it is in a photograph or on film." Regarding contemporary New York as "virgin territory," he walked the city in search of source material and to reinforce the concept he and Prince had formulated. At Lincoln Center, he came upon the theatre reference reading room at the Library of the Performing Arts, and it served as a prime example of what he was looking for. An almost bare, glassed-in, steel-edged space with cold lighting and multiple reflections, it did not, in Aronson's words, "convey the slightest feeling of the warmth and concentration of books and reading. Instead, it had an antiseptic air about it—it was a hospital for books." To him, it epitomized an urban environment in which "apartments are like hospitals, antiseptic environments without privacy." The set's open scaffolding also captured the designer's sense that New York has "no patina," but is instead a city, unlike those of Europe, that is "constantly demolishing and rebuilding itself."

To impress upon himself the city's pace and behavioral patterns, Aronson kept a daily record of how many buttons he pushed in going about his daily activities. "I was interested in what the city does to you in life today in New York," he said. "If you wrote down how many places you found yourself in one day, from the moment you woke up how many buttons you pushed, how many places you walked to, it would be staggering. You wouldn't believe it was possible—that that's the way we function today." Aronson also wanted the set to express "the confinement and obstruction in city living—the human being battling to cross a traffic-clogged street. . . . Movement in New York is vertical, horizontal, angular, never casual. In Versailles, you bow. In New York, you dodge cabs. You save your life from one car to another by moving from place to place not to be run over. The final *Company* design gave my feeling of how the city affects people."

If the set for *Company* was primarily composed of cubic spaces, the entire basic unit was placed at an angle on stage. This decision added to the plasticity, depth, and dynamic visual rhythms of the design—and in turn reinforced the agitated, neurotic tempo of the musical's New York as expressed in its characters, direction, and choreography. As the performers moved around and about the platforms, or in and out of elevators, *Company* gained in urban excitement as well as theatrical fluidity. The actual building of the set represented a technical challenge, as Aronson insisted on no visible

diagonals in its construction. "You need diagonals to get strength that will support the structure," said J. J. Moore, an Aronson assistant. "We had to put something in there to keep the set strong. In the end, we engineered diagonal supports into things that no one in the audience would see as diagonals. We added diagonal braces off stage, as soon as the set hit the wings, and we put some behind walls. For strength and to save on cost, we used steel instead of the lighter-weight aluminum, along with the Plexiglas, for the set. The elevators were hung from cables and driven by motors at the top."

The designer did not put in the elevators for effect. "Like a factory without people working in it," said Aronson, "the set is just a lifeless structure without actors. I remember the carpenter who built the set in the Bronx studios looking at the construction on the floor [of the studio] and shaking his head. When he saw it raised up on the Alvin Theatre stage, he turned to me and remarked that he'd had no idea how beautiful it would be with the actors at work. It was the finest compliment I ever had received. After all, my sets are designed for actors. The stage is their home away from home. . . .

"I don't believe in gimmicks, not from my point of view or that of actors, critics, or audience. By making a totally mobile unit set, I could make it seem as big as a city street or as intimate as a one-room apartment. I wanted to give the feeling of total mechanization, so much so that people behaved that way. I think of myself as a painter, and *Company* was the first of more than a hundred shows I designed that didn't have a drop of paint in it. I used projections to represent reflections of the city; New York is a city of reflections, a place where you feel skyscrapers without seeing them." In his own way, Aronson had reinvented the abstract vision of urban life that had so enraptured the designers who had revolted against Stanislavskian realism in the Soviet theatre of the early 1920s.

The designer had other novel ideas, too. He walked all over the city and had photographs taken of the urbanscape—sometimes with special trick lenses—and sent them to Robert Ornbo, who picked the ones which would best lend themselves for use as slides. Ultimately, there were six hundred slides requiring twenty-eight carousel projectors. They could be used to transform the entire compartmentalized set into a nightclub or street; black-and-white projections (some of them negative images) were used for the scripted scenes, color for the musical numbers. In keeping with the high-gloss, high-fashion approach, Aronson also insisted on importing pieces of contemporary plastic Italian furniture—or fabricating copies—that he had seen pic-

16, 17, 18 Models of three designs cut from *Company:*
Central Park, with plastic trees (16); a penthouse scene
(17); and a fragmented drop for multiple projections (18).

tured in the Italian edition of *Vogue* magazine (but had yet to be introduced in America, as would happen after the Museum of Modern Art exhibition "Italy: The New Domestic Landscape" in 1972). D. D. Ryan, the costume designer, provided sources for the latest in both furniture and fabrics. Although cut during the tryout in Boston, even the show's trees, in the end, were made of plastic. Some other fanciful design ideas were also eliminated along the way: the use of Polaroid lens effects to create blackouts, a plastic waterfall for a Paley Park sequence, a fragmented frontdrop on which multiple images could be projected.

Company marked the first time that Prince was able to rehearse the actors on a full-size mock-up of the set, constructed on stage at the Alvin. "It was like looking at an elevated map," the director found. "There were so many elevations, and nothing moved in the mock-up. I had to time everything. But the set was so accommodating that I could go into rehearsal not knowing where everything would be done and just knowing that it could all be done within the set." Early on, Prince discovered that one of the show's biggest, if unexpected, laughs came early in Act II when an empty-headed stewardess visiting Bobby's bachelor pad spoke a flattering line about the décor—in spite of the fact that the stage was empty and the platform containing the apartment's furniture had yet to arrive. Besides working as a joke in the context of the scene, the moment also allowed the audience to relax and have fun with the production's doing away with any pretense to realism. As a result of this discovery, what had been an elaborate bedroom set was stripped down to one piece of furniture, a bed. *Company* was a constant paring down of elements to essentials.

Prince also found that the set enabled him to use "close-ups, cross-fades, dissolves—all the techniques of film and none of the techniques of the stage. When Elaine Stritch stands there and looks down and sings 'It's the little things,' what you've done is you've brought a camera in to a lady and quick-cut to her face." Bennett was ecstatic to be working with a unit set after years of doing musicals with elaborate set changes (*Promises, Promises; Coco*); in fact, it was because the choreographer was always assigned the job of staging set changes that he had begun to think about becoming a director. To his amazement, Bennett found that "the *Company* set had levels, elevators, and still a playing space to dance in. I could move one dancer—Donna McKechnie, the only dancer in the show—all over the set. Because the set and the winches all ran on angles, I had a staging concept for the show—the choreography was all on angles, too." Sondheim saw a model of the finished set at a relatively late date, but had been prepared by Prince about what to expect. Some of Aronson's design conception had even fueled the images governing two long sections in the show's climactic song, "Happily Ever After" (later replaced by another song, "Being Alive," during the production's Boston tryout). Prince had told Sondheim that Aronson wanted the design to reflect an era "surfeited with things that are too easy for too many people to come by—the promises, the amenities of contemporary life, from trips to Florida to girls." In "Happily Ever After," Robert sings, among other things, of "the pretty girls smiling everywhere from the ads and the TV set." Sondheim also had to ask Aronson exactly how long it would take the cast to descend from the set's upper level to the stage floor, in order to construct the opening, theme-setting title song. "I built the climax of the number around the notion of having the cast all over the set," Sondheim subsequently recalled. "I had to gear the amount of bars, the amount of music, to the longest journey anyone would have to make—from the highest level to the lower level and the center of the stage. Boris told me the number of seconds, and I built the climax of the long-held note of 'Company'—the word 'love'—to suit that, so that Bennett would be able to get people from all over the stage and coagulate them in a mass downstage center."

Aronson found the final confirmation of the success of his design for *Company* not in the acclaim that greeted it, but in the ever dismantled and frantic city that inspired it. "I find, after designing *Company*, that the city imitates me," he said near the end of his life. "Everywhere I walk in New York, I see my set."

THE GRANDEUR OF THE EMPTY STAGE

From each production, I learn something new, and the longer I work in the theatre, the more I am convinced that a stage set in sketch or model form cannot convey what its ultimate function must be on stage. The theatre is a collective effort. You must make allowances for that moment when all the ingredients of a play come together. Only then can you say, "It works."

FOLLIES (1971)

In *Follies*, the musical with which Prince, Sondheim, and Bennett immediately followed *Company*, Aronson had what might seem the simplest assignment imaginable: the show takes place on the empty stage of a Broadway theatre that is in the process of being demolished. Yet, as easy as the task might seem, it proved to be a difficult challenge. The "empty stage" he designed for *Follies* was the most technologically complex set he had yet created—a costly, intricate construction that made equally tough demands on the co-directors (Prince and Bennett now shared their billing), the stagehands, the performers, and, in its way, the audience.

Follies confounded an audience's usual expectations. If the musical's title promised a lavish entertainment of the old school—and if its setting was, as described in the program, "a party on stage of this theatre tonight"—the show was actually about disenchantment and decay. It was, in Sondheim's words, "a dream play, a memory play." A meditation on the demise of old-time, pre–World War II show business, *Follies* used the death of vaudeville as a metaphor for the death of American innocence. Like everything else in the piece, Aronson's bleak set uncompromisingly expressed the work's unpleasant, at times harsh, delineation of the decline of a society's optimistic faith in both progress and the success ethic.

The idea for *Follies* had been hatched years earlier, under the title *The Girls Upstairs*, by Sondheim and the book writer, playwright James Goldman. The show unfolds at a present-day reunion of Ziegfeld performers, now middle-aged to aged, who have returned to take one last look at the fabled showplace where they had been glorious fixtures thirty years earlier. The theatre is soon to make way for a parking lot; as the characters socialize at their party, the audience discovers that they are in varying degrees haunted by the past and disillusioned by the present. Goldman's story focused on two once-glamorous Follies girls (Alexis Smith and Dorothy Collins) who had long ago married stage-door Johnnies (John McMartin and Gene Nelson), only to wonder, ever since, if they might not have married the wrong men.

Aronson and Prince collaborated on *Follies* as they had on every project since *Cabaret:* there were months of discussion in the spring, after which the director disappeared for the summer to leave the designer with what he most valued in their partnership—the time to struggle in peace. Aronson had only a very rough, early script to work with, along with a demo record of the four songs Sondheim had written for *The Girls Upstairs:* "Don't Look at Me," "Flowers," "Waiting for the Girls Upstairs," and "Pleasant Little Kingdoms/Too Many Mornings." As was also true of *Company,* Aronson was to send off photographs of a rough model in midsummer, receive and incorporate Prince's suggestions, and then produce final sketches and models by an unofficial Labor Day deadline. Then there would still be more changes, some of them prompted by further rewrites, before a finished design would be ready. Thus was Aronson a full collaborator throughout the show's genesis: as he and Odets had once dreamed of doing, set and play were created in tandem.

But in the problematic case of *Follies* the set would have to be created *before* the play. The initial script, as Prince explained to Aronson, would have virtually no resemblance to the show that would eventually be mounted. It was a realistic script whose detailed architecture contained, among other elements, the theatre's old dressing rooms and box office. Prince didn't want a realistic musical specifically fixed in place; he also wanted the script yanked out of a literal chronology by having the characters' present and past interwoven throughout the show. The authors, who had resisted the notion of flashbacks, warmed to the idea of simultaneous past-and-present action. They decided to give their characters on-stage alter egos—a second set of actors to represent the youthful selves of the principal players.

"When Hal told me that the show takes place on an empty stage, that was immediately worth a million to me," Aronson said. "Then when he said that the theatre is in a state of being demolished, I was delighted, because that would mean Cubism. . . . If it had just been another backstage show, with the back of scenery showing and all, I wouldn't have touched it. But an empty stage is a goldmine—a concept that really fascinates me. A chance for Cubism of the highest order—and not just for the sake of abstraction, but based on something very real."

Aronson had some clues, if not a script, to work with. From the start, Prince talked about surrealism and the use of rubble on stage; there was a plan to include, near the end of the musical, a real old-fashioned Ziegfeld Follies–type show-within-the-show. What most aided Aronson in determining the overall mood of the material were the four early Sondheim songs, which the designer listened to over and over while working; conversations with Sondheim and Bennett which clarified authorial intentions that were not yet on paper; and a few

specific images that Prince and Aronson had discussed in their spring brainstorming sessions. In particular, two photographs defined the atmosphere of both the design and the show's staging. One, which both Prince and Aronson independently discovered in a movie memorabilia book, was the celebrated 1960 *Life* magazine photograph of a glamorously dressed, aging Gloria Swanson standing in the midst of rubble in the skeletal remains of a just-demolished New York movie palace, the Roxy. The other was a still from Federico Fellini's film *Juliet of the Spirits*—a surreal backstage scene which seemed to capture the mixed mood of glamour and gloom, past and present, that *Follies* called for. Two elements in the Fellini scene—a black staircase and a pair of outsized statues of Greek goddesses—figured in the final show. The goddesses were provided by Bennett, who introduced chorus-girl "ghosts," representing the theatre's more romantic past, in the show's opening number. (A goddess-like showgirl's statue, with a crack running through it, also served as the logo for the *Follies* poster, which was designed by David Edward Byrd.)

Still, the full solution was slow in coming. When Aronson received a new outline of *Follies* in midsummer, he found that it didn't so much clarify his assignment as complicate it, for it seemed to depart entirely from the drift of his previous conversations with Prince. As imagined by the author, *Follies'* set would rely on "lots of boxes" to dramatize its time shifts. "The boxes represent the mind," read the outline. "What happens outside them—on top or in front or on stairs built around or above them—is real; it happens at the party. What occurs *inside* the boxes are the memories, fantasies, and thoughts of our characters. . . . The boxes are a kind of house of the past, and at the end our four leads have to move out of that house." Prince told Aronson to ignore this device, but by then Aronson was so stymied that there was little hope of providing any preliminary design ideas to the director prior to his autumn return.

Eventually, the solution did come. "The concept in my design was to make the theatre a place that would elicit very touching memories of the grandeur which took place in that environment," Aronson decided. "I wanted to imagine—to *emphasize*—that great dramas, tragedies, epics took place there. I wanted it to be more than just a music hall." As the designer saw it, "Memories arrive in bits and pieces—they're evocative—strung together into chains, colored by the imagination. I used these leftovers, these remnants, very purposefully. If you see a statue and a hand is missing, or the nose is broken, it leaves so much more to the imagination than if it were complete. This very

1 Gloria Swanson standing in the ruins of a demolished New York movie palace, the Roxy. Long before anyone had thought of *Follies*—whose atmosphere was inspired by this picture—Aronson had written about the Roxy Theatre in a journal: "The Roxy Theatre rose from steelwork with a terra-cotta façade and an ecclesiastical stillness fell over the moving-picture temple. In 1927 the preposterous theatre opened. In 1960 it vanished—all this gold-leaf plaster, frosted glass, etc., was gone. Disappeared forever. That mixture of the social and personal reflects the whole structure of the theatre." The feeling of the Swanson photograph was captured at the very opening of *Follies*, when a brief flash of light, accompanied by a drumroll, revealed the cavernous "empty stage" of the gutted theatre and a single black-and-white showgirl ghost haunting it.

2 A photograph of actual Roxy rubble, used in the set.

[fragmentation] creates a positive-negative relationship between the missing pieces and the elements that remain. The audience helps all evening in re-creating the past, because we only suggest it. I took full advantage of this duality, this juxtaposition, to try to create an image of a monumental theatre of bygone days." At the same time, Aronson had to solve the "great problem" of designing a set "which combined the availability of many performance areas on various levels and yet maintained visually the effect of an empty stage." He solved it "by creating movement—units which moved forward, close to the audience for a particular scene, and then disappeared into the background, again becoming part of the rubble and decay. . . . Bones scattered around a room . . . coming together to create a form and then returning to bones."

The units consisted of several formations of open scaffolding which moved diagonally on and off, making for a variety of elevations, entrances, and exits. Strictly abstract, they could open up or narrow in focus and be used in many different ways, even as a bandstand for the show's on-stage party musicians. (There was an additional full band in the pit.) To avoid the usual heavy platforms of Broadway musicals and to preserve the show's ethereal haunted-house atmosphere, Aronson put the scaffolds on thin legs that were moved mechanically beneath a false stage floor six inches high; performers could enter under, on top of, or through the scaffolding, even when the units were in motion. The stage floor was broken up into chunks—basically, into three jagged areas, all steeply raked—with the area farthest back serving as a stage within the stage, for entrances and exits. By splitting up the floor, Aronson created a sense of distance which would heighten the show's evocation of traveling back into the past and yet allow fluidity of choreographed movement.

"The mechanical problem," said Aronson's assistant, J. J. Moore, who had to help work out the design's technical execution, "was that the floor was not only a series of elevations, but that they were all on a rake, an angle—and not one angle, but different angles! We were faced with a pile of surfaces, none of which were level with each other. We had to take scenery that was basically offstage and slide it onto platforms that sometimes didn't even extend as far as the stage masking and were instead isolated in the middle of the stage." The solution was to find "a common denominator—a common bottom which all the wheels had to travel on" and to design "a special device thin enough to travel from the wheels up through these layers of platforms to the scaffolding at the top, so the wheels always stayed on a level we

3 Federico Fellini's *Juliet of the Spirits*—a surreal backstage scene whose statuary goddesses figured in the *Follies* set.

4

4 A preliminary sketch of the "empty stage," with
its three raked floor areas, rubble, scaffolding, and a
hint of Swanson far upstage center. Aronson wrote to
Prince: "It opens surreal—elements of broken-up
space with Weisman [as the Ziegfeld impresario was
named in the musical] in evening clothes. . . .
Weisman turns [to the band] and [says], 'Maestro!'
Then everything starts to get going. Weisman is
a 'magician-impresario' who conjures up the past—
a past of follies and illusions."

5

5   An early model, with figures for scale and
black-and-white photographic cut-outs for rubble.
Aronson designed the fractionalized stage floor as if
remembering Tairov's preoccupation with the stage
floor from his Russian tutelage in the 1920s.

6, 7   In the thirties, Aronson anticipated his
"Loveland" valentine motif with this design for Radio
City Music Hall (6). Preliminary ideas for "Loveland"
included the first version of the fan (7). Aronson
considered the fan the quintessential shape typifying
a Ziegfeld Follies show set and designed accordingly,
even before "Loveland" had been written by the
Follies authors.

designated as basic floor." As Moore said, "It looked like a very simple thing, but there was so much geometry behind it—several different base lines, of which only one was the stage floor."

Decorating the upper reaches of the stage were the "bits and pieces"—the faded hangings suggesting both gauzy memories of the theatre's past and the already partially demolished proscenium of the theatre's present. Rubble extended to the proscenium arch of the Broadway house where *Follies* was to play, the Winter Garden (itself once a Ziegfeld palace): fake, disintegrating parts were integrated with the actual arch. Unlike the *Cabaret* and *Company* sets, the *Follies* set was to have absolutely no furniture; Prince no longer wanted "wagons bringing on people and couches."

In the final half-hour of *Follies*, there was to be a full flashback—a Felliniesque dream sequence in which the characters were subsumed by their remembered past, as conjured up by a pastiche period Follies spectacle of several numbers' duration. And once this show-within-the-show, titled "Loveland" and arriving without a preceding intermission, had ended, the set within the set lifted to return to the empty stage: *Follies* concluded in the present as the reunion party finally ended at daybreak. Then—and only then—would the audience discover yet another scenic element. To suggest that the back wall of the theatre had already been demolished, Aronson designed a trompe-l'oeil backdrop showing the sunlit New York street outside the theatre, as well as the skeletal remains of the theatre's marquee.

As was his wont, Aronson had designed the basic set of *Follies* with jarring asymmetry. But for the old-fashioned "Loveland" sequence he pointedly designed old-fashioned, two-dimensional, symmetrical sets that typified the entertainments of the Ziegfeld era. The first of them—whose dramatic arrival would magically transform the dilapidated theatre into a bejeweled vaudeville palace—was a fan-shaped collage suggesting a huge valentine in a Fragonard mode. "Loveland" was, as Aronson said, the set's surprise—"valentines and lace . . . symmetrical, sweet, rosy . . . rising out of the rubble and ruin. A flash of color amidst the doom." Wanting more than "just the idea of people crying while a theatre is being dismantled," Aronson felt he had made the show's Proustian theme concrete by providing an intentional letdown for the audience after the excitement of watching "Loveland" come together: by being "banal, predictable, lifeless" (as Aronson wrote to Prince in a note on the set-in-progress), the romanticized Follies sequence would be revealed as dead weight—the psychological burden of the past that the characters must escape. The

removal of "Loveland" and the ensuing dawn would seem liberating by contrast: "When all is broken down again and we see the daylight, it must be like a breath of fresh air!" Not for nothing did *Follies'* final image resemble, in its conception and streams of dawn sunshine, the blindingly lighted liberation of the prisoners that Aronson had designed for the finale of *Fidelio* a few years earlier.

Various rough models were assembled over the summer. Aronson put figures in his models to give a sense of the playing areas and scale; these figures, as well as the use of black-and-white elements in the model, inspired Bennett to conceive of a chorus of ghostly showgirls weaving in and out of the action in black-and-white costumes. Eventually, the entire "past" of *Follies* was kept in black and white until the "Loveland" extravaganza, at which point color took over completely, as befits a sequence when the characters' past at last becomes their present. In what proved to be the show's most famous number—"Who's That Woman?"—Bennett also found inspiration in the set, using its three stage areas to particularly exciting effect: as a chorus line of frumpy, retired Follies "girls" attempts to re-create a legendary tap-dance number from the good old days, the women's younger alter egos suddenly materialize in mirror image behind them to dance the number with the verve of three decades earlier. To make the arrival of the ghost dancers a surprise, Bennett darkened the rear stage level and sent the dancers quietly on stage in rubber-soled shoes. (The sound of the ensuing tap dancing was piped in from the basement, where male dancers executed the steps.)

To coordinate the staging and the various movements of the set with the entire company, the last few rehearsals were held on the set in its final stages of construction at Feller Scenic Studios in the Bronx. Amazingly enough, no scenic adjustments were needed to accommodate some of the actual vaudeville veterans in the show, such as the octogenarian Ethel Shutta. "No one ever complained," said J. J. Moore. "They accepted the extreme angles with no great problem—even when they had to dance on the upper platform, which had the strongest angle. But no one could have worked cold on that stage and dealt with it; we needed that rehearsal period."

The lighting and costumes had to be plotted with care. For the first time, the lighting designer Tharon Musser used side follow spots; to avoid lights that were visible to the audience, she did not place any on the scaffolding, but instead topped the set with an entire ceiling (invisible to the audience) of lights. With her next show, Bennett's *A Chorus Line*, Musser used the newly invented electronic "memory

8

9

8, 9 The basic gutted-theatre set, seen in model (8),
is transformed by the "Loveland" set (9)—a fan-shaped
Fragonard valentine—into a bygone Follies palace.

10

13

11

14

12

15

16

10, 11, 12, 13, 14, 15   In this sequence of photos, the transition to "Loveland" can be seen on stage. In the first picture (10), the scaffolding units are in their closed-in position, with one dream figure on top of the scaffolding and a group of partygoers behind. The transformation into "Loveland" begins as the partygoers move downstage (11). In pictures taken during the Boston tryout, the rest of the "Loveland" transformation—in which the present-day, gutted theatre reverts to the vaudeville palace of 30 years earlier—is seen step by step.

16   Art Deco determined the design of the other "Loveland" sequences.

17

17 The *Follies* finale: After "Loveland" has departed, the reunion party comes to its daybreak conclusion. A drop suggests that the back wall of the theatre has already been demolished, revealing the New York street and a shell of a marquee outside. Aronson: "In this country, cities have no time to develop a patina— as soon as a building goes up, they make plans to tear it down—and they're right!" Prince: "Boris said Americans spend all their lives picketing against aging. Every building is taken down in 25 years, like our metaphor, the Follies. The show was taking place before the demolition of the theatre, but, at the end, the theatre is half torn down and we are halfway onto the street."

board" to mandate fast lighting cues. So demanding was *Follies*, her last musical requiring manually executed lighting cues, that the production's head electrician put his television up for sale after the first technical run-through: he knew that he would not have the usual spells of inactivity, allowed by less ambitious lighting plots, for goofing off. Costumes had to be ordered before songs were written, and, as designed by Florence Klotz, they were elaborate and heavy. Because plastic and synthetics lack the right reflective qualities, Klotz searched exhaustively through the U.S. and Europe for real bugle beads. Because of the scaffolding, the chorus girls had to learn to slither through entrances that were barely two feet wide. As Klotz recalled, "There were very narrow staircases with no railing. I thought, 'Oh, God, I have dresses on these girls that weigh a lot, and the trains will go over the stairwell and take the girls with them.' We tried it out at Feller's to see if the girls could make it—and they did, by practice." Klotz's Marie Antoinette costumes for "Loveland"—six feet wide and seven feet tall altogether—were indeed too wide to get through entryways. They had to be flown in from above in the very limited backstage area so that the waiting chorus girls could step into them and be hooked up.

One of the most thrilling moments for those involved with *Follies* came in Boston, where the musical was to have its tryout at the Colonial Theatre. At the technical rehearsal, the "Loveland" set was flown in for the first time, and, to the amazement of all, the dazzling coordination of scenery, staging, costumes, performances, and lighting worked, in at least rough form, immediately. "It was a miracle," Sondheim later recalled. "It was one of the most complicated set changes in the history of the theatre, and the stage manager, Fritz Holt, in his first major Broadway job, came within twenty percent of making it work." For J. J. Moore, the success of Aronson's work on *Follies* confirmed his conviction that "with Boris' sets, the greatness was that you *felt* their impact."

It was also in Boston that Bennett dreamed up the idea of using the entire set to solve a costume change. At the end of "Loveland," not only did there have to be a dramatic transition from the past back into the present, but there also had to be time for Ben (John McMartin) to change from his "Loveland" costume to the party clothes of the present. Bennett, out of necessity, devised a surreal sequence of "chaos" to return from the gilded Follies to the gutted theatre. "I went to Boris and said, 'What if I took the whole set apart, moved the platforms, lights, and mirrors up and down, and had the whole show fall

18 The New York street drop of the final scene was based on a photograph of an actual construction site on Columbus Avenue.

19 Painters at the Feller Studios hand-painting the Fragonard inserts on the "Loveland" valentine drop.

20

20, 21   Full view of the *Follies* set during rehearsal
in the Bronx (20); and Aronson supervising the
construction (21).

21

23

22, 23   Michael Bennett rehearsing the celebrated
"mirror" number "Who's That Woman?" on the
Follies set as it is being constructed at Feller Scenic
Studios in the Bronx (22). The retired Follies girls are
seen in mirror image as ghost images of their younger
selves dance their old tap number on the upper
platform of the set. "Who's That Woman?" as it
appeared on stage, lighted by Tharon Musser and
costumed by Florence Klotz (23).

24

24, 25   Bronx rehearsal with Michael Bennett, center
(24), and on-stage realization in Boston with Alexis
Smith, center (25) of the "Uptown/Downtown"
number in "Loveland," later to be replaced by another
song, "The Story of Lucy and Jessie."

apart?' " the choreographer later recalled. Aronson and Feller figured out how to do it, and then Bennett accompanied the chaos with the most dissonant music possible: he had the band play different songs from the score simultaneously.

Although Bennett considered *Follies* "the most beautiful show" of his career and "ninety percent realized," he felt that the musical lacked "that ten percent that would emotionally involve the audience." The musical earned mostly favorable reviews, a large cache of Tony Awards, and a decent run (slightly over a year), but the mass public never warmed to it. Some critics misunderstood the musical's ambitions: in the *Variety* notice, the reviewer complained that "scenery is introduced late"—as if the majority of *Follies* preceding the "Loveland" sequence had no scenery. (In fact, the reviewer had been fooled by the effective design—he had fallen for Aronson's illusions without knowing it.) The production didn't come close to paying back its investors, and, while it has posthumously acquired a reputation far exceeding its initial reception, it is unlikely ever to be seen again in a full production with Aronson's lavish empty stage." With its large cast and extravagant sets, costumes, and lighting, *Follies* cost less than a million dollars to produce in 1971, but to reproduce its original staging fifteen years later would have cost six or seven times that amount. (In lieu of such a revival, an all-star concert version, without any of the original staging or production design, was presented by the New York Philharmonic in 1985.) A show about the death of a particular kind of American theatre, the musical was in a sense a self-fulfilling prophecy. "In *Follies*," Aronson said, not without reason, "I wanted to pay tribute to the institution of the theatre, as the process of its dismantling is becoming more than a fantasy."

26 In the depths of the present: Yvonne De Carlo singing Sondheim's "I'm Still Here" at the reunion party of *Follies*.

SCANDINAVIAN WHITE-ON-WHITE

The musical theatre in general appeals to me because it has nothing to do with the naturalistic theatre. In a drama, you have to justify your entrances and exits. You don't just walk out of a set when you finish your dialogue. You have to say what makes you go out, or forget your hat. The difference between a play and a musical is the difference between a painting and a poster. . . . Current musicals are not conceived from scratch, as a rule. They are adaptations. Especially with adaptations, there is a need for newness, freshness, more inventiveness and the use of new scenic materials.

A LITTLE NIGHT MUSIC   (1973)

"Where *Follies* symbolized lost grandeur," Aronson said, "*A Little Night Music* was pure whipped cream."

Prince had long wanted to do a "masque-like" musical—"something that deals with encounters in a country house, love and lovers and mismatched partners." At various times, he had considered Jean Anouilh's *Ring Round the Moon* and Jean Renoir's *Rules of the Game* as source material. The final choice was Ingmar Bergman's film *Smiles of a Summer Night*, but the Prince version (originally titled *Smiles*), with a book by Hugh Wheeler and a score by Stephen Sondheim, treated the material more sunnily than the Swedish filmmaker had. "Although our plot is essentially the same as the film, our tone is light, high comedy," Prince said at the time. "Bergman's was dark, romantic comedy. We needed music because of the tonal change. We needed a light-opera treatment." Once *Night Music* had opened on Broadway, the director added, "In the past, I've lectured on the necessity for abrasion, for things to collide, to set off sparks. [But] I didn't want this show to be rough-hewn. The seams couldn't show. It's like—off a spool." In his memoirs a year later, Prince concluded, "Mostly *Night Music* was about having a hit."

The frothy *Night Music* was a hit and, for its creative personnel, a relatively easygoing experience. This was also true for Aronson, except for some technical glitches with the finished sets. But the designer felt no particular affinity for the nineteenth-century Scandinavian aristocrats who populated the story, and he couldn't immediately see the point of adapting a recent film that was perfect in its original form. Aronson observed that "one of the horrible things which has occurred in playwriting is imitating the technique of the movies, which the stage can't cope with. If we have a room and then go to another one, we have to somehow take away all the furniture and bring in other furniture. It becomes a tremendous problem in the theatre." His fears about the difficulties of translating so cinematic a work to the stage were compounded by the first draft of Wheeler's libretto. *Night Music* was conceived as a play within a play: "In those country houses at the turn of the century, they often had family musicales," according to Prince. "So what we were going to do was put a stage within our stage and play on two levels."

This first script was still very much like the movie, even to the point of including the famous bedroom scene with the trick bed. It

1, 2   *A Little Night Music* (1973): A photograph of
white birch trees that helped inspire the dominant
scenic motif (1), and the birch trees, painted on silk,
being attached to Lexan screens at Feller Scenic
Studios (2).

had realistic interior scenes alternating with less realistic exterior
scenes. The inner stage was to be used essentially for interiors; the
outer stage was to represent the park of an estate, with a "leaf curtain"
(depicting woods) which would cover the inner stage and permit set
changes. In anticipation of a first meeting with Prince, Aronson made
a breakdown of all the scenes as called for by the script. He then discovered that a designer would have to cope with a dizzying profusion
of realistic scene changes: at least nine scenes in Act I, with more in
Act II (none of which repeated a setting from Act I). According to Aronson's analysis, this scheme would necessitate twenty-eight raisings
and lowerings of the leaf curtain in two acts, or one every three and a
half minutes within a two-hour play (not counting the opening and
closing of the house curtain four times). Although the script was
never meant to be realistic, the style for the musical had yet to be
determined.

What eventually convinced Aronson of the show's viability was
the discarding of the original structural concept (and, with it, the elimination of the stage-within-the-stage and the leaf curtain) and a meeting that Prince arranged early in the preproduction period. Years
earlier, Prince had initiated play readings for his associates; actors did
readings of scripts that interested the director, some—but not all—of
which he would end up producing and directing. In the case of *Night
Music*, the entire creative and technical staff attended the reading and
met afterward in the theatre's basement for an uninhibited discussion
on the piece. Aronson found this meeting the most constructive and
successful of any in his career with Prince, and during it he took down
key words and phrases which crystallized his approach to the production: " 'Charade of a time which has passed' . . . delicious, charming,
subtle, funny, Chekhovian country house, Opéra Bouffe, sexy, flirta-
tious, comedy in classic sense . . . Players 'drift' on and off . . . Waltzes
. . . Just a clearing in the woods—a world we create within . . . Beds in
woods . . . Birches . . . Pauses—texture of *Vanya* . . . Sweden—2:30
P.M. already dark . . . Summer—11:00 night is daylight; midnight, light
blue . . . Mysterious daylight—strange not brilliant, white . . . No
horizon. People interested in themselves—self-absorbed . . ." "In
place of the leaf curtain was the notion that the whole musical, even
its bedroom scenes, could unfold in the woods, with no clear distinc-
tion made between exterior and interior scenes. "They would be metaphorical trees, not literal trees," said Sondheim. This plan liberated the
show from realism and allowed Aronson to start thinking in the surre-
alist visual terms of the Belgian painter René Magritte. The notion of

"drifting" actors and a waltz score gave him the notion of gliding scenery—specifically, sliding screens that would prove to be the dominant feature of the design. "All shows have their problems," Aronson said, "and the difficulty with this one is that it calls for a simple, non-mechanical production, yet it takes place in so many different locales. To make it look effortless, furniture has to be moved with ease without interrupting the story, and I had to find modern ways of moving it without distracting the audience." The solution was to have the furniture come on behind the panels and be revealed as the panels moved, thereby creating a continuous, graceful flow.

Aronson wanted to hear some of the score to help discern more of the "flavor" of the show. Although Sondheim hadn't written much of it, "a few scraps" satisfied the designer. "When I heard them, I was enchanted. I stopped thinking about the movie and thought about Mozart. . . . I had a very vivid memory of white birch groves in Russia; one of my dreams had always been to use birch trees in a design for the stage. The birch lends itself to the stylization needed to unify the look of the production. The trees could be used in the form of screens to create entrances and exits and as the method of shifting scenes. Birch trees would give the show the lyrical quality called for." So a forest of white birch trees, emblemizing the long white nights of Sweden, soon became the permanent scenic motif of *Night Music*, and within these woods Aronson planned to accommodate all the story's settings.

But a technical difficulty remained: "How could I make a tree on stage look light?" He ruled out the traditional material for appliquéd stage trees—gauze—which "creates an abundance of wrinkles and moiré effects." Instead, Aronson immediately started to work with plastic in mind and even did some sketches on plastic. "The problem became what *not* to do," he said. "To me, the setting must be like champagne, it must sparkle, and if it doesn't, it is nothing." As designed, the screens turned out to be twenty-four feet high, with no visible framing on the edges. This made it impossible to use Plexiglas, which was available only in twelve-foot panels that would have to be joined at visible seams and reinforced by metal frames. The technical solution was suggested by J. J. Moore, Aronson's assistant, and Peter Feller, the scenery builder. They knew of a new plastic, developed by General Electric and used primarily for bulletproof windows in banks and airplanes, called Lexan. Unlike regular plastic, which might shatter and injure actors, Lexan was sturdy and shatterproof. It was available in panels of the requisite towering height, and, as required by law

3, 4 Magritte's 1965 painting "Blank Signature" (3), and a scene from *Night Music* in which characters disappear behind the birch-tree panels in a similar disruption of conventional perspective (4).

5   The Act I opening, "Night Waltz" in *A Little Night Music:* a Swedish "white night" as reconstituted from Aronson's childhood memories of St. Petersburg. Aronson and the lighting designer, Tharon Musser, fought successfully to prevent the use of any colored light on the drop.

6   A bedroom and living room in the woods. Liberated from naturalism, Aronson set interior and exterior scenes alike among the birch trees, assuming correctly that the audience would quickly adjust to the conceit.

7 "A Weekend in the Country": the Act I finale,
which Sondheim wrote during rehearsals in
accordance with the movements of Aronson's
sliding panels.

8

9

OPPOSITE

8   The opening of Act II of *A Little Night Music*, as seen in London. Antique cars were constructed at reduced scale, with found odds and ends from actual cars mated with newly built pieces.

9   A dinner party in the woods, backed by Madame Armfeldt's "tiny Titian." Aronson saw the scene itself as a Titian, full of dark, rich colors. Although taking place inside the house pictured in the backdrop, it was set, in the show's fashion, in a forest *in front of* the house. "The table," Aronson said, "is a still life." The scene was short but elaborately designed. "It disappears while people still want more."

10   The woods, with the house peeking through.

11 The show curtain, hung in the woods, is a miniature version of the 19th-century house curtain at the 18th-century court theatre in Drottningholm.

12 The last vestige of the stage-within-the-stage concept for *Night Music:* the show curtain doubles as a stage curtain and the woods double as a set for a 19th-century theatrical production in this Act I sequence (as seen in London) in which the actress-heroine, Desirée Armfeldt, performs in a play of the period.

for all scenic materials, it was fireproof. Thus, the birch trees were painted on silk, which was then attached to the Lexan panels.

"There is nothing more old-fashioned than sliding panels," said Aronson, "but these screens—paint and appliqué on transparency without any visible framing—gave a feeling of grace, freshness, and flow. The reflections of the stage lights off the panels increased the theatricality of the effect." Actually, the reflective quality of the panels caused much internal debate among the production team, not all of whom at first accepted the notion that the glittering stage lights should be revealed to the audience.

Simple as the screens looked, their execution was complex. The sliding panels, each driven by a separate motor, hung from tracks over the stage. The motorized panels had to stop at a variety of exact marks during the show. Motors were also required to drive furniture in and out on 150 different cues. This was accomplished with an elaborate system of tracks in the floor, in which different pins guided "plates" (carpeted panels one inch thick bearing the furniture) into the correct grooves, so that the furniture would end up in exactly the right positions on a grass-colored carpet that covered the floor.

During *Night Music*'s Boston tryout, however, a hitch quickly became apparent: Aronson's delicately painted but heavily hung birch-tree screens were emitting a coarse racket. The sound they made in their metal tracks was picked up and amplified by the production's microphones. The solution, again proposed by Peter Feller, was to return to a practice of a generation earlier and redo the tracks in wood. The resulting diminution of the noise level was nearly as pronounced as the contrast in decibel levels between the rubber-wheeled Paris and steel-wheeled New York subway trains.

As had been true with previous Aronson designs, Prince and Sondheim found ideas for their own work by exploiting the finished set during rehearsals. "It was fun to show Boris things that could be done in his set that he didn't expect," said Prince. In the musical's final scenes, the director used the screens cinematically to "wipe" away one pair of lovers and (for the song "The Miller's Son") to reveal another, clandestine couple. To write the most crucial number in the score, an operetta-style Act I finale in which invitations are distributed to the entire cast of characters for a fateful "Weekend in the Country," Sondheim relied on Aronson's set as he had in writing the opening number of *Company*. In rehearsal—and with the song still unwritten—Prince and Wheeler walked through the scene on stage, ad libbing the progress of the invitation from household to household

for the composer's benefit. "Then I went home and started to play around with it," said Sondheim. "The number was written around the scenery. I'd call Hal and ask if I could get a character from here to there with a screen move—and he'd say yes or no, or that he'd need more time for a move. The movement of the screens was what allowed me to feel the sense of flow from place to place." Conversely, Aronson expanded on a Sondheim lyric in designing one of the sets. The grande dame of the musical, Madame Armfeldt, at one point boasts in a song ("Liaisons"), "I acquired some position plus a tiny Titian"—eventhough there are no tiny Titians. In an Act II dinner-party scene, Aronson expanded on the joke by providing a monumental tapestry based on a Titian theme.

A Little Night Music was a departure from Aronson's past collaborations with Prince and Sondheim, especially *Company* and *Follies*. "It's mostly a painted show," Aronson noted after the opening. "Only the furniture on stage is three-dimensional. This differs very much from *Company* and *Follies*, which had Constructivist scenery with elevations, platforms, elevators, and so on. This musical is also, predominantly, done in white. It has a few colored scenes in it, but basically the approach is white-on-white." Even so, Aronson finally pronounced himself satisfied with the results. *Night Music* had not, at least, committed the sin of attempting "a documentary representation of Sweden," but was instead "an American production that attempts to recapture the Scandinavian feeling [of] white nights. And white is just the light touch that this musical needs."

13   An Aronson collage anticipating his *Night Music* design.

A BOLD DEPARTURE

I strongly believe that for each play you first and foremost must create a space which, inherent in its design, already holds the mystique of the entire event. In good design, the only thing expensive is the taste which goes into a production. The rest can be shockingly simple.

PACIFIC OVERTURES (1976)

"What we were trying to do sounded so pretentious," said Stephen Sondheim of *Pacific Overtures.* "It was a Japanese idea of a Western musical of a Japanese subject." Pretentious or not, this Kabuki-style Broadway musical about the first, nineteenth-century encounter between Japan and America was the most esoteric and perhaps the most daring of the Sondheim-Prince-Aronson collaborations. It was also the shortest-lived. *Pacific Overtures* ran only six months—less than half as long as the team's previous commercial failure at the Winter Garden, *Follies.* And, like *Follies* with its "empty stage," *Pacific Overtures* was a spectacle that did not parade its opulence; the show found its aesthetic and budgetary extravagance in the simple imagery of austere Japanese prints. "I felt a great need to go back to illusion for this show," said Aronson about what proved to be the final—and, in the view of some, crowning—achievement of his Broadway career. "I wanted simplicity and a strong Japanese feeling, naïveté mixed with sophistication. . . . But simplicity and lightness on stage can be the most expensive way to do theatre. *Pacific Overtures* was a very expensive simple show."

The complexity of the design came from Aronson's own intellec-

tual approach to the script's historical subject, as well as from the intentionally distorting lens through which that history was presented in the show's libretto and staging. Adapted by John Weidman, Hugh Wheeler, and Sondheim from Weidman's unproduced non-musical play, *Pacific Overtures* told of Commodore Matthew Perry's mission to "open up" an isolated Japan to Western trade and influence in 1853. But *Pacific Overtures* was not to be a documentary treatment of its real-life events. Prince saw it as a "documentary vaudeville," resembling neither a conventional book musical nor the previous Sondheim-Prince experiments. The show would instead meld clashing elements of Western and Eastern stagecraft—predominantly those of Broadway and Kabuki, as it turned out. In this way, the musical's style might in itself convey the authors' sardonic message about the cultural shock that the West inflicted on a once-isolated Japan.

"The show was about the encounter of two forces and the opening of new worlds for each of them" is how Aronson explained *Pacific Overtures.* "The Americans came as pioneers, explorers, showing their 'brass.' The Japanese held back with the inner reserve and suspicion of an insular people while leaning on their great traditions. Just as Amer-

OPPOSITE

3   The show curtain in use and in scale, with the Kabuki reciter (Mako) before it at the opening of Act I.

1, 2   *Pacific Overtures* (1976): A Japanese stencil design (1) that, after being refracted through a color Xerox machine and an Aronson collage, surfaced in the show curtain (2).

3

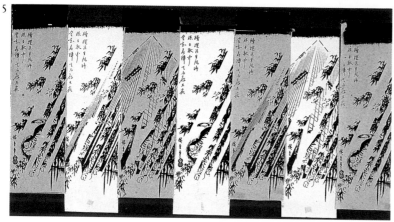

4, 5, 6 Rejected show curtains for *Pacific Overtures* demonstrate Aronson's collage technique. Some of the curtains explicitly mix traditional Japanese and contemporary American elements (including a skyscraper reminiscent of *Company*). An early curtain using repeated stripes is closer to the pattern of actual Kabuki curtains than the show curtain finally chosen. The florid colors were created with the Xerox 6500.

icans introduced Japan to the wonders of mechanization, the 'discovery' of Oriental art and architecture at that time influenced the Occident from then up to the present. Japan lost its culture through the influx of the industrial Western innovations, but in the process became more advanced. America went in reverse—it began without a past and had to become more human." As Aronson brooded over the challenge of rendering so recondite a musical in concrete visual terms, he looked for contemporary applications of its theme. "It is going on today with the Arabs," he concluded. "You see a photo of an Egyptian boy riding a bicycle in his native outfit, but on top he has a modern American coat. He is a product of mixed cultures and mixed traditions. . . . In Japan, the West of today combines with the ancient traditions. How do you have such a synthesis of cultures? I say they are not combinable. That was the problem in the play. How do you present the conflict between an ancient, traditional society and a foreign, mechanized, modern approach to life?" For Aronson, the show's theme was most succinctly and artfully captured by a Sondheim song of Act II, "Bowler Hat," in which the audience watches a Japanese character as he rises through the governmental bureaucracy over a period of decades and increasingly "accommodates" himself to Westernization by adopting Western appurtenances (a bowler hat, a monocle, a pocket watch, a Victorian desk). Fittingly, "Bowler Hat" was the one song in *Pacific Overtures* that could be performed without illustration. "It didn't need scenery," the designer said. "In miniature, it conveyed the conflict of being contemporary and of being of another time."

Set pieces—sometimes in the form of elaborate props—were required in other scenes, however. The designs, like the endlessly revised show itself, were a long time coming. Originally, *Pacific Overtures* opened at a Victorian party and was told in reverse chronology. Later, Prince came up with the idea, also to be abandoned, of "taking the show into the audience, and the audience into the show." The director conceived of the device as a quasi-storyteller's theatre: "Each actor would enter the audience and tell fifteen people the same story, about how Perry's warships arrived in Japan. Each actor would play a different character—a peasant, an aristocrat, a mother—and would tell the story in character. Only in the last five sentences would all the words be timed to be said by the entire cast in unison."

Prince also thought that he would like to employ "every conceivable [theatrical] style" in *Pacific Overtures*—"not just Kabuki, but French farce, melodrama, ballet, commedia dell'arte, rock-and-roll

7 The show curtain as seen in a model which also shows the bleached hardwood floor and Kabuki ramp, the *hanamichi*. The show curtain's bold, stenciled look—patterned with chrysanthemums and butterflies in navy blue, reds, and pink tones—made the audience feel it was entering a Japanese garden. "Beginning with *Company*, I noticed a sort of creeping disease," said Stephen Sondheim. "With each successive show, more and more of the orchestra pit got covered by the set. By the time we got to *Pacific Overtures*, I used to make gallows jokes that the entire orchestra would be in the dressing rooms and we could build the stage right over the audience—which, with the *hanamichi*, of course, is literally what happens. It bothered me, because the music sounds more canned, but I lost those battles. It was a question of what you choose to sacrifice. Hal understood that a musical works better the closer you can get to the audience—which means you don't separate the show from the audience with an orchestra pit. . . . After *Pacific Overtures*, Boris was so impressed by what I did, he said that next time I'd get an open pit."

8 A model showing Prince's plan (later abandoned) for playing the show throughout the auditorium of the Winter Garden Theatre.

9

9   In the opening number of *Pacific Overtures,*
"The Advantages of Floating in the Middle of the
Sea," Sondheim established the show's tone and view
of feudal Japan. The lowered header adds to the Kabuki
look; the ecru backdrop with stylized brushstrokes
suggests watermarked Japanese rice paper.

10, 11, 12   A detail of the header (10), which was created by collage and could be lowered beneath the proscenium arch to achieve the horizontal look of the Kabuki stage. It also could form the Shogun's bedroom for the song "Chrysanthemum Tea" (11)—which was played in front of it, as seen in model form—or, as Prince discovered, could be used to represent a jail when a scene was played behind it, as seen on stage (12).

13, 14   The *Pacific Overtures* kimono curtain was used in the song "Four Black Dragons." A bronze bell (a flat cut-out) heralds the arrival of the American ships, as seen in the model (13) and on stage (14).

15, 16 Later in the same song, the curtain separates, allowing townspeople to make entrances and exits, as seen in the model (15) and on stage (16). The empty spaces in the curtain are as important as the kite-like shapes.

17 The curtain could form a still tighter configuration.

18

19

18, 19 In "Four Black Dragons" in *Pacific Overtures*, the Americans arrived as "dragons" walking down the *hanamichi.* Aronson pictured them in the form of turn-of-the-century industrialists—Dada-style men who walked like machines and represented the influx of the West, which was bringing technology to insular Japan. To design these costumes, Aronson made collages—as seen in front (18) and side (19) views— combining images of ships with those of period inventions, such as steam engines.

revue." While vestiges of this "vaudeville" approach can be found in the final version of the musical (particularly in Sondheim's score and lyrics), the director realized, after the fact, that Kabuki "is so powerful and pungent that, in a weird way, it's shackling. Once we opened the Kabuki door, it controlled us."

But that control was not total. Prince's staging did borrow from Kabuki: he used the traditional *hanamichi* ramp running through the audience, black-clad stagehands, men playing women, and a "reciter." Even so, he never imitated Kabuki slavishly. "He didn't want that look," said Aronson. "Kabuki's costumes and makeup are too elaborate; the colors are often garish. And today Kabuki relies heavily on endless turntables, trapdoors, catwalks. Prince wanted more the feeling of a simple Japanese inn. Yet, everything was to remain traditionally Japanese—even the arrival of the Americans is seen through the eyes of the Japanese."

The overall framework of the design was determined early. "We have to establish a basic set-up within which we do the show," Aronson wrote to Prince after reading an early draft of the script. "This set-up is established already when the audience enters the theatre. It should look as foreign and yet as pleasing as a Japanese garden (not literally)—more like a celebration. Against this light, ephemeral world, the actor would stand out—sharply outlined against a bleached hardwood floor and a white surround—opulent in costume and large in gesture." The set would stress "simplicity" and look as if it was "made of rice paper, origami, kites, bamboo." There would be no heavy scenic units or turntables; screens and other necessary individual scenic pieces would be brought in from the wings (by the Kabuki stagehands) or hung to fly in from above; for some scenes, a "header" lowered underneath the proscenium arch would give the stage the horizontal shape of Japanese theatre. The "surround" would consist of white wings and a white backdrop (done in three sections). The background was marked with two magnified brushstrokes covering the entire width of the stage—suggesting a cloud-like image on translucent, watermarked paper. To augment the lightness of the show's look, the stage floor and its extension, the *hanamichi,* would both be built out of hard, pale, natural wood, like a huge basketball court. Against this environment, any scenic piece, as well as any actor, would be isolated and clearly delineated.

That spareness reflected the design's basis in Japanese prints—a conceit that at first both excited and frightened Aronson, who had long collected and studied Japanese woodcuts. "I had never had an assignment so closely related to an art which I admire," he explained. "But occasionally you have doubts about whether you are on the right track—especially if you have never done [that art], nor been to the country." What ended those doubts was Prince's suggestion that Aronson look at the Metropolitan Museum exhibition "The Great Wave," which documented the influence of Japanese prints on French Impressionist painters in the nineteenth century. "I could see how French artists could take the techniques and essences of Japanese prints and still make them look one-hundred-percent French," said Aronson. "I was elated." No longer would he have to aspire to the impossible—of becoming "Japanese overnight."

More important, Aronson saw a way to combine the timeless traditions of Japanese printmaking with his own modernist art, in a manner that might subtly dramatize the musical's East-versus-West conflict. As he formulated this approach over the summer of 1975, the designer wrote Prince a series of notes explaining his ideas: "I am much taken by the technique of [Japanese] prints—the achievement of recognizable images in the most stylized manner, through the use of outline and a variety of stencil patterns and graphic textures. Technically, [Japanese prints] are exact and accurate in every minute detail. One would think they would be limited in fantasy, but they are not. Although they are absolutely based on almost photographic reality, the reality is not the camera's eye, it is the eye of the artist. . . . It seemed to me only natural to translate that [technique] into collage—rather than imitating Japanese brushstrokes. I thought it ideally suited the show, because I could combine authenticity with a contemporary technique—and in a personal way."

The method by which the designer combined the two art forms in his *Pacific Overtures* designs was a completely unexpected one. Aronson implored Prince to pay for the rental of a color Xerox machine, then a new and costly appliance, for the designer's personal use for a month or so. Prince agreed, and Aronson soon achieved a literal merging of Japanese brushstrokes and modern collage. He Xeroxed Japanese prints to refract the Japanese palette through the Xerox machine's artificial color spectrum. Then he cut up the reproductions and created collages that reflected the abstraction and textual surfaces of his own art at that time. "You misunderstand if you think that I use [the Xerox 6500] merely for the purpose of reproduction," the designer wrote to a somewhat baffled Prince. "I use it as a tool. . . . The machine can be utilized in a creative way." While the audience might never specifically notice the important role played by collage, let alone

20 The "Four Black Dragons" collages realized as costumes: the four industrialists (played by chorus women dressed in black and sporting cigars) walked down the ramp with stylized boats around them (smokestacks included), as seen in a run-through; the ship simultaneously appeared on the opposite side of the stage. This Dada-esque device captured "the spirit of the show," according to Sondheim, but it confused the audience in Boston, the first stop on the pre-Broadway tryout tour. The four industrialized "dragons" were cut immediately.

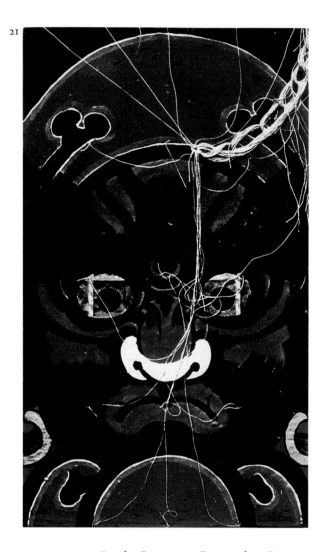

21, 22, 23, 24 *Pacific Overtures:* Commodore Perry arrives in "Four Black Dragons." Research for Aronson's collage included a miniature kite purchased in New York (21) which inspired the ship's eye and face. The ship as it arrives, in a model (22), in a production photo (23), and in its expanded form, in a model (24).

OPPOSITE

25 The ship on stage. In front of the ship at left is the skiff Aronson designed in the Noh theatre style for Perry's Japanese greeter.

OPPOSITE

26 The surrounding backdrop was separated into three panels, the middle of which could rise to allow the sliding on of light set pieces such as this puppet throne (puppet designed by E. J. Taylor). Only at the dramatic entrance of the ship in "Four Black Dragons" was the center panel's rising visible to the audience. Different fabrics, including muslins and linens, were tried to see which had the whiteness and translucency required to make the surround look as close to rice paper as possible. The only fabric that worked was the percale used in bedsheeting.

27 Collage screens as scenery, here in an Act II assassination scene.

a Xerox machine, in his designs, Aronson was certain that theatregoers would sense the thematic contributions made by the scenery even if they couldn't quite articulate what those contributions were. J. J. Moore, one of Aronson's amused assistants on the project, recalled *Pacific Overtures* as "the paper-doll show. . . . Boris kept cutting and pasting more Xerox paper. He talked Xerox into letting him lease a color machine when only corporations could do so, and, with no supervision, he could do whatever he wanted to, just playing like crazy. He kept turning the magenta way up." As Aronson later elaborated: "It is easy to be victimized by the machine—because whatever comes out will surprise you. You have to have a point of view and know why you are using it." Out of these collage experiments came all the drops for the show, including a "kimono curtain" that could spread apart to suggest kimonos hanging from several cords the width of the stage. As he arrived at his final designs, Aronson conducted hundreds of experiments combining Xerox, prints, and painting—some made on paper, some on cotton and silk.

For the mobile scenic elements, Prince and Aronson kept to their plan of using only screens and light structures. "I felt that screens were more harmonious, and that the play is about the struggle to achieve harmony," said Prince. Sondheim regarded his music for the show as "a Japanese screen score [that] came out quite homogeneous and elegant and very spare and Japanese." Both sides of the screens were used. On their faces were representational images, created by collage, suiting the various scenes; the backs were either white or black and showed their bamboo construction.

Prince did not want "a lot of contraptions on stage" for the other scenic pieces. But it was not so easy to preserve the show's light, Oriental aesthetic and accommodate its complicated script demands. To avoid an excess of "contraptions"—to create scenery that could "look light, be simple to handle, and yet perform tricks"—the designer turned to indigenous Japanese mechanisms for inspiration. He played incessantly with inexpensive but ingeniously devised Japanese pocket toys. He studied Japanese kites and fans. He amassed stacks of Japanese papers and studied the Japanese method of wrapping both small and large objects.

Nowhere did this line of investigation pay off more handsomely than in the most important scene, when Perry's warships first arrive in Japan. The main ship went through many incarnations as the script was rewritten. At first, it was a huge, symmetrical behemoth that headed straight downstage toward the audience, then opened up and

28, 29   In the song "Someone in a Tree" in *Pacific Overtures*, Sondheim imagined how speculative history might be written by would-be eavesdroppers, among them a young boy in a tree, who surrounded the treaty house where Perry and the Japanese negotiated their first agreement. Although the number was considered by Sondheim and others to be among the musical's highest achievements, it was never successfully designed or staged in the Broadway production. The first model used a roll-on tree and a house constructed out of rice paper and surrounded by flying kites; the house was to disappear immediately after the negotiation, allowing the Japanese to obliterate any evidence of a foreign presence. "The treaty house was supposed to grow out of the stage floor, magically, from flat pieces," according to Aronson's assistant, J. J. Moore. "We worked for a long, long time trying to figure out how to fold things for it, to telescope the pieces. The tree was going to bloom, with a lot of individual twigs and individual blossoms." In the manner of a traditional magic trick, the blossoms were attached to wires within the thin tubes that made up the tree. But in the face of last-minute budget cuts, the design was eliminated overnight. Also cut, by Sondheim's choice and to his regret, was a quatrain of the song's lyric which depended on the sudden appearance of leaves on the tree. (The quatrain was reinstated by the author in the published version of the score.) In the ensuing and simplified version of the set, the original, costly pop-up design of the treaty house (28) was replaced by soft pieces to be hung and unfolded, like a Japanese lantern. It was to be assembled in full view of the audience, thereby requiring meticulous, time-consuming rehearsals. But the pieces arrived late for the Boston tryout, and there was no time left to rehearse their delicate assembling, so a compromise version was quickly concocted (29).

30

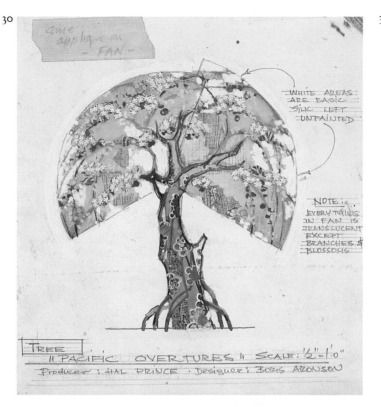

31

32

30, 31, 32 Not satisfied with the treaty house design for "Someone in a Tree," Prince asked that it be rethought and redone for the next out-of-town stop, at the Kennedy Center in Washington. In New York, a new design was tried, in which the blooming of the tree was done in the manner of the opening up of a fan, seen as designed (30) and as occupied by a singer onstage (31). The treaty house became a simple structure made up of three screen-like pieces which could be quickly assembled and removed during the scene (32). The only aspect preserved from the original design was the flying kites above and around the house.

33

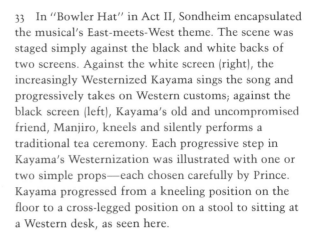

33 In "Bowler Hat" in Act II, Sondheim encapsulated the musical's East-meets-West theme. The scene was staged simply against the black and white backs of two screens. Against the white screen (right), the increasingly Westernized Kayama sings the song and progressively takes on Western customs; against the black screen (left), Kayama's old and uncompromised friend, Manjiro, kneels and silently performs a traditional tea ceremony. Each progressive step in Kayama's Westernization was illustrated with one or two simple props—each chosen carefully by Prince. Kayama progressed from a kneeling position on the floor to a cross-legged position on a stool to sitting at a Western desk, as seen here.

34 Kayama's house, as seen on stage, was typical of the design's delicacy.

34

35

35, 36   One of the almost subliminal motifs of Aronson's design involved the use of eyes—from those that appear on the front of the large ship in "Four Black Dragons" to this model of a set for the finale, "Next" (35). The "Next" set was also a solution to budgetary constraints. There was no money left for the number; the set could utilize the backs of the seven floating screens while upholding the paper-thin look of the show. The eyes, to be pictured on silver reflective paper, would be diverted toward the "next" that might swallow up modern, urban Japan. But the idea was abandoned as too subtle. A year later, Aronson found a photograph in *The New York Times* picturing similar eyes that had been painted as graffiti on rocks by the Kiyotaki River in Kyoto (36). "For many," said the accompanying article, "the painting reflects the decline in group standards and the urbanization that have been overcoming Japanese cities." This was, of course, the same theme that Aronson had hoped to address with his use of the eyes in his finale set. When the designer saw the article, he said, "That's the way the finale should have been done—with graffiti eyes sprayed over the set's pure white background." He kept the clipping, hoping that he might have a chance to redesign the ending should the show ever be revived.

36

THE NEW YORK TIMES, THURSDAY, NOVEMBER 10, 1977

Graffiti, 141 Giant Eyes Along River Bank, Hint at Changing Japan

By ANDREW H. MALCOLM
Special to The New York Times

KYOTO, Japan — Katsuo Nakagawa was strolling along the famous wooded banks of the Kiyotaki River here one day admiring the bright autumn colors when, suddenly, he could not believe what he saw. There, staring back at him from the river were 141 giant eyes —pink ones, white ones and black ones —painted on rocks.

Such incidents, whether merely malicious mischief or artful expression, have been unheard of in Japan, so the mysterious eyes were reported to the police and a full investigation was launched. The result has been a bureaucratic, legalistic and artistic debate that reveals something of the social workings and values of a changing society.

It has also become a severe headache for Yoshihiro Imaeda, a seasoned detective who for a quarter of a century has dealt with simpler wrongdoings like murder and arson. "This," said Superintendent Imaeda, "is a very unusual case."

The complexity arises because almost

Eyes painted last September on rocks on the Kiyotaki River in Kyoto, Japan

everyone with a stated opinion denounces the painted eyes as offensive to the rural river's natural beauty but there does not seem to be any law prohibiting them. While newspapers and officials call for stern action against the culprits, policemen and prosecutors are hesitating since any acquittal could endorse the legality of similar freelance graffiti anywhere.

Avoiding a Bad Loss of Face

"We must be very cautious in this case," a prefectural official explained. "If we lost it would be a bad loss of face, and it might encourage others to pull the same stunt."

The mysterious tale of the painted eyes began in September when Mr. Nakagawa, as he has once or twice a week for three decades, went to the river to sing his favorite folksongs far from complaining neighbors. Like millions of others he regards that particular river area, called Takao, as one of the most picturesque in Japan—especially in fall, when the maples turn the steep hillsides into bright hues of red and gold.

Restaurants, tearooms and sake shops, some built on stilts, line much of the mossy, gracious gorge where the river trickles among the rocks on the northwestern outskirts of this ancient Japanese capital. Though there is a mass of trash—plastic bags, bottles,

A city official called the eyes "awful" and suggested they had been painted by "crazy people."

cans and papers—sloshing there, it is the bizarre eyes, some neat, some sloppy, that offend many.

"One or two might be O.K.," said Akira Asano, a longtime Kyoto resident, "but that many and that bright and in Takao. I mean, really—it's such bad taste."

"They must be crazy people, that's all," said Takeshi Izawa, who is the official in charge of maintenance of the river. "The eyes are awful and primitive. I think they just wanted some media attention. If so, they must be happy because they sure got it."

No Billboards, No Advertisements

He immediately checked the River Law, but found no provision against painting rocks. Similarly the Scenic Preservation Law and the Ancient Capital Preservation Ordinance. Officials even checked the outdoor billboard regulations, but it was decided that rocks are not billboards and eyes are not advertisements.

Superintendent Imaeda, calling the case unprecedented, commented: "The legislators who wrote all these laws never expected this sort of incident. Such crimes were unimaginable here."

The police, the prefectural govern-

ment and the prosecutor are meeting to consider the next move. Only after they have reached a consensus will the prefecture file a complaint, the police launch an official inquiry and the prosecutor place charges.

Overlooked for the moment is that the authorities have no idea who painted the rocks. They know only that the act took about five gallons of oil paint and will likely require blowtorches to undo at substantial taxpayer expense. They speculate that four or five young people were involved, which happens to coincide with the number spotted in the area just before Mr. Nakagawa went out singing.

For many the painting reflects the decline in group standards and the urbanization that have been overcoming Japanese cities.

Cold Cement, Not Beautiful Wood

"For one thing," said Mr. Asano, who has lived all of his 38 years here, "the buildings are getting taller and they're made of cold cement instead of beautiful woods. We're not so kind to each other any more either. Sometimes even local people speak harshly to one another. And people move more often too. We used to know everyone, but now there are some neighbors I don't know. It doesn't seem right."

Superintendent Imaeda sees the changes reflected in crime statistics for this city, whose 1.4 million residents make it Japan's fifth largest. "The total number of felonies is still going down," he said. "The number of murders is staying the same—33 so far this year— but the so-called fun crimes, those committed with no motive other than thrills, they are increasing. I think it's the frustrations of modern life."

Meanwhile, the painted eyes remain on the rocks in case they are needed as evidence. The perpetrators remain at large. The sightseeing throngs come to see the leaves but go away remembering the eyes. Mr. Izawa, sitting in his Government office, shook his head: "I don't understand it. Nothing like this has happened before."

served as a stage set for a party. It also contained a stage for a vaudeville show-within-the-show and a contemplated puppet show. This complicated design was executed in model form and working drawings to the point of being ready to be built. But it was cumbersome and lacked the buoyant feeling of the rest of the production. Fortunately, as it happened, the ship's various secondary uses were stripped away in subsequent script revisions, rendering the original design obsolete, until finally the ship's dramatic import was limited exclusively to its fearsome arrival. At that point, Prince voiced his preference that the redesigned ship enter from the wings and travel across the stage sideways so that it could fill the entire width of the stage. Aronson preferred a perpendicular move, toward the audience. The dilemma was resolved by Peter Feller. He suggested a way by which Aronson could design it to do both, so that it moved forward downstage and opened up sideways simultaneously. In fact, this ship could be designed so that it could be walked on by stagehands, with no mechanization necessary. This appealed to Aronson and freed him in his final design to make the ship look more like the "black dragon" the accompanying Sondheim song ("Four Black Dragons") said it was. In the scene itself, the ship suddenly appeared at the climax of that song, in which peasants sang with mounting horror of the increasing proximity of the Americans. Arriving in giant size on the stage horizon and riding on waves resembling those in Japanese woodcuts, Commodore Perry's ship uncurled and grew larger, like a dragon, as it came toward the audience. The front of the ship, inspired in part by a miniature Japanese kite Aronson had bought in New York, had the image of a Kabuki mask and gave the ship its "eyes." The terrifying, fire-breathing "dragon" contrasted strongly with the delicacy of the Japan it was invading. Meanwhile, the large American ship stood in pointed contrast to the tiny, hand-crafted boat the Japanese sent to greet Commodore Perry: Aronson designed the skiff in Noh style, as a prop that an actor could walk on and off.

However light and translucent the design of *Pacific Overtures* was in theory, it still might have looked heavy on stage. The ideal material for the set—paper—could not be used in scenery that was required by law to be fireproof. But the lightness was successfully simulated with bamboo, cotton, silk, and the bleached wood floor, as well as by elaborate hand painting (all of it supervised by Aronson at the studio). To enhance the crisp look of the show, Tharon Musser, the lighting designer, bathed it in "white" light (achieved with a mixture of colored lights).

For all the elaborate care that was taken with *Pacific Overtures*, it had second-act problems in all departments, scenery included, and they were not solved by the time of the Broadway opening. "Act II seems to go off at a tangent, to minimize the original encounter," Aronson wrote in notes on an early script. Months later, not much had changed. The closing song, an ironic "jump cut" to present-day industrialized Japan, didn't achieve its intended effect. The finale's most important theatrical moment—in which the singing of contemporary Japanese urbanites is interrupted by a pair of Japanese peasants who walk out to "fish" from the *hanamichi*—was lost once the runway, which occupied a center-floor position during the Boston tryout, was shunted off to the side in New York. Monetary shortfalls further damaged the second act. Earlier on, when $50,000 was cut from the scenery budget, necessity required hasty adjustments in fastidiously planned designs.

Whatever went wrong with *Pacific Overtures*, Aronson's scenery received the greatest acclaim of his career. Even a well-received low-budget revival of the musical by Off Off Broadway's York Theatre Company in 1984 could not escape the overpowering influence of the original designs. The last product of the Prince-Aronson partnership, initiated a dozen years earlier with *Fiddler on the Roof*, this project also brought that collaboration full circle. "Now we could do Japan and let it be put through a Russian's head," Prince later recalled. "And it had greater resonance than any imitation Aronson might do of Chagall. In *Pacific Overtures*, we had a Japanese show designed by a Russian and put on for Americans."

37   An Aronson collage of the period of *Pacific Overtures*.

CODA

THE NUTCRACKER (1976)

After *Pacific Overtures*, Aronson had numerous offers to design plays, musicals, and operas. Given his increasingly frail health, he realized he could not undertake such projects. But he was also possessed by the idea of designing a ballet, for he felt that his findings in his latest experiments in collage and mixed media lent themselves to ballet, preferably a modern one. Even as he asked Jerome Robbins about the possibility of such a project, he was unexpectedly approached by American Ballet Theatre to design a *Nutcracker* with and for Mikhail Baryshnikov, in his debut as a choreographer. Aronson had little interest in accepting the invitation. He saw scant point in trying to compete with Balanchine's evergreen *Nutcracker* for the New York City Ballet, and besides, as he put it, he was "the wrong man for a Christmas show." But Baryshnikov, who had seen Aronson's work in *Pacific Overtures*, was persistent and eventually won Aronson over with his ideas about the ballet and with his talent as a dancer (which the designer observed on stage for the first time after they had met). From the start, Aronson felt an electricity between himself and Baryshnikov. The designer relished the familiarity and ease of speaking Russian with the dancer; he wanted to work with an extraordinary, young, blossoming artist who was Russian-born yet cosmopolitan in sensibility. Aronson was also pleased to be working once again in the medium of ballet, which he regarded as particularly hospitable to invention and fantasy.

In his production of *The Nutcracker*, Baryshnikov drew on a standard Soviet version, Vassily Vainonen's for the Kirov, but he also turned back to the original E. T. A. Hoffmann fairy tale and the familiar psychoanalytic interpretations of it. "Yes, I am a Freudian," Baryshnikov explained to *The New York Times*. "I have never considered *The Nutcracker* to be a Christmas ballet. . . . Yes, it takes place on Christmas Eve and it's wintertime, but for me it's really a love story. It's about all those beautiful and frightening dreams a very young girl has when she first wakes up to love. It's that moment in a girl's life when she first experiences all those complicated emotions, some of which she doesn't understand herself, and none of which have anything to do with Christmas. You see, her soul opens and grows, just like the Christmas tree. But the Christmas tree is only a symbol of her growing emotions. So my whole point of view is to show Clara falling in love with her prince. In my version, Clara is never quite certain whether all the strange and wonderful things she is feeling, and the things that are happening all around her, are a dream or reality. Like

I

first love, everything becomes very disturbing and very ambiguous."

For his part, Aronson followed Baryshnikov's approach by consulting two rare books in his possession: a collection of Hoffmann fairy tales illustrated by the author and a book on Russian folk art, *Lubok*. Without copying the old illustrations—"You cannot put tracing paper over a picture and capture its spirit," the designer said—he did develop a close connection between his work and Hoffmann's, whose nightmarish tone belied the cute *Nutcracker* productions that have sprung up on stage in this century. "There is the feeling that children are only affected by beautiful things, but that is not always the case," Aronson said. "They are often much more enchanted with something fearful and dangerous." The entire piece was not a matter of "fantasy versus reality" but "theatre within theatre," with Drosselmeyer's puppet theatre setting the "naïve" flavor of the design.

Aronson, too, saw the ballet as a girl's dream, and noted that "dream images are usually vaguely familiar elements with some details sharply focused and defined in color." He designed the settings as "a continuous breaking through," from the prologue drop (which becomes translucent) to the Stahlbaum home to the growing of the Christmas tree (which causes the walls of the house to warp and vanish as it breaks through the ceiling) to the nightmarish battle of the Mouse King and the Nutcracker. After the Nutcracker's transformation into the Prince, the dark-blue backdrop bleeds through (or fades into) the light, snowy forest for the dance of the Snowflakes and the appearance of the road which Clara and the Prince will follow to his kingdom. In Act II, Clara and the Prince are on visual and musical waves of clouds on the road toward the castle, which appears in the distance at the end of their brief dance. This scene fades into a close-up of the kingdom's gate, which finally opens up into the court scene. Aronson intended this to be a traditional design in the style of eighteenth-century puppet theatres, reflecting the fact that Clara's dreams grow out of Drosselmeyer's puppet show at the Christmas party, yet somewhat vague, distorted, and surreal (if still recognizable).

Baryshnikov gave the go-ahead on the design after seeing a few tentative sketches and a collage for the front curtain. The results were eventually seen on network television, and, a decade later, the production remains in the ABT repertory. To Oliver Smith, who produced the ballet, the sets had the appropriately child-like feel of playing with toys. In his final project, Aronson had returned to what he had often described as the designer's primal joy—of working with "toys, tinsel, cut-outs, and an empty stage."

2

1, 2 A sketch of the show curtain (1), a collage, for Baryshnikov's production of *The Nutcracker* (1976)— and in model form (2) as lighted from behind and rendered translucent during the ballet's prologue. The curtain depicts elements of what is to come (the Nutcracker, mice, etc.), as Drosselmeyer indicates while preparing his puppets for the Christmas party during the prologue. The translucency shows the wheels which work his inventions. To his longtime assistant, Robert Mitchell, this design typified Aronson's "device of back-painting his theater drops in such a way that a change of light from front light to back light revealed new images or reinforced hidden images embedded in the front painting."

3, 4   *The Nutcracker:* The Stahlbaum's living room on Christmas Eve, as seen in model form (3) and on stage (4). To Aronson, the Stahlbaum home was bourgeois and typically domestic, but with an air of mysterious things to come.

5, 6   The Christmas tree gradually and magically expands, obliterating the room with it, as seen in model form (5) and on stage (6). The expansion of the tree signified young Clara's "breakthrough and emotional change." As the tree grows, the room's off-white walls warp and then vanish.

7, 8 The tree fully expanded, in model form (7)and on stage with soldiers and mice (8). The tree grew to a height of 33 feet, at the rate of 8¼ inches for each of the 48 bars of music that Tchaikovsky wrote for the tree-growing interlude in the original scenario for the ballet.

9, 10   The gateway to the kingdom, which was
designed as a castle in the air, as seen in the model (9)
and with Baryshnikov and company on stage (10).

11, 12 The final scene of *The Nutcracker*, in court—
in model form (11) and on stage (12). A traditional but
distorted 18th-century puppet-theatre design, with
the translucent backdrop vaguely depicting enlarged
candle flames.

13   A sketch of the snowy woods on the way to the castle.

14   The model of the road to the castle; Baryshnikov added steam to enhance its cloud-like formations.

15   On stage in *The Nutcracker*, Baryshnikov and
Gelsey Kirkland dance before Aronson's road drop,
seen in the televised version.

16

16   Aronson in front of his road drop in the television
studio as CBS filmed his final project, *The Nutcracker*
(1977).

Chronology

Bibliography

Index

I am fascinated with the empty stage. It is a question not of how you fill that emptiness—but rather of what you can extract from the existing space.

Chronology

Each entry indicates the title of the production; the author(s); the name of the theatre (with the subsequent name of the theatre, if renamed and still in use, within parentheses); the opening date and number of performances (when available); the stars of the production (if any); the producer; the director; Aronson's design contribution (*set, costumes, lighting*); other designers who worked on the production (when known). Ballets and operas are labeled as such.

1924

DAY AND NIGHT by S. Ansky
Unser Theatre, Bronx
set, costumes

1925

THE FINAL BALANCE by David Pinski
Unser Theatre, Bronx
set, costumes

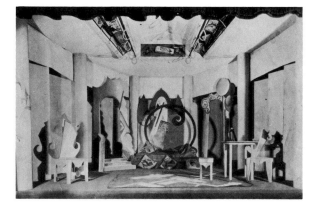

THE BRONX EXPRESS by Ossip Dymov
Schildkraut Theatre, Bronx
Co-directed by Aronson
set, costumes

STRING OF PEARLS by Sholem Asch
Yiddish Art Theatre
set, costumes

1926

THE TENTH COMMANDMENT by
  Abraham Goldfaden
Yiddish Art Theatre (Second Avenue Theatre),
  Nov. 17, 1926
With Maurice Schwartz and Joseph Buloff
Directed by Schwartz; ballet directed by
  Michel Fokine
set, costumes

1927

MENSCHEN STOIB (HUMAN DUST) by
  Ossip Dymov
Yiddish Art Theatre (Second Avenue Theatre)
set, costumes

THE TRAGEDY OF NOTHING by Moisha Nadir
Irving Place Theatre
Produced by the Art Circle
Directed by Aronson
set, costumes

YOSHE MUSIKANT (SINGER OF HIS OWN SADNESS)
  by Ossip Dymov
Yiddish Art Theatre (Second Avenue Theatre)
Directed by Joseph Buloff
set

RED, YELLOW AND BLACK by Adolphe Wolfe
Directed by J. Mestel

$2 \times 2 = 5$ by Gustav Wied
Civic Repertory Theatre, Nov. 28, 1927;
  16 performances
With Harry Sothern
Produced by Eva Le Gallienne
Directed by Egon Brecher
set, costumes

1928

LAG BOIMER by M. Olgin
   (adapted from Sholom Aleichem)
Choreographed by B. Zemach
set, costumes

1929

THE GOLEM by H. Leivick
unrealized project
Yiddish Art Theatre
Directed by Maurice Schwartz
set, costumes

STEMPENYU, THE FIDDLER by Sholom Aleichem
Yiddish Art Theatre (Second Avenue Theatre)
With Maurice Schwartz and Celia Adler
Directed by Schwartz
set, costumes

JEW SÜSS by Lion Feuchtwanger
Yiddish Art Theatre (Second Avenue Theatre),
   Oct. 18, 1929
With Maurice Schwartz and Samuel Goldenburg
Directed by Schwartz
set

ANGELS ON EARTH by Chuno Gottesfeld
Yiddish Art Theatre (Second Avenue Theatre),
   Dec. 10, 1929
With Maurice Schwartz and Samuel Goldenburg
Directed by Schwartz
set, costumes

1930

ROAMING STARS by Maurice Schwartz
   (adapted from the novel by Sholom Aleichem)
Yiddish Art Theatre (Second Avenue Theatre),
   Jan. 24, 1930
With Schwartz
Directed by Schwartz
set

JIM COOPERKOP by Shin Godiner
Princess Theatre, Oct. 17, 1930
Produced by the Yiddish Workers' Art Theatre
set

1932

WALK A LITTLE FASTER by S. J. Perelman (book),
   Vernon Duke (music), E. Y. Harburg (lyrics)
St. James Theatre, Dec. 6, 1932; 119 performances
With Beatrice Lillie and Clark and McCullough
Produced by Courtney Burr
Directed by Monty Woolley
conception and design (costumes by Kiviette)

1934

SMALL MIRACLE by Norman Krasna
John Golden Theatre, Sept. 26, 1934; 117 performances
With Myron McCormick and Ilka Chase
Produced by Courtney Burr
Directed by George Abbott
set

LADIES' MONEY by George Abbott
Ethel Barrymore Theatre, Nov. 1, 1934;
    36 performances
Produced by Courtney Burr
Directed by Abbott
set

1935

BATTLESHIP GERTIE by Frederick Hazlitt Brennan
Lyceum Theatre, Jan. 18, 1935; 2 performances
With Burgess Meredith and Helen Lynd
Produced by Courtney Burr
Directed by Arthur Sircom
set

THREE MEN ON A HORSE by John Cecil Holm and
    George Abbott
The Playhouse, Jan. 30, 1935; 835 performances
With William Lynn, Sam Levene, and Shirley Booth
Produced by Alex Yokel
Directed by Abbott
set, costumes

AWAKE AND SING by Clifford Odets
Belasco Theatre, Feb. 19, 1935; 137 performances
With Jules Garfield, Luther Adler, Stella Adler,
    and Morris Carnovsky
Produced by the Group Theatre
Directed by Harold Clurman
set

RADIO CITY MUSIC HALL STAGE PRODUCTIONS
Radio City, 1935 season
set

THE BODY BEAUTIFUL by Robert Rossen
Plymouth Theatre, Oct. 31, 1935; 4 performances
With Polly Walters
Produced by Sidney Harmon
Directed by Rossen
set

WEEP FOR THE VIRGINS by Nellise Child
46th Street Theatre, Nov. 30, 1935; 9 performances
With Evelyn Varden
Produced by the Group Theatre
Directed by Cheryl Crawford
set

PARADISE LOST by Clifford Odets
Longacre Theatre, Dec. 9, 1935; 73 performances
With Morris Carnovsky, Luther Adler, Elia Kazan,
    and Stella Adler
Produced by the Group Theatre
Directed by Harold Clurman
set

1937

WESTERN WATERS by Richard Carlson
Hudson Theatre, Dec. 28, 1937; 7 performances
Produced by Elsa Moses
Directed by Moses and Carlson
set, costumes

1938

THE MERCHANT OF YONKERS by Thornton Wilder
Guild Theatre (Virginia Theatre), Dec. 28, 1938;
   39 performances
With Jane Cowl
Produced by Herman Shumlin
Directed by Max Reinhardt
set (costumes by Kermit Love)

1939

THE TIME OF YOUR LIFE by William Saroyan
Shubert Theatre, New Haven
With Eddie Dowling and Julie Haydon
Produced by the Theatre Guild
Directed by Robert Lewis
set, costumes (not used on Broadway)

THE GENTLE PEOPLE by Irwin Shaw
Belasco Theatre, Jan. 5, 1939; 141 performances
With Sam Jaffe, Franchot Tone, Sylvia Sidney,
   Elia Kazan, Lee J. Cobb, and Roman Bohnen
Produced by the Group Theatre
Directed by Harold Clurman
set

LADIES AND GENTLEMEN by Ben Hecht and
   Charles MacArthur
Martin Beck Theatre, Nov. 17, 1939; 105 performances
With Helen Hayes and Philip Merivale
Produced by Gilbert Miller
Directed by MacArthur and Lewis Allen
set

1940

THE GREAT AMERICAN GOOF, ballet by
   Eugene Loring (choreography), Henry Brant
   (music), and William Saroyan (libretto)
Center Theatre, Jan. 11, 1940
With Loring, Miriam Golden, Antony Tudor, and
   Lucia Chase
Produced by Ballet Theatre
set, costumes

THE UNCONQUERED by Ayn Rand
Biltmore Theatre, Feb. 13, 1940; 6 performances
With Dean Jagger, Helen Craig, and John Emery
Produced by George Abbott
Directed by Abbott
set

HEAVENLY EXPRESS by Albert Bein
National Theatre (Nederlander Theatre),
    April 18, 1940; 20 performances
With John Garfield
Produced by Kermit Bloomgarden
Directed by Robert Lewis
set, costumes

THE NIGHT BEFORE CHRISTMAS by Laura and
    S. J. Perelman
Morosco Theatre, April 10, 1941; 22 performances
Produced by Courtney Burr
Directed by Romney Brent
set

CAFÉ CROWN by H. S. Kraft
Cort Theatre, Jan. 23, 1942; 141 performances
With Morris Carnovsky and Sam Jaffe
Produced by Carly Wharton and Martin Gabel
Directed by Elia Kazan
set

CABIN IN THE SKY by Lynn Root (book),
    Vernon Duke (music), and John Latouche (lyrics)
Martin Beck Theatre, Oct. 25, 1940; 156 performances
With Ethel Waters, Katherine Dunham, and
    Dooley Wilson
Produced by Albert Lewis
Directed by George Balanchine
set, costumes

CLASH BY NIGHT by Clifford Odets
Belasco Theatre, Dec. 27, 1941; 49 performances
With Tallulah Bankhead, Lee J. Cobb,
    Joseph Schildkraut, and Robert Ryan
Produced by Billy Rose
Directed by Lee Strasberg
set

THE SNOW MAIDEN, ballet by Bronislava Nijinska
    (choreography), Alexander Glazunov (music) and
    Sergei Denham (libretto)
Metropolitan Opera House, Oct. 12, 1942
With Alexandra Danilova, Nathalie Krassovska,
    Igor Youskevitch, and Frederic Franklin
Produced by Ballet Russe de Monte Carlo
set, costumes

R.U.R. by Karel Čapek
Ethel Barrymore Theatre, Dec. 3, 1942;
   4 performances
Produced by David Silberman and I. Daniel Blank
Directed by Lee Strasberg
set

THE RUSSIAN PEOPLE by Konstantin Simonov
Guild Theatre (Virginia Theatre), Dec. 29, 1942;
   39 performances
With Herbert Berghof and Luther Adler
Produced by the Theatre Guild
Directed by Harold Clurman
set

THE FAMILY by Victor Wolfson
Windsor Theatre, March 30, 1943; 7 performances
With Lucile Watson and Carol Goodner
Produced by Oscar Serlin
Directed by Bretaigne Windus
set (costumes by Carolyn Hancock, lighting by
   Moe Hack)

THE RED POPPY, ballet by Igor Schwezoff (choreog-
   raphy and libretto) and Reinhold Glière (music)
Music Hall Theatre, Cleveland, Oct. 9, 1943
With Alexandra Danilova, Frederic Franklin,
   Ruthanna Boris, and Igor Youskevitch
Produced by the Ballet Russe de Monte Carlo
set, costumes

WHAT'S UP by Alan Jay Lerner and Arthur Pierson
   (book), Frederick Loewe (music), and Lerner
   (lyrics)
National Theatre (Nederlander Theatre),
   Nov. 11, 1943; 63 performances
With Jimmy Savo
Produced by Mark Warnow
Directed by George Balanchine and
   Robert H. Gordon
set (costumes by Grace Houston)

SOUTH PACIFIC by Howard Rigsby and
   Dorothy Heyward
Cort Theatre, Dec. 29, 1943; 5 performances
With Canada Lee
Produced by David Lowe
Directed by Lee Strasberg
set

MISS UNDERGROUND by Vernon Duke (music) and
  Lorenz Hart (lyrics)
unrealized project
With the Cristiani family
set

1944

PICTURES AT AN EXHIBITION, ballet by Bronislava
  Nijinska (choreography) and Modest Moussorgsky
  (music; orchestrated by Ivan Boutnikoff)
International Theatre, Columbus Circle; Nov. 3, 1944
With Katia Geleznova
Produced by Ballet International
set, costumes

SADIE THOMPSON by Howard Dietz and Rouben
  Mamoulian (book), Vernon Duke (music), and
  Dietz (lyrics)
Alvin Theatre (Neil Simon Theatre), Nov. 16, 1944;
  60 performances
With June Havoc
Produced by A. P. Waxman
Directed by Mamoulian
set (costumes by Motley)

1945

THE STRANGER by Leslie Reade
The Playhouse, Feb. 12, 1945; 16 performances
Produced by Shepard Traube
Directed by Traube
set, lighting (costumes by Rose Bogdanoff)

THE DESERT SONG by Otto Harbach (book, lyrics),
  Oscar Hammerstein II (book, lyrics), Frank Mandel
  (book), and Sigmund Romberg (music)
Philharmonic Auditorium, Los Angeles, April 30,
  1945
With Walter Cassel, Dorothy Sarnoff, and
  Sterling Holloway
Produced by Edwin Lester, Civic Light Opera
  Company
Directed by Holloway
set (costumes by Walter Israel, lighting by
  Adrian Awan)

THE ASSASSIN by Irwin Shaw
National Theatre (Nederlander Theatre), Oct. 17, 1945;
  13 performances
With Frank Sundstrom, Roger de Kovan, and
  Karl Malden
Produced by Carly Wharton and Martin Gabel
Directed by Gabel
set

1946

TRUCKLINE CAFÉ by Maxwell Anderson
Belasco Theatre, Feb. 27, 1946; 13 performances
With Virginia Gilmore, Richard Waring, and
    Marlon Brando
Produced by Harold Clurman, Elia Kazan, and the
    Playwrights' Company
Directed by Clurman
set (costumes by Millie Davenport)

THE FORTUNE TELLER (in New York, retitled
    GYPSY LADY) by Harry G. Smith (book and lyrics)
    and Victor Herbert (music)
Philharmonic Auditorium, Los Angeles
Century Theatre, Sept. 17, 1946; 79 performances
Produced by Edwin Lester, Civic Light Opera
    Company
Directed by Robert Wright and George Forrest
set (costumes by Miles White, lighting by
    Adrian Awan)

SWEET BYE AND BYE by S. J. Perelman and
    Al Hirschfeld (book), Vernon Duke (music), and
    Ogden Nash (lyrics)
Shubert Theatre, New Haven, Oct. 10, 1946;
    production did not reach New York
With Dolores Gray
Produced by Nat Karson
Directed by Curt Conway
set (costumes by Karson)

1947

THE BIG PEOPLE by Stanley Young
Lyric Theatre, Bridgeport, Conn., Sept. 20, 1947;
    production did not reach New York
With Ernest Truex
Produced by Theatre Incorporated
Directed by Martin Ritt
set (costumes by Rose Bogdanoff)

THE CHANGELING by Thomas Middleton and
    Thomas Rowley
unrealized project
With Beatrice Straight
Produced by Theatre Incorporated
Directed by Norris Houghton
set, costumes

1948

THE GOLDEN DOOR by Norman Rosten
unrealized project
Produced by Kermit Bloomgarden
set

SUNDOWN BEACH by Bessie Breuer
Produced by the Actors Studio
Directed by Elia Kazan
set (not used in final production)

SKIPPER NEXT TO GOD by Jan de Hartog
Maxine Elliott's Theatre, Jan. 4, 1948; 6 performances
With John Garfield
Produced by the Experimental Theatre
Directed by Lee Strasberg
set

THE SURVIVORS by Peter Viertel and Irwin Shaw
The Playhouse, Jan. 19, 1948; 8 performances
With Louis Calhern, Hume Cronyn, and
    Richard Basehart
Produced by Bernard Hart and Martin Gabel
Directed by Gabel
set, lighting (costumes by Rose Bogdanoff)

LOVE LIFE by Alan Jay Lerner (book and lyrics) and
    Kurt Weill (music)
46th Street Theatre, Oct. 7, 1948; 252 performances
With Nanette Fabray and Ray Middleton
Produced by Cheryl Crawford
Directed by Elia Kazan
set (costumes by Lucinda Ballard)

DETECTIVE STORY by Sidney Kingsley
Hudson Theatre, March 23, 1949; 581 performances
With Ralph Bellamy and Meg Mundy
Produced by Howard Lindsay and Russell Crouse
Directed by Kingsley
set (costumes by Millie Sutherland)

THE BIRD CAGE by Arthur Laurents
Coronet Theatre (Eugene O'Neill Theatre),
    Feb. 22, 1950; 21 performances
With Melvyn Douglas
Produced by Walter Fried and Lars Nordenson
Directed by Harold Clurman
set, lighting (costumes by Ben Edwards)

SEASON IN THE SUN by Wolcott Gibbs
Cort Theatre, Sept. 28, 1950; 367 performances
With Nancy Kelly and Richard Whorf
Produced by Courtney Burr and Malcolm Pearson
Directed by Burgess Meredith
set, lighting

THE COUNTRY GIRL by Clifford Odets
Lyceum Theatre, Nov. 10, 1950; 236 performances
With Uta Hagen, Paul Kelly, and Steven Hill
Produced by Dwight Deere Wiman
Directed by Odets
set, lighting (costumes by Anna Hill Johnstone)

THE ROSE TATTOO by Tennessee Williams
Martin Beck Theatre, Feb. 3, 1951; 306 performances
With Maureen Stapleton and Eli Wallach
Produced by Cheryl Crawford
Directed by Daniel Mann
set (costumes by Rose Bogdanoff, lighting by
  Charles Elson)

BAREFOOT IN ATHENS by Maxwell Anderson
Martin Beck Theatre, Oct. 31, 1951; 30 performances
With Barry Jones and Lotte Lenya
Produced by the Playwrights' Company
Directed by Alan Anderson
set, lighting (costumes by Bernard Rudofsky)

I AM A CAMERA by John van Druten
Empire Theatre; Nov. 28, 1951; 214 performances
With Julie Harris
Produced by Gertrude Macy and Walter Starcke
Directed by van Druten
set (costumes by Ellen Goldsborough)

LOVE AMONG THE RUINS by Elmer Rice
unrealized project
Produced by the Playwrights' Company
set

BALLADE, ballet by Jerome Robbins (choreography)
  and Claude Debussy (music)
New York City Center; Feb. 14, 1952
With Nora Kaye, Tanaquil LeClerq, Janet Reed, and
  Robert Barnett
Produced by the New York City Ballet
set, costumes

I'VE GOT SIXPENCE by John van Druten
Ethel Barrymore Theatre, Dec. 2, 1952;
  23 performances
With Viveca Lindfors, Edmond O'Brien, and
  Patricia Collinge
Produced by Gertrude Macy and Walter Starcke
Directed by van Druten
set (costumes: supervision by Burton J. Miller)

1953

THE CRUCIBLE by Arthur Miller
Martin Beck Theatre, Jan. 22, 1953; 197 performances
With E. G. Marshall, Beatrice Straight,
    Walter Hampden, and Madeleine Sherwood
Produced by Kermit Bloomgarden
Directed by Jed Harris
set (costumes by Edith Lutyens)

MY 3 ANGELS by Sam and Bella Spewack
Morosco Theatre, March 11, 1953; 344 performances
With Jerome Cowan, Walter Slezak, and
    Darren McGavin
Produced by Arnold Saint-Subber, Rita Allen,
    and Archie Thomson
Directed by José Ferrer
set (costumes by Lucinda Ballard)

THE FROGS OF SPRING by Nathaniel Benchley
Broadhurst Theatre, Oct. 20, 1953; 15 performances
With Anthony Ross, Hiram Sherman, Haila Stoddard,
    and Barbara Baxley
Produced by Lyn Austin, Thomas Noyes,
    Robert Sagalyn, and Robert Radnitz
Directed by Burgess Meredith
set, lighting (costumes by Alvin Colt)

1954

MADEMOISELLE COLOMBE by Jean Anouilh
Longacre Theatre, Jan. 6, 1954; 61 performances
With Julie Harris, Eli Wallach, and Edna Best
Produced by Robert I. Joseph and Jay Julien
Directed by Harold Clurman
set (costumes by Motley)

1955

THE MASTER BUILDER by Henrik Ibsen
Phoenix Theatre, March 1, 1955; 40 performances
With Oscar Homolka and Joan Tetzel
Produced by T. Edward Hambleton and
    Norris Houghton
Directed by Homolka
set (costumes by Alvin Colt, lighting by
    Lester Polakov)

BUS STOP by William Inge
Music Box Theatre, March 2, 1955; 478 performances
With Kim Stanley, Anthony Ross, Elaine Stritch, and
    Albert Salmi
Produced by Robert Whitehead and Roger Stevens
Directed by Harold Clurman
set (costumes and lighting by Paul Morrison)

ONCE UPON A TAILOR by Baruch Lumet
Cort Theatre, May 23, 1955; 8 performances
With Oscar Karlweis
Produced by the Playwrights' Company and
    George Boroff
Directed by Joseph Anthony
set (costumes and lighting by Paul Morrison)

A VIEW FROM THE BRIDGE, A MEMORY OF TWO
    MONDAYS (previously titled TWO NEW PLAYS)
    by Arthur Miller
Coronet Theatre (Eugene O'Neill Theatre),
    Sept. 29, 1955; 149 performances
With Van Heflin and Eileen Heckart
Produced by Kermit Bloomgarden and
    Robert Whitehead–Roger Stevens
Directed by Martin Ritt
set (costumes by Helene Pons, lighting by
    Leland Watson)

THE DIARY OF ANNE FRANK by Frances Goodrich
    and Albert Hackett
Cort Theatre, Oct. 5, 1955; 717 performances
With Joseph Schildkraut, Gusti Huber, and
    Susan Strasberg
Produced by Kermit Bloomgarden
Directed by Garson Kanin
set (costumes by Helene Pons, lighting by
    Leland Watson)

DANCING IN THE CHEQUERED SHADE by
    John van Druten
McCarter Theatre, Princeton, N.J., Dec. 20, 1955;
    production did not reach New York
Produced by Walter Starcke
Directed by van Druten
set (costumes by Ruth Morley, lighting by
    Leland Watson)

1956

GIRLS OF SUMMER by N. Richard Nash
Longacre Theatre, Nov. 19, 1956; 56 performances
With Shelley Winters, George Peppard, and
    Pat Hingle
Produced by Cheryl Crawford
Directed by Jack Garfein
set (costumes by Kenn Barr, lighting by
    Leland Watson)

1957

SMALL WAR ON MURRAY HILL by
    Robert E. Sherwood
Ethel Barrymore Theatre, Jan. 3, 1957;
    12 performances
With Jan Sterling and Leo Genn
Produced by the Playwrights' Company
Directed by Garson Kanin
set (costumes by Irene Sharaff)

A HOLE IN THE HEAD by Arnold Schulman
Plymouth Theatre, Feb. 28, 1957; 156 performances
With Paul Douglas and Lee Grant
Produced by the Producers Theatre
Directed by Garson Kanin
set (costumes by Patton Campbell, lighting by
    Jean Rosenthal)

ORPHEUS DESCENDING by Tennessee Williams
Martin Beck Theatre, March 21, 1957;
  68 performances
With Maureen Stapleton and Cliff Robertson
Produced by the Producers Theatre
Directed by Harold Clurman
set (costumes by Lucinda Ballard, lighting by
  Abe Feder)

THE ROPE DANCERS by Morton Wishengrad
Cort Theatre, Nov. 20, 1957; 189 performances
With Siobhan McKenna, Art Carney, Joan Blondell,
  and Theodore Bikel
Produced by the Playwrights' Company and
  Gilbert Miller
Directed by Peter Hall
set (costumes by Patricia Zipprodt)

1958

THIS IS GOGGLE by Bentz Plagemann
McCarter Theatre, Princeton, N.J., Jan. 23, 1958;
  production did not reach New York
With Kim Hunter and James Daly
Produced by Otto Preminger
Directed by Preminger
set (costumes by Anna Hill Johnstone, lighting by
  Leland Watson)

THE FIRSTBORN by Christopher Fry
Coronet Theatre (Eugene O'Neill Theatre),
  April 30, 1958; 38 performances
With Katharine Cornell and Anthony Quayle
Produced by Roger Stevens and Cornell
Directed by Quayle
set (costumes by Robert Fletcher, lighting by
  Tharon Musser)

THE COLD WIND AND THE WARM by
  S. N. Behrman
Morosco Theatre, Dec. 8, 1958; 120 performances
With Eli Wallach and Maureen Stapleton
Produced by the Producers Theatre,
  A Robert Whitehead Production
Directed by Harold Clurman
set (costumes by Motley, lighting by Abe Feder)

J.B. by Archibald MacLeish
ANTA Theatre (Virginia Theatre); Dec. 11, 1958;
  364 performances
With Christopher Plummer, Raymond Massey, and
  Pat Hingle
Produced by Alfred de Liagre
Directed by Elia Kazan
set (costumes by Lucinda Ballard, lighting by
  Tharon Musser)

1959

CORIOLANUS by William Shakespeare
Shakespeare Memorial Theatre, Stratford-on-Avon,
  England; July 7, 1959
With Laurence Olivier, Edith Evans, Mary Ure,
  Vanessa Redgrave, Albert Finney, and
  Harry Andrews
Directed by Peter Hall
set (costumes by Riette Sturge Moore)

FLOWERING CHERRY by Robert Bolt
Lyceum Theatre, Oct. 21, 1959; 5 performances
With Wendy Hiller and Eric Portman
Produced by the Playwrights' Company and
    Don Herbert
Directed by Frith Banbury
set (costumes by Theoni V. Aldredge, lighting by
    Paul Morrison)

A LOSS OF ROSES by William Inge
Eugene O'Neill Theatre, Nov. 28, 1959;
    25 performances
With Betty Field, Warren Beatty, and Carol Haney
Produced by Arnold Saint-Subber and
    Lester Osterman
Directed by Daniel Mann
set (costumes by Lucinda Ballard, lighting by
    Abe Feder)

1960

SEMI-DETACHED by Patricia Joudry
Martin Beck Theatre, March 10, 1960;
    4 performances
With Ed Begley
Produced by Philip Rose
Directed by Charles S. Dubin
set (costumes by Helene Pons, lighting by
    Klaus Holm)

DO RE MI by Garson Kanin (book), Jule Styne
    (music), and Betty Comden and
    Adolph Green (lyrics)
St. James Theatre, Dec. 26, 1960; 400 performances
With Phil Silvers and Nancy Walker
Produced by David Merrick
Directed by Garson Kanin
set (costumes by Irene Sharaff)

THE QUEEN AND THE REBELS by Ugo Betti
unrealized project
With Viveca Lindfors
Produced by Marilyn Shapiro
Directed by Gene Frankel
set

1961

THE GARDEN OF SWEETS by Waldemar Hansen
ANTA Theatre (Virginia Theatre); Oct 31, 1961;
    1 performance
With Katina Paxinou
Produced by Ben Frye and Irving Squires
Directed by Milton Katselas
set (costumes by Patricia Zipprodt, lighting by
    Tharon Musser)

1962

A GIFT OF TIME by Garson Kanin
Ethel Barrymore Theatre, Feb. 22, 1962;
    92 performances
With Henry Fonda and Olivia de Havilland
Produced by William Hammerstein, David Shaber,
    and William Snyder
Directed by Garson Kanin
set (costumes by Edith Lutyens, lighting by
    Jean Rosenthal)

JUDITH by Jean Giraudoux
Her Majesty's Theatre, London, June 20, 1962
With Ruth Meyers and Sean Connery
Produced by Roger Stevens, William Zeckendorf,
    and H. M. Tennent Ltd.
Directed by Harold Clurman
set (costumes by Freddy Wittop)

1963

ANDORRA by Max Frisch
Biltmore Theatre, Feb. 9, 1963; 9 performances
With Horst Buchholz
Produced by Cheryl Crawford and Roger Stevens
Directed by Michael Langham
set (costumes by Ray Diffen, lighting by
   Tharon Musser)

1964

FIDDLER ON THE ROOF by Joseph Stein (book),
   Jerry Bock (music), and Sheldon Harnick (lyrics)
Imperial Theatre, Sept. 22, 1964; 3,242 performances
With Zero Mostel, Maria Karnilova, and
   Beatrice Arthur
Produced by Harold Prince
Directed and choreographed by Jerome Robbins
set (costumes by Patricia Zipprodt, lighting by
   Jean Rosenthal)

INCIDENT AT VICHY by Arthur Miller
ANTA Washington Square Theatre, Dec. 3, 1964;
   99 performances
With Hal Holbrook and Joseph Wiseman
Produced by the Repertory Company of Lincoln
   Center (Elia Kazan, Robert Whitehead)
Directed by Harold Clurman
set (costumes by Jane Greenwood, lighting by
   Jean Rosenthal)

1965

L'HISTOIRE DU SOLDAT by Igor Stravinsky (music),
   C. F. Ramuz (libretto), and Anna Sokolow
   (choreography)
Grand Ballroom, Waldorf-Astoria Hotel, Jan. 24, 1965
Produced by the America-Israel Cultural Foundation
Staged by Jerome Robbins
set (costumes by Patricia Zipprodt, lighting by
   Richard Casler)

1966

CABARET by Joe Masteroff (book), John Kander
   (music), and Fred Ebb (lyrics)
Broadhurst Theatre, Nov. 20, 1966;
   1,165 performances
With Jill Haworth, Lotte Lenya, Bert Convy,
   Jack Gilford, and Joel Grey
Produced by Harold Prince and Ruth Mitchell
Directed by Prince
set (costumes by Patricia Zipprodt, lighting by
   Jean Rosenthal)

1967

MOURNING BECOMES ELECTRA, opera by
   Marvin David Levy (music) and Henry Butler
   (libretto)
Metropolitan Opera House; March 17, 1967
With Evelyn Lear, Marie Collier, John Reardon, and
   Sherrill Milnes
Produced by the Metropolitan Opera Association
Directed by Michael Cacoyannis
set, costumes

1968

THE PRICE by Arthur Miller
Morosco Theatre, Feb. 7, 1968; 429 performances
With Kate Reid, Harold Gary, Arthur Kennedy, and
  Pat Hingle
Produced by Robert Whitehead and
  Robert W. Dowling
Directed by Ulu Grosbard
set, costumes (lighting by Paul Morrison)

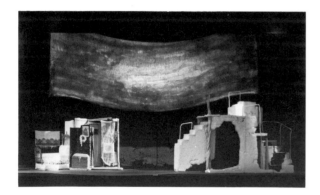

ZORBA by Joseph Stein (book), John Kander (music),
  and Fred Ebb (lyrics)
Imperial Theatre, Nov. 17, 1968; 305 performances
With Herschel Bernardi and Maria Karnilova
Produced by Harold Prince and Ruth Mitchell
Directed by Prince
set (costumes by Patricia Zipprodt, lighting by
  Richard Pilbrow)

1970

COMPANY by George Furth (book) and
  Stephen Sondheim (music and lyrics)
Alvin Theatre (Neil Simon Theatre); April 26, 1970;
  705 performances
With Dean Jones and Elaine Stritch
Produced by Harold Prince and Ruth Mitchell
Directed by Prince
set (costumes by D. D. Ryan, lighting by
  Robert Ornbo)

FIDELIO, opera by Ludwig van Beethoven (music)
  and Joseph Sonnleithner (libretto)
Metropolitan Opera House, Dec. 16, 1970
With Leonie Rysanek, Judith Blegen, Jon Vickers,
  Walter Berry, and Giorgio Tozzi
Produced by the Metropolitan Opera Association
Directed by Otto Schenk
set, costumes

1971

FOLLIES by James Goldman (book) and
  Stephen Sondheim (music and lyrics)
Winter Garden Theatre, April 4, 1971;
  521 performances
With Alexis Smith, Dorothy Collins, Gene Nelson,
  and John McMartin
Produced by Harold Prince and Ruth Mitchell
Directed by Prince and Michael Bennett
set (costumes by Florence Klotz, lighting by
  Tharon Musser)

1972

THE CREATION OF THE WORLD AND OTHER
  BUSINESS by Arthur Miller
Shubert Theatre, Nov. 30, 1972; 20 performances
With Bob Dishy and Zoe Caldwell
Produced by Robert Whitehead
Directed by Gerald Freedman
set, projections (costumes by Hal George, lighting by
  Tharon Musser)

THE GREAT GOD BROWN by Eugene O'Neill
Lyceum Theatre, Dec. 10, 1972; 19 performances
With John Glover
Produced by the New Phoenix Repertory Theatre
 (T. Edward Hambleton)
Directed by Harold Prince
set (costumes by Carolyn Parker, lighting by
 Tharon Musser)

1973

A LITTLE NIGHT MUSIC by Hugh Wheeler (book)
 and Stephen Sondheim (music and lyrics)
Shubert Theatre; Feb. 25, 1973; 600 performances
With Glynis Johns, Len Cariou, and
 Hermione Gingold
Produced by Harold Prince and Ruth Mitchell
Directed by Prince
set (costumes by Florence Klotz, lighting by
 Tharon Musser)

1974

THE TZADDIK, ballet by Eliot Feld (choreography),
 and Aaron Copland (music)
Newman Theatre (New York Shakespeare Festival),
 May 29, 1974
With Feld, Richard Gilmore, and Jeff Satinoff
Produced by the Eliot Feld Ballet
set, costumes (lighting by Jennifer Tipton)

1975

DREYFUS IN REHEARSAL by Jean-Claude Grumberg
Ethel Barrymore Theatre, Oct. 17, 1974;
 12 performances
With Ruth Gordon, Sam Levene, and
 Tovah Feldshuh
Produced by David Merrick
Directed by Garson Kanin
set (costumes by Florence Klotz, lighting by
 Jennifer Tipton)

1976

PACIFIC OVERTURES by John Weidman (book) and
 Stephen Sondheim (music and lyrics)
Winter Garden Theatre, Oct. 11, 1976;
 193 performances
Produced by Harold Prince and Ruth Mitchell
Directed by Prince
set (costumes by Florence Klotz, lighting by
 Tharon Musser)

THE NUTCRACKER, ballet by Tchaikovsky (music)
 and Mikhail Baryshnikov (choreography)
Kennedy Center, Washington, D. C.
With Baryshnikov, Marianna Tcherkassky, and
 Alexander Minz
Produced by American Ballet Theatre
set (costumes by Frank Thompson; lighting by
 Jennifer Tipton)

1977

THE NUTCRACKER, ballet by Tchaikovsky (music)
 and Mikhail Baryshnikov (choreography)
CBS Television
With Baryshnikov, Gelsey Kirkland, and
 Alexander Minz
set (costumes by Frank Thompson)

Bibliography

The editions listed are those consulted by the authors, not necessarily the originals. Unbylined newspaper articles are listed by name of publication; in some cases it has been impossible to ascertain the date or title, if any, of a newspaper article. Yiddish titles are given in English translation.

ALTMAN, RICHARD, WITH MERVYN KAUFMAN. *The Making of a Musical: "Fiddler on the Roof."* New York: Crown, 1971.

AMBERG, GEORGE. *Ballet: The Emergence of an American Art.* New York: Mentor, 1949.

ARONSON, BORIS. "Costume in the Yiddish Theatre." [1923?] (in Yiddish).

———. "Designing *Sweet Bye and Bye.*" *Theatre Arts*, October 1946.

———. *Marc Chagall.* Berlin: Petropolis, 1923 (in Russian), 1924 (in German).

———. "The Modern Art: An Expression." [1920?] (in Yiddish).

———. "Trends: Constructivism and an Egg (Impressions of the International Theater Exposition)." *The Hammer*, April 1926 (in Yiddish).

———, et al. "The Theatre Takes Stock: A Discussion of the Vital Problems of Today's Theatre." *Theatre Arts*, May 1940.

ATKINSON, BROOKS. [Essay on *Detective Story.*] *New York Times*, April 3, 1949.

AUER, JAMES. "*Pacific Overtures:* Another Miracle for Set Designer Aronson." *Milwaukee Journal*, March 14, 1976.

AULICINO, ARMAND. "How *The Country Girl* Came About." *Theatre Arts*, May 1952.

BABLET, DENIS, ED. *Les Voies de la création théâtrale.* Vol. 7, *Mises en scène, années 20 et 30.* Paris: Éditions du Centre National de la Recherche Scientifique, 1979.

BAKER, ROBB. "*Follies:* Broadway Finds Art in Its Own Past." *Chicago Daily News*, April 17–18, 1971.

BANN, STEPHEN, ED. *The Documents of 20th-Century Art: The Tradition of Constructivism.* New York: Viking Press, 1974.

BARNETT, ELLA. "Art and the Yiddish Theatre." *New York Sun*, November 20, 1926.

BARRY, JOSEPH A. "Free Taste: The American Style of the Future." *House Beautiful*, October 1952.

BASINGER, JEANINE, ET AL., EDS. *Working with Kazan.* Middletown, Conn.: Wesleyan University Press, 1973.

BEAUFORT, JOHN. [Interview with Aronson.] *Christian Science Monitor*, June 28, 1947.

———. [Interview with Aronson.] *Christian Science Monitor*, May 16, 1959.

BENTLEY, ERIC. [Review of *Mademoiselle Colombe.*] *The New Republic*, January 25, 1954.

———. *What Is Theatre?* New York: Atheneum, 1968.

BLUME, MARY. "After 50 years and 100 Set Designs." *International Herald Tribune*, July 11–12, 1970.

BOTTO, LOUIS. "Boris Aronson: Designs for a Princely Musical." *Playbill*, May, 1973.

BRAUN, EDWARD. *The Theatre of Meyerhold: Revolution on the Modern Stage.* New York: Drama Book Specialists, 1979.

BROWN, JOHN MASON, ET AL. *Art in the Theatre: An Exhibit by B. Aronson.* New York: Anderson Galleries, 1927.

CAMPBELL, MARY. [Interview with Aronson.] Associated Press, December 26, 1970.

———. "Aronson Designs Intimate, Germanic *Fidelio.*" Associated Press, December 26, 1970.

CLURMAN, HAROLD. *All People Are Famous.* New York: Harcourt Brace Jovanovich, 1974.

———. "A Director Prepares." *Theatre Arts*, April 1963.

———. *The Fervent Years.* Rev. ed. New York: Hill and Wang, 1957.

———. *The Naked Image: Observations on the Modern Theatre.* New York: Macmillan, 1966.

———. *On Directing.* New York: Macmillan, 1972.

COHEN, RONNY H. "Alexandra Exter's Designs for the Theatre." *Artforum*, Summer 1981.

CROSBY, JOHN. [Interview with Aronson.] *New York Herald Tribune*, December 22, 1961.

Dance Observer. [Review of Aronson's Museum of Modern Art exhibit, bylined "G.L."] August–September 1947.

DENBY, EDWIN. [Review of *Pictures at an Exhibition.*] *New York Herald Tribune*, November 4, 1944.

DOWNING, ROBERT. "*J.B.*'s Journeys." *Theatre Arts*, February 1960.

DUKE, VERNON. *Passport to Paris.* Boston: Little, Brown, 1955.

FREED, CLARENCE I. "The Changing Scene: Leaders of the Modern Trend in Stage Design and Decoration." *American Hebrew*, March 23, 1928.

FÜLÖP-MILLER, RENÉ, AND JOSEPH GREGOR. *The Russian Theatre.* New York: Benjamin Blom, 1968. [Originally published in London in 1930.]

FUNKE, LEWIS. "The Rialto." *New York Times*, December 31, 1967.

GENAUER, EMILY, ET AL. *American Ballet Theatre: Thirty Six Years of Scenic and Costume Design, 1940–1976.* New York: Ballet Theatre Foundation and the International Exhibitions Foundation, 1976.

GEORGE, WALDEMAR. *Boris Aronson et L'art du théâtre.* Paris: Chroniques du Jour, 1928.

GLASSGOLD, C. ADOLPH. "Art in the Theatre: Boris Aronson." *The Arts*, January 1928.

GLENNY, MICHAEL, ED. *The Golden Age of Soviet Theatre.* New York: Penguin Books, 1981.

GRAY, CAMILLA. *The Great Experiment: Russian Art, 1863–1922.* London: Thames and Hudson, 1962.

GREEN, HARRIS. "When Will They Stage Opera for Its Music?" *New York Times*, August 22, 1971.

GROVER, STEPHEN. "Bringing a New Show to the Broadway Stage Is High Drama in Itself." *Wall Street Journal*, February 27, 1973.

———. "Building Stage Sets Involves Much More Than Meets the Eye." *Wall Street Journal*, February 26, 1975.

GRUEN, JOHN. "Baryshnikov Tries His Hand at Choreography." *New York Times*, December 19, 1976.

GUERNSEY, OTIS L., JR., ED. *Broadway Song & Story.* New York: Dodd, Mead, 1985.

GUSSOW, MEL. "Prince Revels in *A Little Night Music.*" *New York Times*, March 27, 1973.

HAGUE, ROBERT A. [Review of *Pictures at an Exhibition*]. *PM*, November 5, 1944.

HENDERSON, MARY C. *The City and the Theatre.* Clifton, N.J.: James T. White, 1973.

HOUGHTON, NORRIS. *Moscow Rehearsals: The Golden Age of the Soviet Theatre.* New York: Harcourt, Brace, 1936.

HOWE, IRVING. *World of Our Fathers.* New York: Harcourt Brace Jovanovich, 1976.

HOWELL, BETJE. "A Visual Experience." *Los Angeles Herald Examiner*, September 26, 1976.

INGE, BENSON. [Interview with Aronson.] *New York Herald Tribune*, November 17, 1940.

JENKINS, SPEIGHT. "The Stage Picture." *Opera News*, January 2, 1971.

KANIN, GARSON. "Dialogue from Boris Aronson in Conversation with Garson Kanin." [Videotaped interview, March 20, 1975.] Theatre Collection, New York Public Library at Lincoln Center.

KAUFMAN, WOLFE. "The Story of *Love Life.*" *Love Life* souvenir program, 1948.

KEAN, BEVERLY WHITNEY. *All the Empty Palaces: The Merchant Patrons of Modern Art in Pre-Revolutionary Russia.* New York: Universe Books, 1983.

KENT, LETICIA. "On Broadway, the Spectacle's the Thing." *New York Times*, March 12, 1978.

KERR, WALTER. [Review of *Cabaret*.] *New York Times*, November 21, 1966.

KOLODIN, IRVING. [Review of *The Snow Maiden*.] *New York Sun*, October 13, 1942.

LAND. [Review of *Follies*.] *Variety*, April 7, 1971.

LEE, M. OWEN. "More Than an Opera." *Opera News*, February 2, 1980.

LEONARD, WILLIAM TORBERT. *Broadway Bound: A Guide to Shows That Died Aborning.* Metuchen, N.J.: Scarecrow, 1983.

LEWIS, EMORY. "He Sets the Stage and Mood." *Sunday Bergen (N.J.) Record*, May 23, 1971.

LIFSON, DAVID S. *The Yiddish Theatre in America.* New York: Thomas Yoseloff, 1965.

LITTLE, STUART. [Interview with Aronson.] *New York Herald Tribune*, December 22, 1961.

MACGOWAN, KENNETH. "Stagecraft Shows Its Newest Heresies." *The New York Times Magazine*, February 14, 1926.

MALCOLM, ANDREW H. "Graffiti, 141 Giant Eyes Along River Bank, Hint at Changing Japan." *New York Times*, November 10, 1977.

MANTLE, BURNS, ET AL., EDS. *Best Plays.* New York: Dodd, Mead, 1932–77.

MARLATT, HARRY. "Scene Painting with Light: New Techniques Challenge Realism in the Theatre." *Musical Digest*, September 1947.

MARTIN, JOHN. [Review of *Pictures at an Exhibition*.] *New York Times*, November 4, 1944.

MICHELMAN, FRAN. "Boris Aronson, Painter and Stage Designer: *The Nutcracker*." *On Point*, Fall 1976.

MIELZINER, JO. *Designing for the Theatre.* New York: Atheneum, 1965.

MILLER, MARGO. "The Making of a Set." *Boston Sunday Globe*, October 27, 1968.

MILLIER, JEAN, ET AL. *Paris–Moscou, 1900–30.* Paris: Centre Georges Pompidou, 1979.

MITCHELL, ROBERT. Unpublished essay on Boris Aronson.

NACHMAN, GERALD. [Interview with Aronson.] *New York Post*, February 17, 1965.

NAKOV, ANDRÉI B. *Alexandra Exter.* Paris: Galerie Jean Chauvelin, 1972.

New York Herald Tribune. [Interview with Aronson.] July 3, 1949.

New York Times. [Interview with Aronson.] December 26, 1929.

———— [Interview with Aronson.] October 27, 1940.

OENSLAGER, DONALD. *Stage Design: Four Centuries of Scenic Invention.* New York: Viking, 1974.

————, ET AL. *Artist of the Theatre: Alexandra Exter.* New York Public Library, 1974.

Opera News. "Mourning Becomes an Opera." [Bylined "F.S."] April 1, 1967.

OSBORN, MAX. [Interview with Aronson.] *Palestine Post*, December 8, 1933.

PARKER, H.T. [Review of *Walk a Little Faster*.] *Boston Evening Transcript*, November 25, 1932.

PENDLETON, RALPH, ED. *The Theatre of Robert Edmond Jones.* Middletown, Conn.: Wesleyan University Press, 1958.

PRINCE, HAROLD S. *Contradictions: Notes on Twenty-six Years in the Theatre.* New York: Dodd, Mead, 1974.

"PROTEUS" [pseudonym]. "Jewish Ballet." *Midstream*, August–September 1974.

RASCOE, BURTON. [Interview with Aronson.] *New York World Telegram and Sun.* February 17, 1945.

REINHARDT, GOTTFRIED. *The Genius.* New York: Knopf, 1979.

ROOSE-EVANS, JAMES. *Experimental Theatre: From Stanislavsky to Today.* New York: Avon, 1971.

RUDNITSKY, KONSTANTIN. *Meyerhold the Director.* Ann Arbor, Mich.: Ardis, 1981.

SANDERS, RONALD. *The Days Grow Short: The Life and Music of Kurt Weill.* New York: Holt, Rinehart and Winston, 1980.

SHANLEY, J. P. [Interview with Aronson.] *New York Times*, November 26, 1950.

SIMONSON, LEE. [Review of *L'Art du théâtre* by Waldemar George.] *The Nation*, June 12, 1929.

————. *The Stage Is Set.* New York: Harcourt, Brace, 1932.

The Stage. [Review of *Coriolanus*, bylined "E.J.".] July 16, 1959.

STEINBERG, DAVID. [Review of Aronson's Museum of Modern Art exhibit.] *Newark News*, July 27, 1947.

TAIROFF, ALEXANDER. *Das entfesselte Theater: Aufzeichnungen eines Regisseurs.* Potsdam: Gustav Kiepenheuer Verlag, 1923.

TERRY, WALTER. "Impossible Dream." *Ballet News*, May 1980.

Theatre Arts Monthly. [Review of *The Tenth Commandment*.] January 19, 1927.

————"The Men Behind *J.B.*" April 1959.

Theatre Crafts. "Pacific Overtures: Veteran Designer Boris Aronson Creates a Personal View of 19th-century Japan." January–February 1976.

Time. [Review of *The Great American Goof*.] January 22, 1940.

TOLLER, ERNST, ET AL. *Das moskauer judische akademische Theater.* Berlin: Verlag/Die Schmiede, 1928.

TRAUBE, SHEPARD. "Boris Aronson." *Theatre Guild Magazine*, January 1931.

TYNAN, KENNETH. *Curtains.* New York: Atheneum, 1961.

WATERHOUSE, ROBERT. "Direction and Design, the Partners, no. 4: Two's Company." *Plays and Players*, March 1972.

WELSH, ANNE MARIE. "How This *Nutcracker* Is Different—and Why." *Washington Star*, December 22, 1976.

WHITTAKER, HERBERT. [Interview with Aronson.] *Toronto Globe and Mail*, January 17, 1970.

WILLARD, CHARLES. "Life's 'Progress': *Love Life* Revisited." *Kurt Weill Newsletter*, Fall 1984.

WOOD, THOR E., ET AL. *Boris Aronson: From His Theatre Work.* New York Public Library, 1981.

YOUNG, STARK. *The Theatre.* New York: Hill and Wang, 1958.

Index

Photographic Credits

COLLECTION OF LISA ARONSON: 8; 9 (center and right); 11 (right above); 14 (right above); 16; 18 (right above); 24; 27 (below)—Photo by Halley Erskine; 33; 35 (left above center and below); 36 (above); 38; 39 (right center); 42; 43; 44 (below); 45 (above and below); 46; 49; 50; 51; 52; 61 (above); 65 (right above)—Photo by Alfredo Valente; 67 (below)—Photo by Alfredo Valente; 70 (left above)—Theatre Collection of The Museum of Modern Art; 71; 72; 78; 82 (right center); 83 (above and below)—Photos by Fred Fehl; 84 (left); 90 (below)—Photo by Vandamm; 92 (below) —Photo by Vandamm; 98 (above)—Photo by Arnold Weissberger; 100 (below); 101; 112 (below)—Photo by The Art Institute of Chicago; 119 (below); 122—Life photo by Gordon Parks; 125 (above)—Photo by Maria Austria, Particam Pictures; 126 (left above and below) —Photo by Henk Jonker, Particam Pictures; 128 (right)—Photo by Henk Jonker, Particam Pictures; 130 (below); 134—Photo by Angus McBean; 144 (above)—Life photo by Robert Frank; 146; 150 (above); 152 (below)—Photo by Angus McBean; 154 (below); 155 (above); 178—Photo by Eileen Darby; 180 (below) —Photo by Eileen Darby; 181 (below)—Photo by Chris J. Arthur; 182 (below); 183—Photo by Toho Company; 184—Photo by Chris J. Arthur; 190—Photo by Chris J. Arthur; 191 (above)—Photo by Friedman-Abeles, (below)—Photos by Arnold Weissberger; 193 (above)—Photo by Chris J. Arthur; 195 (above)—Photo by Chris J. Arthur, (below)—Photo by Arnold Weissberger; 196—Photo by Chris J. Arthur; 197 (above)—Photo by Chris J. Arthur; 198 (right above and below)—Photo by Arnold Weissberger; 200; 201 (below)—Photo by Arnold Weissberger; 206 (below) —Photo by Arnold Weissberger; 208 (left below)— Photo by Louis Melancou; 209—Photo by Louis Melancou; 211—Photo by Louis Melancou; 212 (above); 215; 216 (top); 217 (above and right); 218; 221 (below); 227 (left); 233 (right above); 234; 236 (left below); 252 (above); 253 (below)—Photo by Arnold Weissberger; 254 (below)—Photo by Arnold Weissberger; 258—Photo by Theater Van der Wien; 259 (above)—Photo by Theater Van der Wien; 265— Photo by Martha Swope; 269 (above)—Photo by Martha Swope; 272 (left above); 277 (below)—Photo by Stephany Durkins; 279 (below); 287 (below)— Photo by Arnold Weissberger; 293; 294; 295 (left above)—Photo by Vandamm, (right below)—Photo by Lincoln Center Library; 296 (left below and center below)—Photos by Vandamm, (right above)—Photo by The Museum of Modern Art; 297 (center below) —Photo by Life magazine, (right below)—Photo by Fred Fehl; 298 (center above, center below and right above)—Photos by Fred Fehl; 299 (left below)—Photo by Fred Fehl; 300 (left above)—Photo by Fred Fehl; 301; 302 (center above)—Photo by John Seymoor Erwin; 303 (center below)—Photo by Library at Lincoln Center, (right above)—Photo by Galbraith; 304 (center below)—Photo by Friedman-Abeles, (left above and below, right above and below)—Photos by Galbraith; 305 (left above)—Photo by Galbraith, (center above)—Photo by Vandamm, (right above)— Photo by M. Sekita, (right below)—Photo by Angus McBean; 306 (left above)—Photo by Friedman-Abeles, (center above)—Photo by Arnold Weissberger, (right below)—Photo by Angus McBean; 307 (left below)—Photo by Eileen Darby, (center above) —Photo by Inge Morath, (left above, center below, right below)—Photos by Galbraith; 308 (right below) —Photo by Inge Morath, (left above and below, center above and below, right above)—Photos by Galbraith; 309 (right above)—Photo by Z. Dominic, (left above, center above and below)—Photos by Galbraith, (left below and right below)—Photos by Martha Swope.

COURTESY OF CAMERA FIVE—KEN REGAN AND CHRIS-TOPHER LITTLE: 284 (right above and below); 285; 286 (below); 289.

COURTESY OF ZOE DOMINIC: 175 (left below); 177; 182 (above); 193 (below); 197 (below); 225 (below); 256; 259 (below); 263; 267 (right below); 271; 273; 274; 276 (below).

COURTESY OF ROBERT GALBRAITH: 11 (left); 18 (left above and right below); 19 (below); 20 (left above and right); 27 (above); 28 (below); 41 (right above); 44 (left above and right center); 110; 111; 115; 116 (below); 119 (above); 120; 125 (below); 126 (right above and below); 127; 128 (left); 131 (below); 132; 138; 141; 142; 143; 150 (below); 153 (above); 155 (below); 158; 159; 160; 161; (below); 162 (above); 164 (right above)—Photo by The Whitney Museum, (below); 168 (above and below); 170; 173; 176 (above); 180 (above); 185; 186; 201; 202; 203; 204; 205; 206 (above); 208 (above); 213; 214; 216 (below); 217 (below); 220 (above and center); 222; 224; 225 (above); 226; 229; 236 (above and right below); 239; 240; 241; 242; 243 (above and below); 244; 245; 246; 248; 250; 252 (below); 272 (right above and below); 279 (above); 283; 284 (left above, center and below); 286 (left above); 287 (left above); 288 (below).

PHOTOGRAPHED BY TONY HOLMES: 6; 7; 9 (left); 14 (left above and right below); 17; 19 (above); 30 (left below), 32 (above and center); 34; 35 (right); 37; 39 (left above and below); 40; 41; 48; 59 (right below); 64; 67 (above); 70 (left below and right above and below); 74; 75 (above and below center and right); 76; 77 (above); 79 (right below); 80; 81; 82 (left above and right); 83 (below); 84 (right); 86; 87 (left above and right); 88 (left above and right); 89; 90 (above); 91; 92 (above); 93; 94; 96 (above); 98 (below); 99; 100 (above); 102; 104; 105 (above); 106; 107; 108; 114; 116 (above); 118; 123; 130 (above); 131 (above); 133; 137; 144 (below); 148; 149 (above and left); 152 (above); 153 (below); 154 (above); 156; 161 (above); 164 (left above); 167; 172; 174; 175 (right below and above); 176 (center and below) 179; 181 (above); 189; 192; 194; 198 (left above); 208 (right below); 210; 212 (below); 221 (above); 235; 253 (above); 260; 262 (above and below); 264; 267 (left); 270; 277 (above); 280; 282; 290 (above).

COURTESY OF LIFE MAGAZINE: 77—Photo by George Karger; 103—Photo by Eliot Elisofon; 105 (below)— Photo by Gjon Mili; 113—Photo by Leonard McCombe; 233 (left)—Photo by Eliot Elisofon.

COURTESY OF INGE MORATH: 162 (below); 165; 169.

COURTESY OF THE MUSEUM OF THE CITY OF NEW YORK: 36 (below); 81 (center); 149 (right below); 151.

COURTESY OF THE NEW YORK PUBLIC LIBRARY: 32 (below); 54; 55; 58; 59 (above and left below); 61 (right below); 62 (above and right below); 65 (right below); 87 (below); 88 (below left and right)—Photos by Vandamm; 96 (below); 109; 117.

COURTESY OF MIKIO SEKITA: 20 (below); 233; 238.

COURTESY OF MARTHA SWOPE: 22 (top); 227 (above and below); 247; 249; 254 (above); 255; 257; 266; 267 (right above); 268; 269 (below); 272 (center); 275; 276 (above); 277 (right); 278; 290.

A NOTE ABOUT THE TYPE

The text of this book was set in Ascot, a film
version of Trump Mediaeval. Designed by Professor
Georg Trump in the mid-1950s, Trump Mediaeval
was cut and cast by the C. E. Weber Typefoundry of
Stuttgart, West Germany. The roman letterforms are
based on classical prototypes, but Professor Trump
has imbued them with his own unmistakable style.
The italic letterforms, unlike those of so many other
typefaces, are closely related to their roman
counterparts. The result is a truly contemporary
type, notable for both its legibility and its versatility.

Composed by New England Typographic Service, Inc.,
Bloomfield, Connecticut.
Halftones shot by Halliday Lithograph,
West Hanover, Massachusetts.
Separations, Printing and Binding by Dai Nippon
Printing Company, Tokyo, Japan.

Design by Dorothy Schmiderer